Department of the Environment

Crime Prevention on Council Estates

Prepared by the Safe Neighbourhoods Unit (SNU)
For the Department of the Environment

London: HMSO

ISBN 0 11 752766 1

Contents

A separate report *Housing and Safe Communities: an evaluation of recent initiatives*, based on more detailed assessments of the schemes (summarised in the present report) in the following areas:

- Pepys Estate, Lewisham

- Mitchellhill Estate, Glasgow

- Highgate Estate, Birmingham

- Broadwater Farm Estate, Haringey

- Kirkholt Estate, Rochdale

- Easton/Ashley, Bristol

- Golf Links Estate, Ealing

- Possil Park Estate, Glasgow

- Niddrie House Estate, Edinburgh

- Chalkhill Estate, Brent

is available from Safe Neighbourhoods Unit, 4th Floor East, 7 Whitechapel Road, London, E1 1DU.

Acknowledgements

This report is the product of a research project undertaken by the Safe Neighbourhoods Unit (SNU) for the Department of the Environment, under the supervision of Dr David Riley of the Department's Social Research Division.

The SNU project team responsible for this report consisted of John Farr, Katy Ferguson, Tim Kendrick and Steve Osborn.

We would like to acknowledge the help provided by Tim Hope, formerly of the Home Office Research and Planning Unit and currently Associate Professor of Criminology at the University of Missouri-St Louis, in clarifying a number of evaluation issues and for supplying additional data.

Steve Osborn
March 1993

Introduction

On the face of it, the 1980s witnessed an explosion of crime prevention activity. Central government departments developed major new programmes, focused wholly or partly on crime prevention. A national crime prevention body (Crime Concern) was created. Multi-million pound advertising campaigns, accompanied by government circulars and widely distributed crime prevention literature, have been initiated by the Home Office. Local authorities have increasingly developed a discrete role, some in partnership with central government and some independently. Two local government associations, the AMA and ADC, have developed crime prevention guidelines for their members (AMA, 1990; ADC, 1990). The Home Office recently commissioned the development of further guidelines on local partnership approaches involving local authorities (Home Office, 1991).

There appears to be a general acceptance of a particular model for crime prevention: a model which stresses local initiative (but sometimes national input), multi-agency working, some element of consultation of local residents, tackling crime problems using social as well as physical measures, and using local analyses of crime to specify the action to be taken. A great deal of this activity has been focused on residential areas.

Despite the scale of this activity, questions still need to be asked about the rationale behind much of what is going on. Is there a theoretical basis to the work? Is the work based on proven evidence of success? These questions are particularly relevant as, notwithstanding the scale of activity, crime rates continued to rise into the 1990s.

This report brings a spotlight to bear on *housing-related* crime prevention. This field of crime prevention accounts for a large part of crime prevention theory and practice and occupies much of the attention of policy makers. Doing something about crime in residential areas, where its impact is most obviously damaging to the public, has tended to take precedence over crime related to work, travel and leisure.

Structure of report

The report is in two parts.

Part One - Review of Research and Information is a review of published (and occasionally unpublished) material on the topic, mostly from the UK but referring to American and continental European publications where appropriate. A framework for evaluating crime prevention initiatives is put forward as a guide to the various approaches and the evidence they present. Conclusions are drawn on the value of this evidence and the lessons for future initiatives.

Part Two - Assessing Costs and Benefits is a review of cost benefit analysis and cost effectiveness assessment as it has been applied in the crime prevention and related (public sector) fields. Various attempts to determine the costs of crime to public bodies and the community are described. A methodology is put forward for assessing costs and benefits in the housing-related crime prevention field.

Scope and limitations of report

In the expectation that readers are more likely to dip into the report than read it from cover to cover, we would like to highlight a number of issues about the scope of the report and its limitations issues which are referred to in the body of the report, which we feel are important, but which may otherwise be overlooked.

Focus on housing

The report is restricted to crime prevention theory and practice as it relates to the housing field. It is concerned with housing policy and practice and with schemes for particular estates or neighbourhoods. This focus should be borne in mind when reading the report. It explains the exclusion of certain kinds of schemes, including relatively well-known ones such as the Staffordshire Police Activity and Community Enterprise (SPACE), on the grounds that they are not neighbourhood specific. It also partly explains the prominence given in the report to the role of local authorities and central government support. The almost inevitable concentration on areas of public housing means that the leadership role of the local authority as landlord is highlighted. It does not necessarily follow that local authorities have a monopoly on crime prevention schemes or a lead responsibility for crime prevention in general. Also, the existence of sizeable central government programmes such as Estate Action and the Priority Estates Project dedicated to improving housing estates, including (explicity or implicitly) improving their security, or which (like Safer Cities Project grants) can be used to fund security related estate improvements, means that central government support features in many of the schemes described in this report. This does not necessarily mean that central government support is essential for local crime prevention schemes and it is, at least partly, the intention of this report to draw attention to what local authorities may be able to achieve within existing resources.

Limits of information available

Inevitably, the contents of the report have been shaped by the availability of information. A great deal has been written about some topics but not others. Some organisations such as the Priority Estates Project, which have been funded to record and disseminate findings, are a rich source of material on management focused initiatives . Other potential sources, such as individual local authorities, police forces and community organisations, who do not have this kind of remit, often have little or no information on their initiatives. Given our reliance on *professional disseminators* for much of the information in this report, and bearing in mind that they have their own perspectives and interests to promote, we have no way of knowing the true extent of what is actually happening, and *succeeding,* on the ground.

Forced categorisations

In order to make sense of the field and to place some semblance of order on the report, it was necessary to group initiatives together in categories. Inevitably, few initiatives fit comfortably into the categories - many initiatives are multi-dimensional and some change their character over time - and it was not always easy to choose between categories. It should be borne in mind that the categories assigned to initiatives are not intended to be complete definitions or characterisations of those initiatives.

Difficulties of determining elements of success	At various points in the report we try to identify the common elements of more *successful* schemes. It is apparent, however, that these common elements also characterise many of the less successful schemes. This reflects the existence of a kind of orthodoxy of approach, a general acceptance of a particular model, which emerged in the late 1970s and early 1980s and which has meant that many recent initiatives have adhered to or at least paid lip service to certain ideas or principles such as multi-agency working and resident consultation. In retrospect there might have been a case for examining a range of schemes generally accepted as *unsuccessful,* but which appeared to adopt similar approaches to the more *successful* schemes. This would have enabled us to make judgements on whether their *failure* was linked to problems with the approach or implementation or derived from particular intervening factors.

Evaluation can be expensive	In Part One of the report a framework for evaluating crime prevention projects is put forward. Some might argue that to do the job properly is too expensive and that other less demanding frameworks than the one we propose would be adequate. It is our view, nonetheless, that the basic framework needs to be rigorous so that, where finances limit the scope for comprehensive evaluation, **evaluators are able to highlight the limitations of their findings.**

Crime prevention for whom?	In our overall approach to the study, we have been mindful that discussions about the value of particular techniques for assessing the effectiveness of schemes and arguments over the validity and interpretation of findings should not neglect the community's judgement on what has happened. Observers may conclude, on the basis of changes in recorded crime or other quantitative measures, that a scheme has or has not achieved its objective. But such measures may not truly represent the reality of living in that particular area and, at the end of the day, judgements on the success or otherwise of schemes must reflect the resident's views. Crime prevention schemes are set up to ease the burden of crime on particular individuals and groups of individuals and, without some judgement from them, any conclusions drawn on the effectiveness of schemes may be misleading.

Part One   Review of research and information

Part One of the report is a description of the housing-related crime prevention field. It reviews the literature, describes examples of evaluated crime prevention initiatives and assesses the quality of evidence presented. Initiatives are categorised in terms of their major focus: design, management, physical security, social or policing. However, as will become apparent, most initiatives are multi-focused and not easy to categorise.

Part One has four chapters:

Chapter One - Crime and Housing, describes what is known about the distribution of crime in this country and its impact on certain types of housing area, tenure and social group.

Chapter Two - Assessing the Evidence, develops a framework for assessing the quality of evidence presented on the impact of crime prevention initiatives.

Chapter Three - Theory into Practice, describes the literature and the initiatives taken in the housing-related crime prevention field.

Chapter Four - Reviewing the Evidence, makes some judgements about the quality of evidence presented.

Chapter 1   Crime and housing

Residential crime is unevenly distributed across the country and throughout the population. It is concentrated in inner urban areas and on large public housing estates. Its impact is often most severe for low income households, some ethnic groups and young women.

In the past, most regular information about crime has come from the official crime statistics, which include only those crimes reported to and recorded by the police. Not only do crime statistics under represent the volume of crime but their presentation on the basis of police administrative boundaries (force areas, divisions, subdivisions and beats) tends to mask the relationship between crime and particular types of area.

More recently, however, our understanding of the distribution and effects of crime has improved; this is partly because the police have been increasingly prepared to present crime figures on the basis of more clearly understood geographical boundaries (for example, wards, enumeration districts or particular estates or neighbourhoods) but more so, given the limitations of official crime statistics, because of the more widespread use of crime or victimisation surveys.

A large number of surveys have interviewed people about their experiences as victims of crime. These types of surveys began to be used widely in the USA in the 1960s. In Britain, an OPCS survey in 1966 was the first to ask questions about victimisation (Durant et al., 1972) and, since then, the General Household Survey has occasionally included questions about burglary. An important test of crime survey methods was undertaken in 1972 (Sparks et al., 1977). However, crime surveys did not emerge as a common feature of the British scene until the 1980s. The three British Crime Surveys of England and Wales (Hough and Mayhew, 1983; Hough and Mayhew, 1985; Mayhew, Elliott and Dowds, 1989) and of Scotland (Chambers and Tombs, 1984) interviewed nationally drawn samples. Other surveys have addressed victimisation in:

- Counties - eg Merseyside (Kinsey, 1984).

- Districts - eg Islington (Jones, Maclean and Young, 1986; Crawford, Jones, Woodhouse and Young, 1990) and Edinburgh (Anderson, Smith, Kinsey and Wood, 1990).

- Sub-districts - eg East Spitalfields (Safe Neighbourhoods Unit, 1989a).

- Estates or neighbourhoods - eg Hilldrop Estate, Islington (Lea et al., 1988) and Lansdowne Green Estate, Lambeth (Safe Neighbourhoods Unit, 1986a).

- Single residential blocks - eg Trellick Tower, Kensington and Chelsea (Safe Neighbourhoods Unit, 1986b).

And it is now very common for victimisation data to be gathered when surveys are being carried out for other purposes. For example, many *customer satisfaction surveys* intended to investigate public perceptions of local authority (and other)

7

services include sections on crime, as do most surveys of residents on improvements to their estates or neighbourhoods.

A major feature of national and local crime surveys has been the issue of the *fear of crime*. The term is now widely used to describe any anxiety about becoming a victim, but it is important to distinguish fear of crime from assessment of risk. As pointed out by Hough and Mayhew (1985): 'One person may believe his or her chances of being burgled are high and yet remain unworried; another may know the chances are remote, but worry nonetheless. Anxiety about victimisation is determined not just by the perceived likelihood of falling victim, but also by the expected consequences, and people have differing reactions to similar incidents - they are differentially vulnerable'. It is worth bearing this in mind when surveys claim that levels of fear, for instance amongst women, the elderly or in particular neighbourhoods are unrealistic or unjustified in the light of levels of crime.

The prominence given to *fear of crime* has its origins in the perceived *failure* of many American crime prevention programmes in effecting reductions in crime rates. As Curtis (1988) points out: '. . . reduced crime as a measure of success began to be de-emphasised, in favour of reduced fear of crime, a perception measure with a better track record for showing positive results'.

From the wealth of data contained in national and local crime surveys, most of which have not been drawn together for descriptive or comparative purposes, it is possible to develop a more accurate picture of the extent and distribution of crime.

However, it is important to recognise that survey based measurement of crime in neighbourhoods has limitations. For example, the picture of crime presented by surveys is sometimes based on just one type of residential crime - domestic burglary. This is often described as the *major residential crime* because of its volume and because it is exclusively related to the neighbourhoods concerned. Autocrime, whilst it may affect a large number of residents, need not be related to the specific neighbourhood. Other kinds of crime, such as assaults, are relatively low in volume (as far as we can tell) and/or not specifically related to the victims homes or immediate neighbourhoods (for example, autocrime). The problems of measurement presented by crime surveys are discussed in more detail in the next chapter (see p.14).

Crime and residential area

Some types of residential area are more prone to crime than others. On the basis of the ACORN classification of area, the British Crime Survey 1984 identified three *high risk areas*. Hope and Hough (1988) define these areas as follows:

- ACORN I - high status non-family areas - one archetype of the inner city - split between the homes of the rich and the more twilight areas of the urban transients - privately owned buildings in multiple occupation.

- ACORN H - multi-racial areas - poor, private rentals mixed with owner occupation - again in inner cities.

- ACORN G - the poorest council estates, located either in inner cities or in the outer rings of conurbations.

Between 10% and 12% of the households in these areas experienced burglary (including attempts) during 1983, according to the BCS, compared with a national average of 4%. Around 4% of the people in these areas experienced robbery or theft from person in 1983, compared with a national average of 1.4% (see Table 1).

Table 1 **Crime rates, by ACORN neighbourhood group, 1983**
(Reproduced from Hope and Shaw, 1988, p.33)

Crime rates	Burglary incl attempts	Robbery & theft from person	Theft of and from vehicles outside home
	% of HHs victim	% persons victim	% owners victim
Low risk areas			
A. Agricultural areas (n=476)	1	1.3	5
C. Older housing of intermediate status (n=2001)	2	0.8	10
K. Better-off retirement areas (n=463)	3	1.1	6
J. Affluent suburban housing (n=1659)	3	1.1	7
B. Modern family housing high incomes (n=1537)	3	0.9	8
Medium risk areas			
E. Better-off council estates (n=1018)	4	1.4	14
D. Poor quality older terraced housing (n=759)	4	1.4	18
F. Less well-off council estates (n=1175)	4	1.4	15
High risk areas			
I. High status non-family areas (n=609)	10	3.9	15
H. Multi-racial areas (n=400)	10	4.3	26
G. Poorest council estates (n=543)	12	3.3	21
National average	4	1.4	11

Source: 1984 BCS Weighted data

The British Crime Survey 1988 (Mayhew, Elliott and Dowds, 1989) shows a slightly different picture, at least in respect of domestic burglary (the only crime for which ACORN breakdowns are so far available). The latest Survey shows that two areas - *high status non family areas* and *poorest council estates* - are high risk with between 11% and 13% of the households burgled (including attempts) in 1987. The previously highly rated category - *multi-racial areas* - was little different from the national average, with 6% of the households burgled as against 5% nationally.

So-called high risk areas do not necessarily have high rates of all types of residential crime. The British Crime Survey 1984 (Hough and Mayhew, 1985) found that assaults, vandalism to personal property and thefts were more evenly distributed across types of residential area.

Local crime surveys have shown that there are residential areas with exceptional rates of victimisation. For example, in 1988 one in five households on the Stockwell Park Estate in Lambeth were said to have experienced a burglary (excluding attempts) (Safe Neighbourhoods Unit, 1989b, unpublished). Many households experienced multiple victimisation and the ratio of burglaries (including attempts) to households was three for every four households in 1988. On the same estate, nearly one in ten of the sample had been robbed and nearly half of the vehicle owners had had their vehicles stolen, stolen from or damaged in 1988.

The crime profiles of what are regarded by the police, local authorities or the media as high crime estates differ markedly. Table 2, taken from the Stockwell Park study report previously referred to, shows how a range of London estates with high crime reputations differ markedly in their crime profiles. Of course, as one would expect, the extent of victimisation in different parts of the same estate also differed markedly.

Table 2 **Proportions of households or individuals victimised annually, according to surveys, on a selection of inner city *high crime* estates**

	Stockwell Park 1988	Mozart Estate 1988	Lansdowne Green 1987	Hilldrop Estate 1987
Burglary	21%	8%	15%	7%
Attempted burglary	29%	18%	20%	8%
Robbery	9%	8%	12%	5%
Assault	5%	-	9%	4%
Threats	11%	13%	14%	6%
Sexual assault*	2%	1%	4%	1%
Sexual harassment*	11%	1%	7%	5%

* asked of women only

In general, and as one might expect, fear of crime tends to increase with crime. According to the 1984 British Crime Survey, as many as 27% of those living in *high crime areas* felt very unsafe in their area, compared with 12% of the sample as a whole and as few as 3% in the least victimised area category - *agricultural areas* (Hough and Mayhew, 1985).

Fear of crime in particular neighbourhoods, it has been argued (Osborn and Bright, 1989) '. . . causes those who can to move away from what are seen as crime prone areas and those who cannot to retreat into their homes'. The impact of fear on behaviour can be dramatic, particularly amongst women and the elderly, and can result in what many regard as unacceptable levels of avoidance behaviour. On the Lansdowne Green Estate in Lambeth, over a quarter of the male population and nearly two-thirds of the female population regularly avoided going out after dark because of fear of crime (Safe Neighbourhoods Unit, 1986a).

Crime and tenure

Surveys also show a relationship between victimisation and tenure type. Council tenants are nearly twice as likely to be burgled as homeowners, as shown in Table 3 (taken from Hope, 1990 unpublished).

Table 3 **Burglary rates according to tenure type**
(from 1988 British Crime Survey)

	Burglaries (inc attempts) per 100 households	unweighted sample size
Owned or being bought	44	7092
Council rented	92	2445

Note: Rates are calculated using weighted data from the core sample of the 1988 BCS - definitions of terms can be found in the Glossary of the 1988 BCS report; definitions of burglary and attempted burglary are also contained in the Glossary.

As pointed out by Hope and Hough (1988), the relationship between tenure and crime has more to do with the mix of tenure types in different neighbourhoods than the vulnerability of council tenants per se. They found that council tenants in council areas face a risk of burglary considerably higher than the national average, whilst council tenants in non-council areas and owner-occupiers in council areas have a risk of burglary around the national average.

However, as they go on to point out, the variation in burglary rates within the council sector is wider than the overall variation between council tenure and owner occupation. Council tenants in the poorest council areas have a burglary rate five times that of tenants on the better off estates (as defined by ACORN).

Crime and dwelling design

People who live in purpose-built flats and maisonettes appear to be more vulnerable to residential crime than those who live in other forms of accommodation (with the exception of the very small proportion of the population living in property attached to business premises). 5.1% of these households were burgled in 1985, compared with 3.4% living in other forms of accommodation (source General Household Survey 1986, Table 7.3).

However, the higher rate of burglary for purpose-built flats and maisonettes is mainly explained by tenure distribution - about two thirds of these properties are rented from a local authority (or New Town). Owner occupiers living in flats and maisonettes experienced a similar burglary rate in 1985 (2.1%) to owner occupiers in houses (2.5%), and a significantly lower rate than (mostly local authority) tenants in houses (4.2%) or flats and maisonettes (5.4%; op. cit. Figure 7F).

Notwithstanding the fact that differences in crime rates do not seem to be related to differences in dwelling design when looked at nationally (Hope, 1986), some claim links between dwelling design and crime rates in particular local areas (Coleman, 1985). However, the picture is confusing and often contradictory. A survey carried out on the Mozart Estate in Westminster in 1988 (Safe Neighbourhoods Unit, 1988a unpublished) found that the burglary rate was somewhat lower (1 in 16) amongst houses and smaller blocks with under 12 dwellings than for medium size blocks with between 13 and 30 dwellings (1 in 12) but little different from the rate for the largest blocks with 57 or more dwellings (1 in 15). The survey found little relationship between the presence of walkways or interconnections and burglary rates - in fact, the lowest burglary rate was found in blocks with three walkways - and found (contrary to popular perceptions) that households with access from internal corridors serving eight or less dwellings were more prone to burglary and vandalism than households with internal corridors serving between nine and 18 dwellings. Interestingly, the fear of crime expressed by residents bore little relationship to the actual levels of crime - concern about burglary was most apparent in blocks served by walkways and interconnections and in blocks served by long internal corridors.

This divergence between fear of crime and actual crime is evident elsewhere. For example, on the Milton Court Estate in Lewisham, residents in linked maisonette blocks were very much less likely to be burgled than residents in tower blocks, freestanding maisonette blocks or houses but at least as fearful of burglary (Safe Neighbourhoods Unit, 1990).

Crime and social group

Some of the variation in victimisation rates reflects differences in income, socio-economic status, race, gender and *lifestyle*.

In Sheffield in the 1960s, council areas where the majority were skilled manual workers had lower crime rates than those housing the unskilled and the poor (Baldwin and Bottoms, 1976). Unskilled workers are twice as likely to be burgled as professional workers; young men tend to be the most vulnerable to assault (Hough and Mayhew, 1985). When sexual assault and domestic violence are taken into account (which is notoriously difficult for crime surveys), young women are more vulnerable to violence than young men. For most categories of crime, both Afro-Caribbeans and Asians are more vulnerable than whites (Mayhew, Elliott and Dowds, 1989).

Crime and incivilities

Links have been drawn between levels of residential crime and the prevalence of so-called *incivilities* - behaviour which is not defined as crime (at least officially) but which, for many people, is part of the crime problem. Littering, dog fouling, noisy parties and young people hanging about and behaving aggressively are often described as incivilities.

The *Broken Windows* model of crime generation put forward by Wilson and Kelling (1982) describes a developmental or incremental relationship between incivilities and crime. Increasing incivility is accompanied by rising crime rates until, after a certain level is reached, a spiralling cycle of decline sets in. The explanation for this is seen to be the effect that visible signs of neighbourhood deterioration have on residents' perceptions of their area - feelings that the area is in decline leading to withdrawal from community life, fear of venturing out and reduced levels of informal social control.

Wilson and Kelling advocate intervention at an early stage to improve the environment and police deployment to make up for absent informal social controls. Taub, Taylor and Dunham (1984) advocate investment in the local economy to persuade residents to stay. Some commentators also see elements of the *Broken Windows* model behind initiatives undertaken by the Priority Estates Project and by NACRO, the former advocating intervention to improve management and maintenance and the latter intervention to reinforce informal social controls.

Hope and Hough (1988), in their analysis of the 1984 British Crime Survey, see some support for the idea that 'as perceptions of incivility increase, so does worry about crime; satisfaction with the neighbourhood diminishes and crime begins to grow at an increasingly rapid rate'. But, as they go on to point out, this does not prove that there is a causal relationship between incivilities and crime. The British Crime Surveys are cross-sectional studies and, unlike longitudinal studies, are not able to test out processes over time (see *Chapter Two* for further discussion of methodological issues).

Focus on public housing

Concern about crime has tended to focus on public housing, both in this country and elsewhere. Much of this derives from the publication twenty years ago of Oscar Newman's pioneering study *Defensible Space* (Newman, 1972) which drew attention to the links between crime rates and the design of public housing projects in the USA. This concern was expressed most clearly in the multi-million dollar Urban Initiatives Anti-Crime Programme (US Department of Housing and Urban Development, 1980). The Programme initially targeted 39 public housing authorities in the USA.

Although there is now a widespread acceptance of the links between crime and public housing in this country, it was not always so.

A Home Office report on the proceedings of a conference on crime and public housing in 1980 (Hough and Mayhew, 1982) drew a sharp distinction between the American and British experience. American public housing projects (housing 2% of Americans) were seen as 'breeding grounds for delinquency and drug abuse and magnets for crime from surrounding areas'. In contrast, British public housing (catering at the time for about 30% of the population) were seen 'not to suffer to the same extent from a welfare image . . . and often carefully designed to meet the needs of residents . . . there are very few estates where risks of criminal victimisation approach those of may American housing projects. Indeed, it is not at all certain that crime is any more concentrated in public housing . . . than it is in private sector housing' (op. cit. p.1).

In the same report, Mayhew and Clarke say that, despite the research evidence (for example, Baldwin and Bottoms, 1976) that offenders tend to live on council estates and commit their crimes locally, the same research indicates that 'there is no evidence that council tenants are more vulnerable than anyone else . . . For offences likely to be concentrated in residential areas, the evidence suggests that neither burglaries nor household thefts (excluding thefts from gas and electricity meters) are more prevalent than elsewhere; and indeed, for burglary at least, council areas may suffer less than where property is of very high rateable value . . . It is only in regard to vandalism that one can say firmly that council housing is more subject to attack than other dwellings'.

Much of the research on public housing in this country in the 1970s and early 1980s was concerned with vandalism in preference to other forms of crime. The Department of the Environment, whose interest in vandalism was linked to concern about design, management and maintenance on public housing estates, conducted research on related topics such as children's play, children living in flats, housing layout and difficult-to-let housing (see Wilson et al., 1980, and HDD Occasional Papers 3/80, 4/80 and 5/80) and produced an advisory paper on vandalism in 1981 (Wilson, 1981). At the same time, the Home Office focused its research directly on vandalism in an attempt to find effective preventive measures (see Clarke, 1978). The Home Office also funded (through Urban Aid, 1976-79) the first pilot project linking estate improvements to crime prevention this country - the Cunningham Road Improvement Scheme in Halton (Hedges, Blaber and Mostyn, 1980) which was billed as an *anti-vandalism* project.

And so, much of the earlier research into crime and public housing in this country focused on vandalism and, whilst recognising that public housing estates tended to have high offender rates, did not recognise the overall prevalence of residential crimes in these areas.

During the 1980s, however, increasing attention was paid to crime on public housing estates. The concept of the *difficult-to-let* estate emerged unpopular, poorly managed and run-down council estates with a range of inter-related problems of crime and deprivation. The rather limited earlier concern with vandalism gave way to broader concerns about quality of life and more serious crime problems on housing estates. This came about for a number of reasons, not least the growing evidence from the British Crime Survey and elsewhere that estates had high rates of victimisation as well as high rates of offenders. As Hope and Shaw (1988) point out, 'with only a little exaggeration, the problem estate has now come to represent, rightly or not, the modern British image of the high crime community'.

However, it is clear that areas other than public housing estates suffer from high crime rates and there appear to be other reasons for the public housing focus.

Firstly, public housing estates tend to be readily identifiable neighbourhoods with clearly demarcated boundaries. This makes estates easy to characterise as areas with distinct crime problems which are resolvable within their boundaries. This is not often the case for mixed tenure inner city areas (which include areas of relative affluence) which may also suffer high crime rates.

Secondly, the impact of crime on relatively disadvantaged communities (which are over-represented in the Council sector) is likely to be greater, and therefore more deserving of attention, in that residents are less able to ameliorate the effects of crime (through insurance/ replacement), protect themselves (through home/ personal security) or escape (through moving elsewhere).

Thirdly, and practically, the presence of a single landlord may mean that problems are more readily amenable to resolution.

The public housing focus is reinforced by the Department of the Environment's programmes. Crime prevention is one of the criteria of both Estate Action and the Urban Programme and the Department estimated that £38m was spent on security works in 1989/90 under the former and nearly £10m on crime prevention projects in 1988/89 under the latter programme.

Summary

- Certain types of residential area appear to suffer higher rates of criminal victimisation - most obviously, those described as the *poorest estates* and certain categories of inner city area.

- Council tenants are, it appears, more often victims of residential crime than homeowners and, related to this, so too are residents in purpose-built flats and maisonettes.

- People on low incomes, black people and young adults are more often victims of crime and young women suffer most from violence.

- In general, it appears that the fear of crime increases with crime levels, but it may be that some environmental features evoke fear even where crime levels are low.

- Visible evidence of neighbourhood decline may affect residents' perceptions of their areas, reduce informal social controls and contribute to increases in crime rates.

- Notwithstanding the above, outwardly similar residential environments with equally disadvantaged residents have remarkably different crime profiles.

- In qualification, most of these assessments are based on distributions of property crimes and much less is known about the extent of violent crimes.

Chapter Three aims to provide a comprehensive description of housing-related crime prevention initiatives carried out in the UK, making reference where appropriate to initiatives in other countries as well. Claims have been made about the various initiatives described in Chapter Three. The evidence put forward to substantiate those claims varies from, at one end of the spectrum, the subjective judgement of those closely involved to, at the other, seemingly comprehensive and exhaustive evaluations carried out by independent researchers.

In the light of the wide variation in evaluation *methodology* used to assess crime prevention initiatives, how can we draw conclusions about the efficacy of particular initiatives? In this chapter, we will try to develop a set of criteria against which to assess whether project reports in Chapter Three contain sufficient information to make a judgement about their crime prevention effects. In developing the criteria we will be guided by practical considerations of what it is possible to achieve given the methodological constraints of having to operate in the real world rather than the laboratory.

Methodological issues

Notwithstanding the claims which are made about the success of particular crime prevention initiatives, we can never say with complete certainty that they did work. We can only be more or less confident about the evidence presented by the *evaluators,* and the research methods they used to arrive at their conclusions.

Much of the literature on evaluation research is designed to be read by researchers rather than practitioners. Apart from the impenetrability of some of the research jargon, the literature can be off-putting because of its preoccupation with theory, research critiques and research purity. Many of the evaluation models being advocated by social researchers appear to be unattainable in the real world. It is easy to understand why so much of the literature is ignored by practitioners and policy-makers.

But even if the evaluation models being advocated by social researchers appear to be out of step with the reality of programme implementation, that does not mean that the methodological issues raised do not have some value. Too often, claims are made about the success of particular initiatives without any attempt to seek out even a modicum of confirmatory data (which may be readily available) or to at least qualify the findings on the basis of methodological limitations. Just as important, initiatives may be too readily dismissed as failures on the basis of limited data of dubious validity.

Nothing works, everything works

Central to the argument over what constitutes evidence of success is the tension between scientific and pragmatic approaches to evaluation. Scientific procedure is founded on the principle of falsifiability and scientists are trained to avoid concluding that a finding is true when it is false. This means that the scientist is often enticed towards the conclusion that *nothing works* and needs a good deal of evidence to be persuaded otherwise. Practitioners and policy-makers, on the other hand, devote substantial resources to their programmes and policies and want researchers to confirm their effectiveness.

It is easy to see how a pragmatic approach to evaluation can lead too readily to concluding that initiatives are successful. The emergence of a favourable set of recorded crime figures, for instance, is often seen as evidence that an initiative is working with no consideration given to contextual issues such as crime trends in the area, the length of monitoring period or to any external factors which might have contributed to a fall in recorded crime. A case in point is the Home Office's *5 Towns Initiative* which was heavily promoted as a model crime prevention initiative on the basis of reductions in recorded crime at some of the sites (Home Office, 1989), and before a more thorough and independent evaluation was commissioned from the Cambridge Institute of Criminology. Pragmatists may also be accused of selectivity in their presentation of confirmatory material, highlighting data which supports the contention that the initiative was successful and ignoring or explaining away contradictory data. Of course, *quick and dirty* pragmatic evaluations may also show that initiatives **do not** work. But these rarely explain the reasons for failure and practitioners are left to wonder what went wrong and what to do next.

The scientific approach, on the other hand, may lead too readily to concluding that there is no evidence that initiatives are successful. As pointed out by Hope and Dowds (1987):

> . . . social researchers tend to elevate significance testing from the relative to the absolute. In consequence, stringent, probabilistic criteria are brought in to assess programme effectiveness. Much less attention is paid to the sensitivity of the evaluation research design and its power to detect marginal effects. Perhaps the social scientist, preoccupied with theory, tends to deal most of the time in the absolutes of true and false . . . evaluation research which will be useful to policy, ought to be able to detect marginal as well as absolute effects . . .

It is clear that a balance needs to be struck between the two agendas.

Recorded crime as a measure of crime reduction

Recorded crime statistics are an attractive measurement tool. They are relatively easy to collect. They allow for continuous measurement during the life of a project. They can be collected at any point after the start of a project and they allow for retrospective assessment. Consequently, they are regularly used and often quoted as evidence of success.

And yet, the problems of using recorded crime statistics are well known. In the first place, the public's willingness to report crimes may change over time. In particular, it is said that the presence of a project which aims to prevent crime (as a major or subsidiary goal) encourages people to report crime because of improved relations with the police and greater confidence that something will be done (Skogan, 1984).

In fact, this reasoning is sometimes behind attempts to explain away disappointing recorded crime statistics. Hedges et al. (1980), for instance, when describing the outcome of a crime prevention project in Widnes in which survey data showed some fall in crime but police statistics none, say:

> . . . improved patrolling and better relations between police and community almost automatically signal an increase in recorded crime . . .

Interestingly, the recorded crime rate on the project *control* estate fell by 36%.

There is some evidence for increased reporting rates being associated with crime prevention initiatives. Schneider (1986), describing a crime prevention programme in Portland, Oregon, found that the proportion of surveyed burglary victims who said they reported their incidents to the police rose from 50% to 70% during the course of the programme.

Differential reporting rates for different types of crime also present major difficulties. The 1988 British Crime Survey (Mayhew, Elliott and Dowds, 1989) indicated that about a third of all crimes covered by the survey were reported to the police. However, some crimes are less frequently reported to the police because they are relatively trivial (less than one in four incidents of vandalism were reported to the police) or because of victims' fear of reporting (only about one in five sexual offences were reported to the police). More serious property crimes are routinely reported to the police - nearly 90% of burglaries with loss and over 90% of motor vehicle thefts. Changes in crime rates for crimes with low reporting rates are not likely to show up in any significant way in recorded crime statistics and will be swamped by changes in high volume well reported crimes. This could lead to a situation in which an initiative is judged as a success on the basis of overall crime trends, despite increases in violent or sexual offences which may have a disproportionately damaging impact on the local community.

Police recording practices may also vary. Differences between police forces are evident. Farrington and Dowds (1985) concluded that about two thirds of the differences in crime rates between Nottinghamshire, long reputed as a high crime area, and two neighbouring counties was explained by differences in police recording practices. And practices may change over time because of Home Office modifications to the *Rule Book* (which gives guidance on what and how recording should take place) or because of changes in police policy. In fact, the research carried out by Farrington and Dowds in Nottinghamshire led to police policy changes. There is also scope for different recording practices within any one force area. It may be, for instance, that where police officers are involved in a local crime prevention initiative they deal with incidents informally or with greater latitude as part of a local strategy to improve relations with young people.

It seems, therefore, that total reliance on recorded crime statistics may be misplaced and that, where they are used, there should ideally be supporting data from victimisation surveys or elsewhere. This is particularly so where reductions in recorded crime are modest, numerically or proportionately. But can the more **dramatic** reductions in recorded crime levels be challenged on the basis of *contamination* by the initiatives themselves? Could, for instance, the 60% reduction in recorded crime rates on the Pepys Estate in Deptford between 1983 and 1988 (568 fewer crimes in 1988) be explained in terms of any changes in public reporting or police recording practice. Although it is worth exercising caution before accepting even dramatic results at face value, there seems little doubt that this represented a real reduction in levels of crime, although arguments still remain over which specific interventions contributed to this.

Survey data as a measure of crime reduction

The problems associated with the use of recorded crime statistics have led to a greater reliance on information from victimisation surveys. Public surveys can potentially obtain information on all crimes committed against individuals, including those not reported to the police and therefore omitted from recorded crime statistics. They should provide a truer picture of the full extent of crime against individuals. Their use also removes any concern about changes in reporting or recording practices which, as we have said, undermine the value of recorded crime statistics. But how much better are surveys at providing a true picture of crime in residential areas?

The most obvious limitation of victimisation surveys is that they only obtain information on crimes committed against **residents** in the study area. Crimes against **organisations** and **non-residents** in the study area are ignored. This may be most significant for public housing estates, where the local authority as landlord may be heavily victimised in terms of criminal damage and theft of its property. These kinds of offences are not routinely reported to the police and will not be fully represented in recorded crime statistics either. The victimisation of non-residents (people visiting, passing through or working in an area) is a generally neglected area of investigation, although occasionally highlighted in media reports on high crime estates where, for instance, milk and postal deliveries have been suspended because of fear of theft or assault on personnel.

Furthermore, interview based studies have been criticised for giving a distorted picture of the distribution of the effects of victimisation because they use samples which reflect narrow definitions of *crime* and *victims*. First, there is the issue of repeated victimisation. Crime surveys tend to arbitrarily count repeated incidents of, for example, domestic violence or systematic vandalism as just one or two offences (see Genn, 1988). Secondly, there is the problems of hidden violence. Brief interviews tend to be unsuitable for asking people about their experiences of violence, particularly where violence is part of a domestic relationship (see Stenko, 1988). Remarkably, the 1984 British Crime Survey uncovered only **one** attempted rape. Thirdly, surveys tend to ignore crimes committed against young people. The British Crime Surveys interviewed people aged 16 or above and the great majority of surveys have been principally concerned with crimes against the household, with the expectation that the *head of household* or other adult member of the household can speak for young residents (or for that matter other dependants, such as the elderly).

The most striking criticism of crime surveys is handed out by Young (1988), himself a major exponent of crime surveys, who argues that survey data is normally unable to get at the 'subjective meaning of events'. The British Crime Surveys, and many others, highlight the petty, opportunistic nature of crime, the low level of violent offences and the relationship between non-reporting and the *trivial* nature of the incidents concerned. Young challenges these conclusions on the basis that such surveys underestimate crimes of violence, ignore repeated victimisation and define some incidents as *trivial* or *petty* without reference to the actual impact of such incidents on people's lives. He argues that the public should define *crime* and what constitutes *serious crime* if a meaningful picture of the extent and distribution of crime is to be developed.

Surveys have one other major disadvantage when set against the use of recorded crime statistics. Recorded crime statistics can be used to interpret trends in the data over time. For instance, fluctuations in monthly crime statistics can be related to the introduction of particular measures. This is very difficult, if not impossible, to achieve through analysis of survey data.

One issue which needs to be considered in the development of surveys is the definitions of crime to be used. Most local surveys have adopted the British Crime Survey methodology and Home Office Criminal Statistics definitions of crime. However, as pointed out by Hope and Dowds (1987), the measurement system used by the British Crime Survey (to match figures as closely as possible to Home Office counting rules) is time-consuming and may squeeze other more important questions off the questionnaire. They conclude that 'what is relevant for an evaluation study is the change in the number of informants answering "yes" to the screening questions and the seriousness of the event they report. It may also be unnecessary to collect masses of detail on individual offence characteristics if good approximations, rather than exact crime classifications, are required.'

Quantitative versus qualitative measures of effect

The issues raised above by Jock Young and others about the way crimes are counted deserve further expansion. Most studies measure crime in quantitative rather than qualitative terms - adding up the total number of crimes committed in the study area within given periods and assuming that a lower count is *better* than a higher one. Underlying this approach is an assumption that all crimes within a given offence category are roughly equivalent - one playground bully forcing children to hand over their dinner money (robbery) equals one armed man forcing a security guard to hand over a payroll (robbery), and even that crimes committed within different offence categories are roughly equivalent - one domestic burglary equals one rape. This way of counting also assumes an equivalent impact on victims from identical events and yet we know, for instance, that a burglary can be a far more serious event for an elderly person on a pension than for a young professional.

The following are some illustrations of how lower crime rates may not be synonymous with reduced crime **problems**.

- Improved home security measures lead to a reduction in the number of domestic burglaries. Prior to improvements, most burglaries occurred whilst homes were unoccupied but there are now a smaller number of violent forced entries to occupied homes.

- Improved home security measures reduce thefts of property from homes but some of this activity is displaced into increased street robberies.

- Do-it-yourself home security improvements reduce burglary rates amongst the more affluent who can afford the cost but some of this activity is displaced to the homes of poorer residents who cannot afford improvements and are not insured against losses.

If crime prevention initiatives are intended to make crime less of a problem for victimised communities, it seems clear that they need to consider the impact that different incidents have on victims. This means paying attention to changes in all categories of offence (even if the project is concerned with preventing only one type of crime) and collecting better information on the precise nature of the incidents and the circumstances of the victims.

Studies at one point in time

A great deal of what has been said about the relationship between crime and social and environmental factors has been based on studies involving the collecting of information from different estates or neighbourhoods **at one point in time** in order to discover factors which account for their differing crime rates. Studies may seek to show, for instance, that estates with walkways have higher crime rates than those which do not and that there are no other factors which could account for the difference in crime rates. These kinds of studies go on to make claims that, because the absence or presence of a particular feature in a neighbourhood is associated with levels of crime, its addition to or removal from a neighbourhood will induce changes in crime levels. This is an imaginative leap rather than a logical one. As such studies do not measure changes over time, they are not able to separate cause from effect. Mayhew (1984) illustrates this by pointing out that, for instance, households with burglar alarms are likely to have higher rates of victimisation than those without because installing a burglar alarm is often a response to victimisation. A study of this kind might falsely conclude that burglar alarms encourage burglary.

To be persuasive, such studies also have to convince us that there are no socio-demographic or other differences between estates or neighbourhoods, other than the salient factor, which could account for differing crime rates. This is a difficult task. Controlling for these other factors requires a great deal of information on the populations concerned, information which is rarely readily available and, even if it is obtained through detailed investigation, questions will always remain over whether some important factor has been missed. And researchers do not always provide the detail needed for others to make a judgement on their studies. Newman and Frank (1982), for instance, in their study of the effects of building design on crime, make no mention of how the sample of blocks was selected.

Hope and Dowds (1987) argue strongly against the use of these kinds of studies in neighbourhood-based evaluation research and also draw attention to the problem of *systematic variation* or, more plainly, running out of numbers. Hope and Dowds note the difficulty of, for instance, evaluating the effect of high rise dwellings on crime after controlling for socio-economic factors. There is such a close relationship between these factors and dwelling type (ie those living in houses and low rise dwellings tend to be economically better off and those living in high rise dwellings less well off), that there are too few cases of better off people living in high rise to make any meaningful comparisons. Hope and Dowds are dismissive of attempts to deal with this systematic bias through large samples - too costly and generally inappropriate to neighbourhood-based evaluation, or through representative designs (over-sampling to increase the number of cases) - too dependent on readily available indicators which subsequent data collection may show as inaccurate.

Before and after studies

The *before and after* study, the most commonly used research design, is one in which an area is selected and measures taken both before and after the introduction of an initiative. The main feature of this method of research is that a population is compared against itself over time.

The simplest form involves tests on a single neighbourhood without any attempt to collect data on other neighbourhoods for *control* purposes. The widespread use of this method is illustrated by Lurigio and Rosenbaum's (1986) review of 111 citizen-based crime prevention programmes, which found that 92% collected their data through this methodology.

There are a number of problems with these kinds of studies. Where sample surveys are used to measure change, different samples are taken for their before and after studies - and differences in sample characteristics may account for any apparent change. Some problems can be overcome by adding control neighbourhoods to the design, but difficulties remain. Hope and Dowds (1987) review three British evaluations involving surveys to illustrate some of these difficulties: an evaluation of a crime prevention project on an estate in Widnes (Hedges, Blaber and Mostyn, 1980), a study of the installation of security devices on an estate in Newcastle with a high burglary rate (Allatt, 1984a; 1984b) and an evaluation of Neighbourhood Watch schemes in two areas of London (Bennett, 1987). They highlighted the following methodological differences:

Panel and cross-sectional designs

Allatt used a panel design for her before and after surveys ie she attempted to interview the same people at both surveys. The advantage of panel surveys is that changes in victimisation rates cannot be put down to differences between the two samples. They are also more sensitive to marginal changes. For instance, the evaluation of the Seattle Programme (Lindsay and McGillis, 1986) found that, although there was only a small overall reduction in burglary rates in the programme area, greater reductions were experienced by active participants in the Neighbourhood Watch type scheme than non-participants. Cross-sectional designs employed by Hedges et al. and Bennett did not yield this level of sensitivity, although Bennett could have used a panel element if he had chosen to as he attempted a 100% census at two points in time.

The main disadvantage of panel surveys is *attrition* - the likely fall in response rate second time round because not all those interviewed first time round will still be available for interview. The main worry is that some residents may have moved away because of their crime experiences and that this might account for reduced levels of victimisation.

Hope and Dowds conclude that 'there are both advantages and disadvantages to each type of sample and perhaps the most useful design would be to incorporate a panel element within a cross-sectional design'.

Monitoring the implementation

All three studies monitored the project implementation to a certain extent. Allatt found that there had been delays in fitting security devices and quality control problems which could go some of the way towards explaining disappointing results. Hedges et al. delayed their *post test* survey by one year because progress monitoring revealed that further time was required for full implementation. Bennett recorded details of, for example, the timing and content of Neighbourhood Watch meetings and when street signs were erected.

The need to describe progress on implementation is often neglected but is crucial, not only so that others can replicate the programme if it successful but also because of the need to distinguish between implementation failure and theory (or concept) failure. Too often, assumptions are made in before and after studies that the programme was implemented as originally intended and without significant delays and quality control problems.

Monitoring outside influences

Both Allatt and Hedges et al. were aware of the need to take account of external factors which could influence the outcomes of their studies. Allatt, for instance, noted the introduction of two new initiatives which could have affected the outcome of her study: a community policing project on the target estate and an estate based housing management project on the control estate.

Response bias

Bennett's surveys suffered higher rates of non-response than was the case for Allatt or Hedges et al. and were more open to non-response bias. None of the studies looked at the nature of the non-response in the first round of surveys to try to find out whether, for instance, non-responders were refusing to open their doors because they had been victimised and were fearful of it happening again. Bennett did attempt to deal with differences between response bias in the two round of interviews by matching on variables such as home ownership and employment.

Theory testing

Whether a project was successful or not, it is valuable to know how and why it worked or did not work. To do this, it is important to have developed some theoretical framework against which the outcomes can be tested.

Hedges et al. were concerned to find out why certain aspects of their project did or did not work in the context of their clearly stated theory that 'if people have a sense of belonging and responsibility for the place in which they live, they will want to look after it and improve it'. They did not use surveys for this purpose, although they could have, but relied on qualitative impressions from meetings with residents and agencies and their own observations of local conditions.

If surveys are to be used in explanation, there need to be appropriate questions on the questionnaire. Bennett gave priority to questions required to clarify and count crimes and gave little room to other topics on the questionnaire. The study was therefore limited in what it could be said about changes apart from crime, although one additional outcome theory - that Neighbourhood Watch would reduce fear of crime - was clearly tested.

Allatt, on the other hand, had little to offer in terms of a hypothesis for the unanticipated outcome of her study - a significant reduction in the fear of crime on the target estate despite no change in the burglary rate.

Table 4   **Summary of three British evaluation studies**

	Allatt (1984)	Bennett (1987)	Hedges et al. (1980)
Used crime surveys	Yes	Yes	Yes
Used police figures	Yes	Yes	Yes
Type of sample	Panel	Cross section	Cross section
Monitored the implementation	Yes (crudely)	Yes	Yes
Used control groups	Yes	Yes	Not for survey
Monitored for outside influences	Yes	No	Yes
Adjusted for non-response	No	Partly	No
Theory testing	No	Yes	Yes
Wave 1 response rate	85%	69% (55%*)	84%
Wave 2 response rate	60% (of 85%)	65% (59%*)	81%

*   Percentages after matching for non-response
Source: Hope and Dowds (1987), Table 2

Some practical issues

Apart from the methodological difficulties, there are some practical obstacles to a thorough and considered assessment of what has been undertaken in the housing-related crime prevention field. First of all, much of what is happening in this field is not recorded or described and is, therefore, not accessible for investigation purposes. Secondly, there is little commitment to and no generally accepted approach to evaluation, which means that sometimes very different kinds of evidence are presented in a wide variety of forms.

We have no real idea of how many physical security schemes, design-led schemes or any other sort of schemes there are. We do not know how many have been evaluated. We may be able to get an idea of the scale of the activity by piecing together information from a range of sources. The Home Office carried out a survey of local authority and police initiated crime prevention projects in 1984 (Home Office, 1985), although it only secured responses from 44 local authorities.

A crime prevention *research sweep* of University departments, research bodies, government departments and the local government associations was carried out by the Department of the Environment in 1988. The purpose of the *sweep* was to identify examples of research being undertaken in the crime prevention field relevant to broad DoE interests. 32 questionnaires were completed, but these identified only nine residentially based schemes.

66 local authorities gave examples of initiatives in a Safe Neighbourhoods Unit survey in 1990 (Osborn and Shaftoe, 1991) of all local authorities in England and Wales, but most had not been written up in any form. Only a small proportion of the responses from both surveys referred to residentially based schemes. We know something of the scale of crime prevention related funding from Estate Action and Urban Programme sources (where crime prevention is one of the criteria) and some detail about Estate Action schemes will appear shortly (see *Department of the Environment Estate Action Handbook of Estate Improvement*, Volume 2, 1991). The Home Office recently published examples of 27 *model* crime prevention schemes (Home Office, 1990), most of which were gleaned from other published sources rather than from any new investigation and few of which related to residential-based initiatives or even mentioned evaluation.

Initiatives are carried out by a large number of different organisations using a wide variety of funding sources so, what information there is, tends to be held in different places and for different purposes. What appears to be missing is a clearing house facility for collating information on crime prevention initiatives. Some might argue that this should be the function of the Home Office Crime Prevention Unit or the Home Office Crime Prevention Centre and that resources should be made available for this purpose. However, the Centre, for instance, keeps no records of evaluated security schemes, despite the fact that it is responsible for disseminating good practice and providing training on physical security measures.

The situation is somewhat different in the United States. Documentation of crime prevention initiatives is more common, and greater attention has been paid to the way initiatives are evaluated. In the community crime prevention field, for instance, a great deal of information is available on the nature of schemes and the techniques used to measure their outcome. Yin (1986), for example, describes in some detail the outcomes of 11 evaluation studies (see Table 5 overleaf). Yin's assessments are investigated in detail in Chapter Four (p.99).

An attempt has been made to establish an international clearing-house through the International Crime Prevention Network (ICPIN) but this, so far, provides few examples of British initiatives in this field.

A paper presented to the 1991 British Criminology Conference by Barry Poyner (1991) cites 122 evaluation studies of crime prevention projects, mainly from Britain and the United States but does not describe the initiatives. The paper attempts to categorise initiatives and come to some conclusions about the effectiveness of various approaches.

Table 5 **Summary of 11 evaluation studies**

Study authors	Intervention sites and period	Type of crime addressed	Description of intervention	Types of outcomes examined	Nature of outcomes	Analytic criteria used to test outcomes
Fowler & Mangione	Hartford, Connecticut, 1973-1979	Residential	*Hartford Project*: physical redesign, police redeployment and community organising	Informal social control; burglary and robbery victimisation rates; fear of crime	Crime reduction when whole intervention in place	Statistical significance
Lavrakas	Evanston, Illinois, 1981 Houston, Texas, 1983 Newark, New Jersey, 1983	Residential	*Crime Newsletters*: distribution of community newsletters in target neighbourhoods	Awareness of newsletter; perceived crime problem; fear of crime	Positive changes at one of three sites	Statistical significance
Lavrakas & Kushmuk	Portland, Oregon, 1974-1975	Commercial	*Portland Project*: physical redesign, police assistance and business organising	Reported burglaries; fear of crime; quality of life	Burglary reduction	Statistical significance
Lindsay & McGillis	Seattle, Washington, 1974-1980	Residential	*Seattle Community Crime Prevention Program*: block watch, security inspections and property engraving	Burglary victimisation rate	Burglary reduction	Statistical significance
O'Keefe	Nationwide campaign, 1979	Residential	*McGruff National Media Campaign*: information used in mass media and in pamphlets	Awareness of announcements; reported learning; reported preventive actions	Reported learning and actions increase	Data in supplemental report
Pate	Newark, New Jersey, 1973-1979	Residential	*Newark Foot Patrol*: foot patrols from 4pm to midnight	Reported crime victimisation rates; perceived crime, safety and satisfaction with police	No crime reduction; changed perceptions	Statistical significance
Rosenbaum et al	Chicago, Illinois, 1983-84	Residential	*Urban Crime Prevention Programme*: block watches and related neighbourhood meetings	Victimisation rates; perceived crime; fear of crime; perceived efficacy; social disorder; physical deterioration	Crime reduction at only one of four sites; increases at others	Statistical significance
Schneider	Portland, Oregon, 1973-74	Residential	*Portland Anti-Burglary Program*: street lighting, property engraving and community education.	Reported burglaries; victimisation rates	Burglary reduction	Statistical significance
Tien & Cahn	Denver, Colorado, 1981 Long Beach, California, 1981 St Louis, Missouri, 1981	Commercial	*Commercial Security Field Test*: security surveys undertaken by business proprietors	Burglary victimisation rates; fear of crime	Burglary reduction at one of three sites	Statistical significance
Trojanowicz	Flint, Michigan, 1979-82	Residential	*Neighbourhood Foot Patrol*: foot patrol and community organising	Reported crime; satisfaction with police	Crime reduction; increase in satisfaction	Descriptive data only
Wycoff & Skogan	Houston, Texas, 1983-84	Residential	*Storefront Police Office*: location of storefront office, staffed by police, in local neighbourhood	Fear of crime; perceived crime, safety and satisfaction with police	Fear reduction; improved perceptions	Statistical significance

The lack of consistency in approach to collecting evidence is not surprising given the low priority given to evaluation in this country. Limited resources are dedicated to programme evaluation. It is interesting to note, for instance, that the substantial programme of housing estate crime prevention projects initiated by NACRO in the early 1980s, which also served as a model for a large number of projects run by other organisations, was built on just one evaluated project (Hedges et al., 1980). NACRO had no difficulty in securing funds from a wide variety of sources to develop these projects but was unable to secure the resources to replicate (and thus confirm the results of) its first evaluation. Most of NACRO's subsequent *evaluations* had to rely, therefore, on obtaining cheaply gathered information such as recorded crime statistics (where the costs of collection are borne by the criminal justice system). A review of the effectiveness of the NACRO initiatives in the 1980s was carried out by the Tavistock Institute (Poyner, Webb and Woodall, 1986). However, the adequacy of the evaluation itself has been called into question. For example, NACRO pointed out that the Poyner et al. study failed to understand or to accurately represent the nature of NACRO's work and did not fully consider the possible effects of these initiatives on offences, such as criminal damage and racial harassment, which tend to be under-reported.

Problems also stem from an absence of dedicated programmes. There are few resources specifically set aside by Government for funding community-based crime prevention initiatives. The Home Office's Safer Cities Programme, as the title signifies, is principally directed at 'the creation of safer cities in which economic enterprise and community life can flourish' although, within its broad remit, it does provide funds for specific estate or neighbourhood-based initiatives. Given their remit, individual Safer Cities Projects have only a relatively small amount of funding at their disposal - £250,000 per annum - an amount which can easily be spent on tackling the problems of a single tower block.

In order to pursue crime prevention initiatives, many agencies have had to rely on *programme bending* - using programmes principally directed towards other objectives. The best example of this has been the widespread use of Government employment and training schemes for the long-term unemployed. For example, the Home Office Five Towns Initiative* (Home Office, 1989) relied on the (now defunct) Community Programme to fund local crime prevention projects, as did many local authorities and police forces. Whilst there is a commitment to monitoring and evaluation in these Government programmes, the outcome measures of interest are those which relate to their principal objectives and not those of the *programme-benders*. And initiatives can quickly peter out before there is an opportunity for evaluation if programme criteria change and do not accommodate what the programme is *additionally* being used for.

Of course, crime prevention initiatives can more easily be accommodated in some other Government programmes: the Urban Programme and Estate Action for example. But here too, crime prevention as an outcome measure is inevitably subsidiary to outcome measures related to their principal objectives.

---

* A retrospective study of the Five Towns Initiative has been undertaken for the Home Office by the Cambridge Institute of Criminology. Although not yet published, the report indicates that some significant crime reductions did occur on project estates but that there were real uncertainties over interpreting the results. For example, the results of the North Tyneside project, most often cited as leading to crime reductions, are confused by the Council's prior and unrelated decision to demolish the problematic tower blocks in one of the areas (Killingworth) cover the project. It seems clear that, if evaluation had been built into the initiative from the start, the task of assessing the impact of projects would have been less difficult.

More thought appears to have gone into the planning of evaluations in the United States. This may be because there have been more programmes specifically dedicated to community based crime prevention, initiated by both Government and by private bodies such as the Eisenhower Foundation. That is not to say that the same inconsistencies in approach have not emerged in the United States. Curtis (1990) notes that 'some initiatives even claim success based on whether the public merely recognises their presence, not on whether they actually reduce crime and drugs'. In his review of a decade of the Eisenhower Foundation's national demonstration programme, he is critical of some of the evaluations sponsored by the Foundation in the past and goes on to set out a structure for information collection which will form the basis of future evaluations. In particular, Curtis advocates the following:

- Making use of community survey supplied information on crime;

- Collecting *process* information on day-to-day implementation;

- Using a *case study* format for writing up initiatives;

- Allowing a minimum of 36 months for evaluation;

- Collecting data on control groups/areas;

- Making use of qualitative, street-level observations and judgements;

- Involving practitioners in the design of surveys and evaluations.

In particular he calls for evaluators to 'play less the role of experts and more the role of collaborators in the future'.

Developing the assessment criteria

The methodological and practical issues we have raised provide the context for developing a set of criteria against which to assess the crime prevention initiatives described in this report. A number of different questions need to be asked about the initiatives. Not only do we want to know whether the incidence and impact of crime was reduced, and whether the initiatives (or elements of the initiatives) were responsible, we also want to know if the effect will last and if the lessons learned are generalisable. Not all these questions will be answerable and, as will be seen, many of the initiatives we describe in the next chapter do not even show convincingly that the incidence of crime was reduced.

Did crime go down?

There are different ways of measuring crime reduction and none is entirely satisfactory. As we have seen, recorded crime statistics only *capture* about one third of the crimes reported in victimisation surveys (and an even lower proportion of some crimes) and at least some of the fluctuations in crime rates assessed in this way are explainable in terms of changes in public reporting and police recording practices. On the other hand, recorded crime statistics may be the only way of capturing crime data retrospectively (which is necessary if an evaluation is planned after a project starts) and obtaining data not available from other sources (such as crimes against visitors to the study area). Recorded crime statistics also provide an opportunity for continuous monitoring which may help with the process of interpreting the impact of different measures. We return to this issue later.

Notwithstanding the difficulties, there may be a case for believing recorded crime statistics where reductions are very large, both numerically and proportionately, on the grounds that such reductions are unlikely to be explained away by reporting and recording artefacts. However, there can be no precise guide to what constitutes a very large reduction in crime. It may be obvious in a few cases, but there are likely to be many more cases where it is far less clear.

For many evaluators, the use of surveys of residents represents an answer to the difficulties of measurement through recorded crime statistics. Surveys are able to capture crimes not reported to the police. If *before and after* surveys include a *panel* element - with a proportion of the *before* sample being interviewed again - then many of the difficulties of controlling for differences between the samples are removed. However, difficulties remain. Surveys rely on the respondent's memory which will often be rather imprecise. They usually fail to pick up on crimes committed against non-residents. They may produce misleading results if respondents and non-respondents differ markedly in victimisation rates (and the findings are not *weighted* to take this into account) or if any difference between non-respondents at two points in time are not controlled for. And the different ways in which incidents tend to be counted may artificially boost the incidence of one-off crimes such as domestic burglary and theft (where every incident is counted) at the expense of on-going crimes such as domestic violence or systematic harassment (where several discrete incidents may be amalgamated for counting purposes).

In general, a combination of recorded crime statistics and survey data appears to be the minimum required to judge whether crime has gone down in the study area. The two measurement tools are able to compensate, to some extent, for their individual inadequacies. Where both point to crime reduction, and where there are no obvious sampling difficulties, it seems safe to assume that crime has in fact gone down. Where the results are contradictory, then a great deal is required of the evaluators if they wish to explain the negative findings.

Of course, survey based crime data can be obtained for groups other than residents. It may be appropriate, depending on the nature of the area, to collect information on people who work in the area: for example, local authority field staff and local businesses. Shop thefts and burglaries, in particular, may be a serious problem in residential areas.

However, it is not always possible to use survey data to measure reductions in crime. In many cases, the need for evaluation is only registered once an initiative begins to show encouraging results, by which time it is clearly impossible to mount any pre-test exercises. It is in these circumstances that the value of other data sources becomes most evident; although, inevitably, these other sources will only provide a partial or indicative measure of crime reduction.

In the housing-related crime prevention field, and particularly where public housing is under the microscope, it makes sense to utilise data held by the housing authority. The housing authority may hold data, for instance, on the incidence and cost of criminal damage to its property. A number of local authorities do have the management information systems in place to enable them to capture this kind of information, although there is little evidence that it is systematically used. For example, Nottingham City Council's housing department has a *vandalism code* on its computerised repairs logs but how little this is activated is evidenced by the trifling cost (£25,000 in 1989/90) they are able to attribute to vandalism in this way (see KPMG Peat Marwick/Safe Neighbourhoods Unit, 1990). Local authorities may also monitor incidents of domestic violence and racial harassment, crimes committed against their staff on site and thefts from local offices. This is particularly so where responding to such incidents is part of a specific management initiative.

Time spent on dealing with crime by local authority staff or staff of other organisations such as the police could, in theory, be costed and reductions in these costs over time used to support other evidence of crime reduction. Attempts have been made to determine these kinds of costs in the past, with some difficulty, and the issue is covered in more detail in Part Two of this report.

There is also a strong case for using qualitative measures of crime reduction. Views on whether crimes have reduced can be gathered from surveys or meetings with residents and from interviews with the police and other local agencies. Qualitative data provides a useful counterpoint to the usual reliance on quantitative data, although it should be used in addition to rather than as an alternative to quantitative measures.

Were crime problems reduced?

Just because the incidence of crime has been reduced in the study area, does not necessarily mean that crime is less of a problem. The impact of a smaller number of crimes could be at least as great if the incidents are more serious and/or the victims less able to cope with the effects.

Traditional methods of measurement are not particularly sensitive to this issue. Crime figures produced from police records and surveys tend to highlight overall changes in crime levels or changes in the levels of higher volume crimes such as burglary and autocrime and pay less attention to changes in levels of crimes against the person. But as practitioners are only too aware, even a small number of crimes involving violence can have a devastating effect on community life. It seems clear that changes in the incidence of low volume crimes involving violence need to be given greater weight than their numbers dictate when the impact of an initiative is assessed.

There is also a tendency for burglary figures to include attempted burglaries as well as actual burglaries. This is not always helpful. An increase in attempted (ie failed) burglaries may be an indication of the success of opportunity reduction based burglary prevention measures, if this is accompanied by a reduction in actual burglaries, rather than an indication of worsening crime problems. If reductions in actual burglaries are balanced out by increases in attempted burglaries, a successful outcome may be overlooked. This issue is generally ignored in the literature.

It is also important to ensure that survey data are able to reflect the seriousness of particular incidents rather than focusing on comparability with definitions in the criminal statistics. We might expect, therefore, that survey-based project evaluations should contain some assessment of changes in the severity of crime problems and how different groups in the community have fared.

Changes in residents' perceptions of local crime problems may also confirm that crime problems have been reduced. Survey evidence of reduced worry or concern about crime, particularly if it is accompanied by modified behaviour, is strongly supportive data. The same can be said for evidence of this kind obtained from local agencies and people who work in the area.

Was the initiative responsible for the changes?

Having ascertained that crime has fallen and that crime problems have been reduced in the study area, we still need evidence that it was the crime prevention initiative which was responsible for the changes rather than some other unconnected factor.

It may be that changes in the study area are just a reflection of more general trends in the wider locality. It may be that they reflect changes in the make up of the local population over the period of the study or unaccounted for differences between survey samples. It may be that some other, unrelated initiative introduced in the study area has had an effect. It may be that those who had been responsible for much of the local crime are now older and no longer in the peak offending age range or, more directly, that they have been arrested and are out of harm's way in penal institutions. The last point is important to bear in mind. A handful of individuals can commit a large number of crimes in a short period of time and account for a very high proportion of the crimes committed in small areas such as housing estates.

Evaluations which aim to take these factors into account need to provide the following kinds of information:

- Evidence from *control* areas that reductions in crime were not just a general feature of the locality. Ideally the same kinds of information should be obtained for the control area(s) as for the study area.

- Confirmation that, where evidence for crime changes relies on survey data, changes cannot be explained by differences in the make up of the two samples or by response rate difficulties. Adequate matching of the samples and controlling for non-response is needed. More ideally, the study might be expected to incorporate a panel element within the cross-sectional design.

- Evidence from demographic data (from surveys or the housing authority) that the make up of the population has not changed.

- Evidence from descriptive accounts of the implementation of the initiative (including details of other initiatives and policy changes happening at the same time) that external factors are unlikely to have accounted for the changes.

Which specific measure led to the changes?

One dimensional initiatives are rare and, in practice, may be impossible to achieve. Even where initiatives are conceived of as being limited to a single, discreet and uncomplicated measure (say, the fitting of security hardware to dwelling doors or windows), there are often unintended by-products such as improved liaison between the police and local residents or a closer working relationship between the police and housing authority. These may have an influence on crime in their own right or may lead to other measures being introduced.

Many initiatives are conceived of as being multi-dimensional or are inevitably so from the very beginning. It seems obvious, for instance, that management and other changes will have to accompany major design changes on estates. Re-modelling of block entrances, alterations to pedestrian routes and to road layouts and redesignation of public and private spaces will inevitably affect maintenance, caretaking and housing management arrangements and may also require modifications to security arrangements.

Some might argue that it is a pointless exercise to attempt to identify which specific measures were responsible for crime changes because there is no way of adequately separating out their effects. In most cases this is likely to be true, if only because of the absence of information about when and how individual measures were introduced.

However, it is sometimes possible to draw conclusions about the effects of individual measures, particularly where measures have been introduced **at different time points**. Recorded crime statistics allow for continuous monitoring of crime figures on a weekly or monthly basis. Data held by other agencies, and particularly by housing authorities, may afford a similar continuous monitoring facility. For instance, information on repair costs attributable to vandalism may be accessible on a weekly or monthly basis. Through analysis of these kinds of data, it may be possible to discount measures which were introduced after crime reductions took place and could not, therefore, account for them; although it may be that the measures introduced at a later stage were responsible for maintaining crime at the lower level once the initial crime reduction had been achieved and that they are therefore an essential element of the overall crime prevention package.

To begin to get some idea of the relative impact of different measures, the implementation needs to be closely monitored and well-documented. There is no point in undertaking continuous monitoring of crime-related data, if we do not know when measures came on stream and whether they were introduced properly. It could be, for instance, that the phone entry system was theoretically designated as operational on a specific date but in practice, because of early system failure, was not operational until much later, if at all.

Does the effect last?

A large number of claims about the success of initiatives are based on evidence collected not long after the implementation of the measures. And yet we know from experience that many improvements do not survive. A case in point is the Priority Estates Project on the Tulse Hill Estate in Lambeth, where dramatic improvements were evident during the course of the three year project but the estate reverted to pre-improvement conditions within a year of the project finishing.

It may be inevitable that many of the initiatives set up in run down areas with multiple disadvantage only secure improvements in the short term. It could be argued that most initiatives do not, or cannot, tackle the underlying causes of the problems these areas suffer - poverty, poor education, ill-health and so on. Whilst it may be possible to ameliorate some of these problems and manage the situation in the short term, by the concentration of attention and resources which projects allow, in the long run the focus has to move elsewhere - to some other area in need. We return to the issue of why projects may fail in the long-run at the end of the report (p.164).

Clearly, a reasonable amount of time needs to have elapsed after the introduction of a measure before a proper assessment of its effect can be made. What constitutes a reasonable time period is difficult to gauge. Measures of effect taken after a few months (as some are) do not provide acceptable evidence of success, although they do provide encouragement for further evaluation at the right time. One might expect that at least one year should have elapsed before an evaluation is carried out. As we have seen, Curtis (1990) advocates a three year follow-up period as the standard for evaluations. However, there can be no hard and fast rules about this, not least because policy makers are not always in a position to wait around before having to make decisions about where to focus resources. The length of follow-up period is an important contextual issue when it comes to assessing the quality of the evidence on the success of initiatives, and should be brought into play when judgements are made about that evidence.

Is the initiative replicable or generalisable?

We need to know from the evidence presented about particular initiatives whether the lessons learnt are applicable in other situations. There are two key issues:

- *Circumstances*

  Are the circumstances in which the initiative was mounted unique or unusual and, therefore, unlikely to be reproduced elsewhere? For example, does the finding that removal of coin operated gas meters was partly or wholly responsible for burglary reductions on an estate have general or even limited applicability, given the fact that most homes do not have coin operated meters any more? Similarly, is the success of an initiative so dependent on one particular individual, whose qualities are unique, that it is unlikely to prosper elsewhere?

- *Cost*

  Is the cost of the initiative so prohibitive that it is unlikely to be afforded elsewhere? Even if the cost of an initiative seems affordable, it may not be cost-effective in relation to the likely benefits. The initiative may have been introduced at a time when finance was less of a problem or costs were considerably lower. The eventual cost of the initiative may have been far greater than had been originally envisaged, meaning that the initiative would not have been mounted if this had been known. This is particularly a concern with regard to expensive redesign measures where decisions to proceed have to be balanced against the benefits of other options such as demolition and rebuilding. However, whilst it may be relatively easy to identify the capital programme costs of initiatives, it is often more difficult to attribute any revenue costs. Any savings accruing from the initiative should ideally be set against the costs, but these kinds of cost benefit exercises are difficult to mount and rarely delivered.

A structure for assessment

On the basis of the previous discussion of the issues involved in developing assessment criteria, the following assessment structure is proposed for judging the evidence presented in this report.

Evidence of reduced crime problems

We are interested in evidence of reduced incidence of crime and confirmation that fewer crimes means a reduced problem. This evidence may be presented in a variety of forms:

- *Subjective assessments* - by those involved in the initiative or by outside *assessors*, clearly not acceptable as evidence except as supporting data.

- *Recorded crime statistics* - which need to be supported by other crime-related data, except (with caution) where the *size of reduction* is judged to outweigh reservations about reporting and recording artefacts. These statistics should ideally show *reductions for all relevant offence categories*.

- *Crime survey data* - which are best looked at in conjunction with recorded crime statistics. These should also indicate *changes in the severity of crime* and *the variable impact on different groups* in the community. Where appropriate, they should also record effects on *local businesses* and *local staff* as well as *residents*.

- *Cost of crime data* - which is likely to provide only partial data (for example, on criminal damage costs), needs to be supported by other data, but may be a crucial measure of outcome for funders.

- *Qualitative data* - from surveys and meetings, on *concern about or fear of crime*, particularly where changes in perceptions are backed up by *changes in behaviour*. Again this data needs to be supported by other crime related data.

- *Other data on crime* - where *particular offences* (for example, domestic violence, racial harassment) are being monitored as part of a local management initiative. These will generally need to be heavily qualified as there is unlikely to be supportive data.

Evidence of initiative's effect	We are interested in evidence that the initiative was responsible for the reduction in crime problems rather than some other external factor. Ideally, all of the evidence below should be available.

- *Control group data* - from the wider locality or from a control estate/neighbourhood, to show that reductions in crime problems were not just part of a local trend.

- *Demographic data* - from surveys or agency statistics, to show that reductions in crime problems were not due to changes in the make up of the population.

- *Sampling data* - where surveys are carried out, to show whether surveys were *cross-sectional* or *panel* or both, and to show that *adequate matching of samples* and *controlling for non-response* was undertaken.

- *Descriptive accounts of implementation* - to show that no external factors could account for reductions in crime problems.

- *Significance testing* - to show that the effect did not occur by chance and particularly to take account of the wide variation in population and sample sizes.

Evidence of effect of individual measures	We are interested in evidence that any individual measure(s), within the overall package, accounted for the reductions in crime problems.

- *Continuous monitoring data* - from recorded crime statistics or other recorded data, to show more clearly when crime reductions took place.

- *Descriptive accounts of implementation* - to show when and how particular measures were implemented, to be used in conjunction with above.

Evidence of permanence	We are interested in evidence to show that the improvements will not be short-lived.

- *Follow-up period* - needs to be a *minimum of 12 months* to provide an *adequate period for data collection* and *ideally 36 months or more to indicate some permanence*.

Evidence of replicability	We need to know whether there are any features of the initiative which reduce its potential for implementation elsewhere.

- *Descriptive accounts of implementation* - should indicate whether there are any special local circumstances which may not be found elsewhere.

- *Details of capital and revenue costs* - with *cost benefit evidence* if available, should provide guidance on its general applicability.

Chapter 3   Theory into practice

This chapter attempts to provide a comprehensive description of the housing-related crime prevention field, focusing on British experience but, where relevant, drawing on material from North America and Europe. Information was obtained from published reports and from various forms of unpublished material such as council committee papers and material directly solicited for the purposes of this report.

The foregoing chapter *Assessing the Evidence* provided a framework for our commentary on the material in this chapter. However, this chapter is essentially descriptive and a more thorough assessment of the initiatives described here is provided in the following chapter *Reviewing the Evidence*.

The material has been assembled into five categories on the basis of what appeared to be the major focus in preventing crime in residential areas:

    A.   Design-led initiatives

    B.   Management-led initiatives

    C.   Security-led initiatives

    D.   Social development-led initiatives

    E.   Policing-led initiatives

It was not always easy to place initiatives in an appropriate category as, notwithstanding how they were originally conceived or continue to be described, many have adopted a multi-pronged approach in practice.

A great deal has been written about the relationship between design and crime. This chapter is a necessarily selective review of the literature, focused primarily on the investigation of examples of design-led initiatives. More extensive literature reviews have been produced by other authors - for example, by Poyner (1982) and Bannister (1991).

Design-led crime prevention has been described as *creative demolition* on the basis that, once executed, design changes are invariably permanent. For this reason it might be expected that practitioners and policy makers would be slow to pursue expensive design changes. Paradoxically, there are many examples of practitioners wholeheartedly embracing the notion of designing out crime.

Research on the relationship between design and crime is rooted in ideological assumptions and has often led to tentative conclusions with numerous qualifications attached. Unfortunately, when practitioners are considering design changes on estates or in areas with high crime levels, the assumptions and qualifications are often forgotten. Publicity can turn specific research conclusions into an accepted *common sense* quite removed from a single study or drawing from a number of different, if not contradictory, theories.

One particular problem in comparing research conclusions is that researchers may concentrate on one particular crime and ignore others. And yet the implications of design changes for each crime may be utterly different. Design changes which aim to eliminate one form of crime, such as burglary, may make people feel more vulnerable to another crime, such as assault. For example, limiting access to through-block routes on estates may force people to use potentially more threatening areas such as ground level car parking areas, which are often not designed as pedestrian routes.

In this chapter we will try to separate out the main strands of thinking about the link between design and crime. In order to simplify as far as possible we will concentrate on areas of difference between approaches rather than areas of overlap. We will examine the main facets of each theory in turn and try to assess the evidence when they have been used in practical neighbourhood and estate projects. It will become clear that most projects draw from a number of theoretical approaches rather than just one and very few projects have been seriously evaluated.

Defensible space: encouraging public vigilance and surveillance to prevent crime

This theory, which makes a causal link between design and crime was first expounded in America by Jane Jacobs (1961) and popularised by Oscar Newman (1972).

Newman's theories concern the way in which design can nurture people's crime prevention inclinations. By studying the New York City Authority's crime records and the design of residential areas, he identified statistical correlations between design features and crime. Newman then translated his findings into four principles (1976):

- Territoriality, the capacity of the physical environment to create a feeling of neighbourhood and encourage residents to exercise surveillance over the area of *defensible space;*

- Surveillance, the capacity of physical design to enable residents to casually and continually survey a public area;

- Image, the capacity of design to improve building image and avoid stigma;

- Environment, the influence of a neighbourhood's geographical juxtaposition with *safe* or *unsafe* areas.

Newman went on to prescribe design changes or features that would reduce a housing estate's vulnerability to crime. These were:

- Reduce the size of a housing estate or block;

- Reduce the number of people (dwellings) sharing an entrance way to reduce the level of anonymity;

- Reduce the number of storeys in a block;

- Group dwellings to encourage social contact;

- Minimise the degree of shared public space inside and near blocks;

- Make the boundaries between public and private space very clear so that an intruder feels conspicuous;

- Make public areas clearly visible to nearby housing so that residents can see intruders;

- Use external rather than internal corridors in blocks of housing so that they are visible;

- Make entrances flush with the street rather than set back;

- Do not have entrances facing away from the street as they are not open to surveillance;

- Landscaping and vegetation which impedes surveillance should be avoided;

- All open spaces should be assigned to and overlooked by adjacent housing;

- Reduce escape routes for criminals such as interaccessible lifts, staircases and exits.

These design features are assumed to act on the behaviour of residents and/or the behaviour of potential offenders.

As identified by Jenks (1987), there are inherent pitfalls in translating a research example into a model in this way:

> Once turned into that epitome of certainty, a standard or guideline, the rationale, the reasoning and the careful qualifications tend to get lost.

Newman's methodology was challenged by others in the field. Further research on other comparable projects within the same area did not find the same strength of correlation (Kaplan, 1973). It was also felt that Newman's theory was based on the premise that crime is committed by outsiders rather than people living within the same block and, as Adams states, 'it must be recognised that residents of public housing often victimise their own neighbourhoods' (1973). Mayhew (1979) and Taylor et al. (1980), both question the notion of *defensibility* of space and point to a sense of community as a more likely reason than building form for residents to engage in active surveillance. Smith (1987) points to the practical difficulty of surveillance as a means of observing and preventing crime.

Wilson (1978) found that the correlation between child density and the incidence of crime was stronger than that found between design and crime. Research by criminologists posed Newman's questions from a different perspective. What do criminals say discourages them from committing crimes in an area? Do residents know what they are looking out for or what to do with the information they get from surveillance? Bennet and Wright (1984) found that, when interviewed, burglars said that surveillance and occupancy were the most important considerations in their choice of target. Shapland and Vagg (1988) pointed out that residents may be unwilling to use the information gathered by their surveillance due to lack of guidance or a clear decision not to co-operate with policing authorities.

Newman later modified many of his claims about the link between crime and environment and began to emphasise the role of tenant participation and good management. However, there were researchers on this side of the Atlantic who took up the principles and extended them.

Poyner (1983) in the UK did more work on boundaries between private and public space. He suggests using clear barriers or a narrowed access to create a symbolic gateway to a non-public area. He advocates the grouping of housing closer together with restricted vehicular movement. He also lays great stress on residents having *a community of interest* through being a fairly homogeneous group.

The following descriptions of design-led initiatives in Britain illustrate the approach to crime prevention.

Stockbridge Village, Knowsley

A recent publication (1989) by the Institute of Housing (IoH) and the Royal Institute of British Architects (RIBA) assesses five design-led crime prevention projects. Unfortunately, assessment is based on the subjective judgement of one architect who visited each project and selective presentation of recorded crime statistics.

One estate assessed is Stockbridge Village in Knowsley, an estate of some 3,000 dwellings. It experienced a high crime level in the early 1980s and a general lack of community cohesion. The Stockbridge Village Trust, part of the government's Merseyside initiative, took over the estate in 1983. Recorded burglaries fell from 458 in 1984 to 205 in 1988 but thefts from and of cars rose.

Built in the early 1960s, the estate had low, medium and high rise housing. By using a combination of private and public funding the Trust began to improve the estate along what appear to be (although it is not stated) Newman principles. Changes included the following:

- *The maisonette blocks were demolished (reducing size of the estate);*

- *The low rise housing was redesigned to produce closes of houses with car parking at the front of each house. Houses that were in terraces were turned back to front so that entrance doors face a common close. Extra houses have been built at the hammerhead of the cul-de-sac to complete the enclosure. The closes are described by the working party as allowing surveillance and defensible space.*

- *The **labyrinth of pedestrian paths** which may have been seen as providing a surfeit of escape routes was reduced;*

- Some of the paths used to go under first floor bedrooms built to bridge the paths. It was felt that because these areas were hidden, they encouraged gangs of youths to congregate. The paths were bounded by one high and one low fence to allow both privacy and surveillance;

- Underpasses were filled in because they were not open to surveillance.

A number of additional initiatives were developed in parallel with these design changes:

- The backlog of jobbing repairs was dealt with by the Trust when it took over the management of the estate;

- The high rise tower blocks have been provided with additional physical security measures and concierges;

- Homewatch schemes were started in a number of areas;

- Extensive consultations with tenants were carried out by the Trust on its predetermined plans;

- A new shopping parade with security guards was opened.

No mention is made of the effect of the scheme on fear of crime, although it is stated that the estate is now more popular with residents and potential residents. However, it was found that houses which were planned for shared ownership were difficult to sell and, remaining empty, they became vandalised.

Source: Institute of Housing and Royal Institute of British Architects, 1989

Woodchurch Estate, Wirral

A second case study in the same working party's report is the Woodchurch Estate on the Wirral, a post-war estate. It contains houses with gardens and an additional development in the centre, comprising seven four-storey maisonettes, two 14-storey high rise blocks and a parade of shops - all of which were added in the 1950s and 1960s. There are more than 3,500 dwellings in all.

High crime rates in the late 1970s and early 1980s contributed to the Council's decision in 1983 to refurbish the central area of the estate. The crime rate then dropped over a period of three years. The number of burglaries reached a peak of 570 in 1983, but dropped back to 264 in 1986. By the time the case study visit was made in 1989, the number of burglaries had increased again to around 400 and there had been unspecified increases in thefts from cars.

Changes, which appear to be based on Newman principles, include:

- The five-storey flat and maisonette blocks were demolished, reducing the size of the estate;

- The number of storeys in the maisonette blocks was reduced from four to two by demolishing the top floors and making terraces of two-storey houses.

The working party notes that all tenants were rehoused and many bought the houses they moved into but, 'On the debit side we were told of the local disruption that some of the original tenants had caused in areas where they had been rehoused and we saw for ourselves that the initial assessment of the value of the two-storey housing project had proved optimistic':

- The layout of the low rise housing was redesigned and 'the rearrangement of roads, footpaths, dwellings and fences created small domestic closes with between 15 and 32 dwellings in each. Car parking is in front of the dwellings, the space behind is enclosed as private gardens.' The working *party found that the 'arrangement had been effective ... However, during the last year (1988), there had been problems. Security arrangements were no longer effective. Where houses were empty the weakness of the layout was becoming apparent.'*

At the same time, construction defects affecting a number of properties were corrected. At the time of the improvement project, some of the houses were for sale. Due to a prices slump, a rise in interest rates and re-possession from mortgage defaulters, about half of the houses were empty and subject to extensive vandalism. The tower blocks had had security measures installed, together with concierges. They had been refurbished and, in line with the growing practice of selective allocations, they were only let to the 55+ age group. Security locks were also fitted throughout the estate with funding from the Victim Support Group. The arcade of shops was refurbished but there was continuing vandalism at the rear of the shops. This was thought to be due to the shops being on a through route and not being overlooked

Although it was thought that the above initiatives contributed to a reduction in recorded crime on the estate, there were fears that security may deteriorate due to lack of funding for further improvements and ongoing maintenance. There was evidence that recorded burglaries and thefts from cars had already started to climb sharply.

Source: Institute of Housing and Royal Institute of British Architects, 1989

Adswood Estate, Stockport

A review of design changes to this estate was outlined by Stollard et al. (1989). Unfortunately, the evidence is again anecdotal rather than empirical.

Adswood is a pre-war estate of houses. It gained a high crime rate and a poor reputation. The Director of Housing for Stockport described the solutions as follows:

- *Making the houses warm and secure;*

- *Enclosing areas around the house with walled gardens with a gate, giving the **ownership** of that space to the resident;*

- *Creating car hard-stands within gardens for cars - allowing surveillance. The intruder would have to enter this private space to commit autocrime;*

- *Changing crescents of streets into culs-de-sac. This, he said, would allow safer play for children, reduce easy escape routes for criminals and create enclosures of **privatised space**;*

- *Removing hedges to reduce hiding places, increase surveillance and increase conspicuousness of intruders.*

There was no additional information on the scheme, except that it was considered to be successful.

Source: Stollard et al., 1989

Brinnington Estate, Stockport

Brinnington Estate in Stockport has a combination of houses and three-storey flats. Between the dwellings were wide open spaces which became vandalised, dirty and unused. The area was unpopular with tenants.

The Council made a number of improvements, which included:

- *Enclosing the entire area with a w-ll;*

- *Making private garden areas adjacent to dwellings;*

38

- *Building a secure fenced children's play area that is visible from dwellings;*

- *Installing planting and landscaping.*

Community programme funded workers were employed to carry out the improvement work; most were local people, some from the estate. Front doors to all dwellings were made more secure and the properties were extensively re-painted.

*It appears that residents now identify the area as their own, as they complain when people from outside the area come in to use their facilities. They have taken **care and control**, although no monitoring of recorded crime levels has been undertaken.*

Source: Stollard et al., 1989

Environmental design: physical factors can encourage crime

The theory of crime prevention through environmental design considers the way in which the urban environment can exert an influence on crime and potential criminals. Although researchers used much of Newman's work, their philosophy sprang from a different premise. Newman saw design as a way of encouraging the public to feel protective and vigilant against criminal activity in their immediate area. Crime prevention through environmental design, say researchers such as Altman (1975) and Jeffrey (1971), sees urban design as a major factor which can promote or deter criminal activity by individuals.

The main thrust of this theory centres on design influences alone, although there are a few researchers who incorporated social factors. Gardiner (1978) and Taylor and Gottfredson (1986) saw social measures and citizen participation as part of a crime prevention strategy through environmental design.

Birenbaum (1983) identified facilities that might be seen to encourage or attract crime, which he called 'offender hangouts'. These included places like bars or drug dealing centres and he recommended their removal.

Moffat (1983) used concepts of the 'urban fortress' and 'urban village'. The former was created by *target hardening* through using physical security measures and the latter by creating small self-policing communities within cities. By combining the two concepts, citizens would be protected but not isolated.

The effect of the spatial layout on crime prevention

Crime prevention through environmental design considers the spatial patterns exhibited by groups of dwellings suffering from high crime rates. A study by Brantingham and Brantingham (1975) attempted to assess the relationship between the spatial use of land and the incidence of burglary. They concluded that, where there were groups of residential buildings, those blocks on the outside had higher burglary rates than those in the interior. They recommended that developments should minimise the number of exterior blocks by designing in squares or circles. Unfortunately, the study took no account of any other crimes, such as assault, which may be affected in a completely different way by spatial layouts.

The public use of spaces between housing units has been examined in the United States and the UK. In the United States, Angel (1968) postulated that the amount that a public area is used influences the likelihood of an individual being a victim of crime. He said that areas with very little public use would not be a target for crime as there was little chance of finding a potential victim. Areas with high public presence would also reduce the likelihood of a person becoming a victim of crime as there would be so many potential witnesses around. He identified a 'critical intensity zone' which was somewhere between the two extremes, where the level of public presence increased the likelihood of crime.

In the UK, Hillier (1987) pointed to the tendency of modern design to create 'undistinguishable and underused space'. Underused space, he said, increases the risks of personal victimisation and burglary of property. Hillier et al. (1983) use *space syntax* techniques to analyse spatial layout patterns and then converts the patterns into numerical form. The *pattern numbers* are then correlated with other pattern numbers which relate to crime rates and vandalism patterns. Another measure, 'encounter fields' (Hillier and Hanson, 1984), relates to the level of use of public space - where the encounter rate was low he found a correlation with high rates of burglary.

The following examples of design-led initiatives illustrate the approach.

Maiden Lane Estate, Camden

Built in the 1970s, all dwellings on the Maiden Lane Estate are low rise.

*The crime prevention needs of the estate are described by a representative of Hunt Thompson architects in **Safer Neighbourhoods** (Stollard et al., 1989). The report by the architects appears to follow the **urban design and deviance** school of thought pioneered by Coleman (see below), and talks of social **malaise** brought on by the design of the physical environment. A second opinion on the proposals relating to **the architecture** of the estate was later given by Hillier et al. of the Bartlett School of Architecture (1989a).*

Hunt Thompson's approach

*Hunt Thompson architects felt that because of the design there was **negative social behaviour** amongst young people. For example, the design does not allow surveillance of young people and children by adults. Children can congregate in unsupervised areas. There are numerous pedestrian networks with low **encounter rates**. Service vehicles cannot get onto the estate because the access routes are **under-designed**, which means that rubbish accumulates in pedestrian areas which look unkempt and attracts rats.*

The crime prevention through design solutions suggested by the architects included:

- *Turning dwellings around so that gardens are back to back;*

- *Removing some pedestrian alleys which some residents are fearful of using because they are not overlooked. This would also increase pedestrian density on a smaller number of paths;*

- *Individualising parking spaces and redesigning bays to make private secure garages.*

Because of the very high child density on the estate, major management, maintenance and allocation changes were also recommended. Architects suggested that the caretakers should take on a more active role in removing the rubbish to the side of the estate where it can be removed by service vehicles. It was also recommended that estate lighting should be extensively improved.

Hillier's approach

*Research by Hillier et al. re-examined the social survey carried out by Hunt Thompson with a view to identifying links between the residents' location on the estate and their attitudes and experiences. Secondly, a study of the estate was made using the **space syntax** method.*

Hillier found that levels of dissatisfaction peaked for residents living in the centre of the estate and that this could not be explained in management or social terms. Space syntax methods revealed that there was a very low level of adult movement and a very high level of child presence around the estate. There was little opportunity for the natural surveillance of children by adults.

It was also found that the centre of the estate lacked **integration** (a direct relationship between spaces or points), while the outer parts of the estate were integrated with the surrounding area. The problem was assessed as being that of a lack of clear internal structure in the estate's layout.

Solutions proposed included:

- In order to create integration with the surrounding area there needed to be routes leading to, from and through the estate into the surrounding area;

- The estate's internal roads should be remodelled to give continuous uninterrupted routes, and vehicular and pedestrian routes separated. This would provide a structure for estate routes and allow natural movement patterns.

Hillier et al. believe that the Hunt Thompson plans did nothing about the segregation of various parts of the estate but, rather, reinforced it. In a final comment about the plans they say, 'One suspects that the [Hunt Thompson] proposals may owe more to current conventional wisdom than to an analysis of the problems specific to the Maiden Lane Estate.'

Source: Safe Neighbourhoods Unit and Institute of Advance Architectural Studies, 1989 Hillier et al., 1989a

Studley Estate, Lambeth

Hillier et al. (1989b) undertook a study of the relationship between crime and spatial layout for the Home Office Crime Prevention Unit in 1988.

As with other estates studied, the Studley Estate was not aligned with surrounding street patterns.

Hillier et al. found that the routes within the estate were 'extremely complex, requiring numerous changes of direction'. The unpopularity of these routes caused problems of access without use and low encounter rates. The urban average for encounter rates between moving adults in non-shopping streets was 2.6 pphm (people passed per hundred metres walked). On the estate, the encounter rate was a quarter of the urban average.

Areas with low encounter rates had poor levels of natural surveillance and these segregated were attractive to children and, in certain situations, to the potential criminal. Encounter rates appeared to decrease towards the centre of the estate.

The report found that the juxtaposition of highly integrated routes with segregated areas may make the latter vulnerable to crime. A crime survey of the estate carried out by Harris Research Centre showed a concentration of crimes against the person towards the outer edges of the estate. The areas were described as 'relatively segregated, but close to and easily accessible to the outside of the estate' - attractive to the potential offender because there was a reasonable chance of encountering a victim and a nearby escape route.

Another finding related to the incidence of theft from the person, much of which occurred on the edge of the estate next to an underground tube station. Here it seemed the theory floundered: high integration and encounter rates were found to coincide with high crime rate. This was put down to poor policing, a factor not previously mentioned.

Burglary showed a different pattern. It was stated that, '. . . in a normal street-with-houses layout, burglary tends towards segregated locations, but with strong influence from more localised design factors. In estates, more complex spatial design made these more localised factors stronger.' The localised factors tend to relate the relationship between dwelling entrances and access routes. It seems that street front entrances next to integrated access routes are good (they allow surveillance), but indirect dwelling entrances with integrated access routes are bad (they provide escape routes without surveillance). On these tentative conclusions Hillier et al. recommended:

- Making internal public segregated spaces private;

- Creating more direct entrances to ground floor homes;

- Restoring the street structure, creating integrated routes through the estate;

- Using entryphones at concealed entrance halls;

- Building some additional dwellings.

Policing near the tube station was raised as an important issue, whilst the congregation of unsupervised children was also considered to be important.

Source: Hillier et al., 1989b

Stockwell Park Estate, Lambeth

A study carried out by the Safe Neighbourhoods Unit (1989b) on this inner city estate made use of a variety of design evaluation studies. Work on the estate's spatial layout had already been carried out by a student at the Bartlett School of Architecture (1989), and this was used to enhance the data gained by SNU's own survey and consultation work.

The estate was described as 'a hole in the surrounding urban fabric'. Tenants expressed a preference for using perimeter (well integrated) routes and then the shortest route to their own front door, rather than using what might be a more direct route which crossed the estate. This preference was even more pronounced after dark and most commonly expressed by women.

The original design of the estate had created streets for pedestrians (walkways) **in the sky**, with access for vehicles and garages on ground level. The Council had redesigned parts of the estate by knocking down some walkway bridges and cutting off direct ground level routes through the estate used by pedestrians by erecting barriers of tall iron railings. The aim had been to reduce the number of escape routes. The effect, it was suggested, was to make the situation worse.

The **localised design factors** included a complete absence of direct dwelling entrances onto ground floor level routes. Most dwelling entrances abutted directly onto walkways which had originally been integrated routes through the estate. Loss of bridges had increased the frequency with which tenants had to go up and down from ground to walkway level using stairwells - areas which caused a high level of fear of crime. Ground floor routes adjacent to both vehicle access roads and garage entrances or blank walls were also quite well used. The lack of dwellings opening out onto the ground floor routes appeared to increase residents' fear. A balance had to be struck between residents choosing the quickest, as opposed to what was considered to be the safest, routes.

On most of the estate there were no windows overlooking the walkways. As a result, they had a very poor level of natural surveillance. Segregated areas were also found to attract groups of unsupervised children.

The report recommended that the ground floor level routes which were currently widely used by residents should be improved with pavements, better lighting, improved litter collection, and by closing off garage entrances. The report also recommended the creation of direct integrated routes to the perimeter roads, particularly on routes to bus stops. It was recommended that, after these changes had been made, pedestrian movement, pedestrian preferences, and the location of crimes should be monitored, before making any further design changes or carrying out further demolitions.

A core group of tenants had a high degree of input into the formulation of recommendations, which covered management and maintenance as well as design.

The report also highlighted a number of other factors:

- *Lighting on the estate was inadequate in many places;*

- *Previous failure to monitor or evaluate the effect that bridge removal had had on crime levels had complicated the assessment process;*

- *The Council had begun a pilot project of ground floor level porches, including rearranging the internal layout of dwellings which would make the walkways redundant;*

- *There was a widespread view amongst tenants that housing management and policing were inadequate;*

- *The estate was unpopular, and a sizeable proportion of tenants had applied for a transfer off the estate.*

Source: Safe Neighbourhoods Unit, 1989b (unpublished)

Urban design and deviance

The work of Oscar Newman was taken up and extended by Alice Coleman (1985), who postulates a relationship between urban design and various forms of deviance and treats design as a criminogenic factor. She analysed London inner city blocks of flats in Southwark and Tower Hamlets (over 106,000 dwellings in all) and an out of town estate in Oxfordshire consisting of just over 4,000 houses.

A large number of features of design were tested against six indicators of *lapses in civilised behaviour* and social malaise. The indicators were litter, graffiti, vandalism, family breakdown resulting in children being taken into care, and *pollution by excrement* - urine and faeces. Coleman ranked them in terms of social taboo and the degree of seriousness in breaching each social taboo - with dropping litter as the least serious and faeces the most serious.

She also carried out some interviews and informal talks with some residents. Her analysis identified 15 features of block design which she claimed were highly correlated with *social malaise*. She also laid a strong emphasis, as Newman had before her, on the way that anonymity allowed crime to occur and was to be reduced through design. Coleman claimed that all indicators of social malaise were found more frequently in and around the inner city flats than on the estate of houses.

The design features which Coleman found to be associated with social malaise and requiring removal or modification included the following:

- Overhead walkways should be removed because they are escape routes and knit together blocks and routes, so increasing anonymity;

- The number of blocks on a site should be reduced, ideally to a single one;

- Clear delineations should be made between private and public space. Windows should allow surveillance over shared space. Confused space should be avoided;

- A site should be walled all round to deter intruders;

- Play areas should be removed, as children teach each other unsociable habits when unsupervised. Children should stay in their own gardens;

- Facilities should be located outside the walled site;

- The number of dwellings in a block should be reduced to combat anonymity;

- Each block or self-contained section of flats should be served by just one staircase;

- Where a block of flats requires a second exit because of fire regulations this should be situated in such a way that it does not appear to be a through route;

- The number of storeys per block should be reduced, as natural social interaction can only take place at street level;

- Private space and gardens should be created in front of entrance doors wherever possible;

- Dwellings raised above stilts or ground floor garages should be avoided or filled in with accommodation because they impede surveillance;

- The number of dwellings served by one entrance should be minimised. The more dwellings served, and the more space shared and not private, the more prevalent were the indicators of social malaise;

- Each dwelling should have its own garden and gate, communal entrances should not be recessed so that they allow surveillance;

- Traditional streets of houses should be created between blocks, as they will be a stabilising social influence.

She considered socio-economic factors as a possible reason for the association between design and social malaise but asserts that design is the stronger influence. Coleman's prescription is that no more flats should be built and that, in order to reduce crime, communal areas on estates should be divided to provide gardens to ground-floor flats.

An interesting difference between Coleman and many other *determinists* is that she has objections to the introduction of culs-de-sac. She says that they give children a false sense of security from the dangers of road traffic and thus fail to provide appropriate road safety experience.

There has been criticism of Coleman's methods and conclusions. Smith (1987b) and Hillier (1987) question the statistical basis of the research. Malaise is measured by the number rather than the rates of crimes or events and could be explained by the sheer weight of numbers housed in the flats when compared to those found on the estate of houses. Her graphs and statistical correlations between malaise and design are criticised as being misleading and far weaker than she portrays. Dickens (1988) questions Coleman's assumptions and says that social interaction between residents in a building must have at least as much relevance as design alone. Spicker (1987) points out that environmental neglect is often the fault of the landlord rather than the residents.

A particularly contentious part of Coleman's theory is that removing overhead walkways will reduce crime by reducing the number of escape routes for criminals.

Coleman was able to put some of her ideas into practice when she studied the Mozart Estate and her design recommendations were subsequently implemented.

Mozart Estate, Westminster

Mozart Estate in Westminster had a poor reputation in the early 1980s because of crime. The Council commissioned Coleman to put her design research into practice and draw up design improvements for the estate in 1984. Westminster City Council went on to implement Coleman's proposals. In 1986 Hillier and Penn of the Bartlett School of Architecture evaluated the effect of walkway removal. In 1987 the Safe Neighbourhoods Unit (SNU) was asked to consult residents living on the estate with a view to testing the effectiveness of the design proposals and Alice Coleman's theory.

The design changes

After studying the estate, Coleman recommended that the walkways should be removed. She stated,

> *'The walkways are the most vicious "open sesame" making the block vulnerable to outsiders . . .The demolition of the walkways and the provision of staircases where necessary, is an important first step in making each building the preserve of its own inhabitants.' (1985)*

Her subsequent aim was to make all areas of the estate private to individual blocks and dwellings and to limit access to and from the estate. Four bridges were removed in 1986.

Evaluation of walkway removal

Hillier and Penn used systematic observation of pedestrian movement to assess their effect on movement patterns. It was their contention that,

> *'If the likely presence of people is predictable from spatial layout, then learning how an area is structured means that we also learn to anticipate where people will be. The sense of safety that we feel in streets depends a good deal on predictability.' (Hillier and Penn, 1986)*

*They also looked at **encounter rates** and found these to be low when walking around the estate at ground level. They asserted that encounter rates fell lower as a person moved towards the centre of the estate and that this meant, 'the sudden presence of a stranger, which would not cause a moment's disquiet in a more public place can seem quite frightening'.*

*Hillier and Penn believe that vulnerability to burglary is reduced by being in areas with a reasonable level of pedestrian movement and not being isolated. As they saw it, Coleman's design proposals would create a **labyrinthine villagey layout** with a number of culs-de-sac which would force pedestrians to use routes adjacent to garages rather than adjacent to the front doors of dwellings. The proposals would divide the estate into isolated, segregated areas which are cut off from the surrounding area.*

Hillier and Penn also found that young people gathered in the areas where there were no adults. Their final proposals stated that 'change in design can as easily increase vulnerability (to crime) as decrease it' and that a study of the pattern of crime and consultation with residents was necessary. They claimed that the proposed layout would cause the estate to be 'disintegrated as a unit without being re-integrated into the local community'.

The Safe Neighbourhoods Unit (SNU) carried out survey and consultation work in 1987 (Safe Neighbourhoods Unit, 1988a). This synopsis is solely concerned with tenants' views on design.

SNU found the estate to have an average crime level when compared with the levels found in inner city areas by the British Crime Survey.

*Correlations between the impact of the removal of walkways and some of Coleman's **disadvantagement variables** (indicators of social problems) were sought. As already described in Chapter One (see p.11), the survey found little relationship between the presence of walkways or interconnections and block size and burglary rates. Levels of crime reported to the police before walkway removal were compared with figures after removal. Coleman had claimed that crime levels had dropped, but SNU found the claim to be unjustifiable. Burglaries and attempted break-ins had appeared to fall, but further examination showed that the figures only covered a five months period. Secondly, police figures for assault and street robbery showed a rise in incidents.*

When residents were asked whether walkway removal had been a good idea, opinions were divided. 42% thought it had been a good idea, 32% did not and 15% said it made no difference. When residents were asked what impact it had made with regard to noise, privacy, fouling, vandalism and sense of community the percentage who felt that it had made no difference went up to 64%.

It seemed that the research did not bear out Coleman's theories and SNU concluded that they thought that the estate's problems were as much related to socio-economic and housing management factors and cuts in funding and resources as they were to design.

Source: Hillier and Penn, 1986
Safe Neighbourhoods Unit, 1988a (unpublished)

Lisson Green Estate, Westminster

Poyner et al. (1986) produced a report on bridge removal on this Westminster estate about the same time as Coleman's assessment of the same issue on the Mozart Estate.

Lisson Green had a chain of walkways linking blocks. It began to suffer from high crime rates, major repair problems, inadequate rubbish disposal, through traffic and parking by outsiders on the estate. The Council installed entryphones on walkways, opened a local office on the estate and then removed some of the bridges linking walkways in 1982.

*It was claimed that these changes reduced crime. Kenneth Baker MP took credit for the changes saying that he had been a pioneer in the field of 'creative demolition' **(Architect's Journal**, 26th March 1986). A national newspaper article headlined 'End of Walkways Cuts Crime' claimed that crime and vandalism had reduced by 50% after the removal of walkways.*

Poyner's evaluation of the effects of walkway removal on crime included the examination of police crime records for the estate for 1981-85 and consultation with the Council's housing officers.

The research found that, in the case of burglaries, 'the risk of burglary may increase with an increased number of vacant flats' rather than being related to walkway removal. In the case of street robberies, they stressed the need to examine incident levels over a substantial period in order to make sense of the real crime trends, rather than relying on short term fluctuations. They found that *street robberies declined dramatically about seven months **before** walkway removal and continued to stay at a low level. The reduction in robberies seemed to coincide with the three areas of the walkway which had entryphones.*

In short, the report did not find a link between walkway removal and crime levels. They concluded, 'not that one crime prevention method is better than another, but that it is important to monitor crime prevention measures with great care'. In their opinion, had the installation of entryphones been carefully monitored, the Council may well have chosen not to take the expensive step of demolishing the walkways, 'at least they might have postponed it to see if it was really necessary'.

Source: Poyner et al., 1986

Designs which require a person presence

There were high hopes for high rise blocks in the 1950s. It was thought that by having tenants in close proximity to one another a sense of community would be fostered (Central Housing Advisory Committee, 1952), that the blocks looked attractive (Sharpe, 1955) and that the 'building of tall flats gives more pleasure to more people' (Gibberd, 1955). By the 1970s tower blocks were commonly regarded as a costly mistake.

As we have already seen, theorists such as Newman and Coleman stated that there was a relationship between the number of storeys in a block and crime. Proposed solutions included reducing the number of storeys or simply blowing the blocks up. Many have been blown up but more remain. The increasing pressure on the public housing stock will ensure their continued existence. For some the solution is seen to be a human presence.

Jones (1987) argues that:

> . . . the use of some controller of entrance to a building has a long history . . . There is, however, a marked difference between gatemen in different economic relationships with the occupants of the complex. Those gatemen employed in middle class private accommodation, or where occupants and gateman are employees of the same organisation, behave differently from gatemen where the occupants are tenants of the local authority. In the former the gateman is seen as servant . . . in the latter as supervisor.

Jones also suggests that the use of gatemen (or porters) in the past was widespread because labour was relatively cheap. Modern multi-storey blocks of the 1960s and 1970s did not make provision for gatemen, but new technological devices such as CCTV mean that the number of people required to keep surveillance is reduced, making it more economical for gatemen to be re-introduced.

Newman did consider the use of a doorman but dismissed the idea as costly. In Canada, Waller and Okihiro (1978) stated that, 'Our findings for apartments question the conclusions drawn from the "defensible space" literature. The location of the apartment in the building, affluence, and the presence of a doorman were much more important factors in determining the likelihood of victimisation than items such as social cohesion.'

Local authorities in this country have taken up the opportunities offered by new technology in crime prevention (Osborn and Bright, 1989). CCTV involves the use of video cameras to monitor activity inside and outside blocks. Such a system requires a human presence to make use of the surveillance information. In some cases this is the tenant who can use CCTV to see the caller. It is, however, unusual to use an expensive system such as CCTV without some form of receptionist, guard or officer involvement because of the risk of vandalism to the equipment. In the United States, Musheno, Levine and Palumbo (1978) looked at a scheme without any *human presence* where tenants could tune into the block's CCTV system on their own television and found that tenants did not bother to carry out surveillance in this manner, so that crime rates were apparently unaffected.

The use of technology to detect and deter criminal activity in a block is a *situational* crime prevention measure. The underlying theory is that by 'manipulating the conditions under which crimes occur, a certain proportion of offences will be prevented' (Bannister, 1988). Situational measures make the potential criminal think again. In practice, as will be seen from the case studies, the gatekeeper's role in managing the fear of crime and the housing management role appear to have a more marked *social* effect than the purely physical measures.

The following examples of design-led initiatives illustrate the approach.

High Street Area, Pendleton, Salford

The High Street area was redeveloped as part of a slum clearance programme in the 1960s and 70s. There are fifteen 22-storey tower blocks, six nine-storey slab blocks and numerous blocks of four-storey family sized maisonettes.

For the purposes of this case study, only the problems identified in the multi-storey blocks, to which crime prevention measures with a person presence were applied, will be examined.

The Council began by holding a series of consultation meetings with tenants which was the beginning of a regular consultation process. The phased improvements began in 1983 and included the following:

- *A 24 hour security guard service in each block. The guard operates from a ground floor office adjacent to the foyer and has a counter and enquiry screen. The guard operates the entry phone and is able to prevent unauthorised access to the block. Callers are only allowed access after their identity has been verified by a resident. The guard also scrutinises people calling to provide services. Residents have their own means of access. When there is no guard the system can revert to an ordinary entryphone system.*

- *Two additional ground floor entrances to the block have been modified to become exits that can only be opened from inside the block. The doors, enclosed stairs and lifts are monitored by CCTV.*

The arrangements have proved popular with tenants and have been paid for out of an additional rent charge. The Council states that crime levels appear to have fallen.

One problem that emerged in 1986 was a high turnover of security guards which tenants complained about. The contract was offered to a different firm in 1987. A major area of potential concern was described as follows: 'It is essential to the success of the scheme that tenants and the security guards are able to strike up a good relationship.' The report does not describe the extent to which this was subsequently achieved.

*In parallel with the above changes, the Council also instituted a modified allocations policy. Each block now contains a high proportion of elderly tenants and new vacancies are let to elderly or **mature** couples.*

Source: Department of Environment, 1991

Chalk Hill Estate, Brent

Built in the 1960s, Chalk Hill Estate is made up of 30 concrete clad blocks of five to eight storeys linked by continuous high level access at every third floor. The blocks form large polygonal courtyards with access from other parts of the development. There are multi-storey car parks in the centre of two courtyards which are linked to the blocks by high level bridges. It is possible to walk along continual covered walkways for over a mile.

*The estate has a high crime rate, particularly for street robbery. Access to dwellings is by **streets in the air**. These **streets**, together with the enclosed staircases, form an extensive network of routes which are not subject to surveillance as no windows overlook the routes. The streets and stairs also provide many escape routes for the criminal.*

In 1980 the Council divided the walkways into sections by installing doors and entryphones. The changes were implemented without tenant consultation, so tenants voted with their feet by propping open or vandalising the doors, rendering the measure useless.

In 1982, after a woman was killed on the estate, there was a second attempt to introduce crime prevention oriented design changes. This time, the Council held a number of large consultation meetings with tenants. By 1986 a design had been agreed for four of the blocks. There was an expectation that success would result in those measures being introduced to all blocks.

The four blocks were first isolated from the adjoining blocks by cutting off inter-connecting routes. New stairs and lifts were installed and two reception booths were provided for two receptionists. The blocks were renamed. The stairs and reception areas are located in a glazed area external to the block. The stairs are open tread and therefore a person going up or down is continuously in view. The openness and visibility would appear to subscribe to two of Newman's prescriptions on visible external entrances and corridors.

The surveillance by receptionists uses two entryphone points and CCTV surveillance cameras outside the entrance and inside the entrance hall. The receptionist can view those approaching the door and any visitor has to identify themselves twice. The improvements appear to have been effective.

Only the first phase of improvements had been completed by the time of assessment. The rest of the estate has not received improvements because of funding problems. Security measures with a person presence are particularly vulnerable when a Council is under financial pressure.

Source: Institute of Housing and Royal Institute of British Architects, 1989

Southwyck House, Moorlands Estate, Lambeth

Southwyck House in Brixton has been dubbed 'the Barrier Block' because of its appearance. The original design brief for Southwyck House aimed to create a buffer or shield between the Moorlands Estate and a planned elevated road - the road was never built.

In 1987 the Safe Neighbourhoods Unit (SNU) was commissioned by Lambeth Council to carry out a survey and consultations with the residents of Southwyck House and local Council and police officers.

Southwyck House has 194 flats in a long curving nine-storey block. There are three long access balconies running along the side of the block with eleven access points. The majority of tenants are relatively young (under 30 years), the block has a history of high crime levels and has been the location for extensive drug dealing.

SNU's survey and consultations identified areas where crime occurred and where tenants were fearful of crimes occurring. There were also extensive consultations with groups of tenants who wanted a direct input into any redesign proposals.

The priorities identified by tenants centred on improved management, maintenance and policing of the block. Their priorities for possible improvements to physical security included:

- Improvements to the security of individual front doors;

- Controlled access to the block, although there was disagreement over how this might be achieved.

The doubts expressed by tenants revealed a number of worries about introducing a person presence, as well as physical measures, to control access to the block. Tenants feared the introduction of a uniformed security presence would label block residents as troublemakers. They feared that security guards would exacerbate tensions in the community by reacting to incidents in a heavy handed way and that guards would make the block **prison like**. Other concerns were that they would be young, inexperienced, poorly trained men on low wages; there would be a high turnover of unsatisfied staff, with resulting instability, and that conflict could erupt between security guards and the police or Council staff.

The report recommended the introduction of a block receptionist service which would control access to the block, with secondary entryphone access to the block supervised by CCTV. The job description of the block receptionist, to be agreed with tenants, was to have a housing enquiries dimension and a role in overseeing cleaning and caretaking in the block.

Recommendations were also made on improving maintenance and repairs, upgrading community facilities and improving policing. Work on this scheme is still in the early stages, although a plan has now been agreed by all parties.

A tenant/officer block steering committee was set up to oversee detailed design feasibility work and an independent tenant liaison worker was employed to enable full consultation with tenants. An on-site office was also established, staffed by Council architects, development officers and the tenant liaison worker, to allow tenants to gain a clear picture of the design proposals and to make their comments. As a preliminary measure, stronger front doors were chosen and fitted in consultation with tenants. The tenant liaison worker also assisted tenants in developing a range of community business initiatives.

Source: Safe Neighbourhoods Unit, 1988b
           Stollard et al., 1989

B.   Management led Initiatives for Residential Areas

In recent years, a number of authors have underlined the importance of taking management considerations into account when assessing problems of crime and fear of crime on housing estates. Some have questioned research and practice which, in their view, overemphasises the relationship between estate design and crime:

> It may be true that certain types of estates (for example, those with large, interconnected linear blocks) are rarely successful; but there are estates of similar design, located in different areas, perhaps with a different history, mix of tenancies or management which work well and where design features exercise less of an effect. The effects of design on crime may have been exaggerated in some areas where housing departments have not developed appropriate styles of management for particular types of property. (Osborn and Bright, 1989)

Some of the principles which underlie local management initiatives were summarised in a 1981 report by the Department of the Environment's Housing Services Advisory Group: *Security on Council Estates* (Department of Environment, 1981).

The report stresses the importance of addressing fear of crime, as well as actual incidence of crime, by developing measures which reduce tenants' feelings of social and physical isolation. The report highlights some of the factors which can result in feelings of isolation among residents on estates: unsatisfactory design features; the unpopularity of certain estates; high child densities; circumstances which result in 'people of different cultural and ethnic backgrounds and/or different lifestyles living in close proximity at high densities, often in unsympathetic and uncongenial environments'; insensitive and remote housing management.

The report concludes:

> Lack of an integrated housing service, combining active supervision with genuine co-operation with tenants, often means that tenants have no sense of belonging to a particular housing scheme. Tenants can face a number of problems, for example, families who have noisy parties or gangs using younger children's playgrounds, yet they feel that there is no-one to whom they can turn who would tackle these problems.

During the last ten years, such problems of anonymity and remoteness in the provision of services have been widely addressed by local authorities in Britain. There a has been a growing trend towards the decentralisation of local authority services, and in particular housing services, to the neighbourhood or estate level in order to improve their accessibility, responsiveness and accountability. This process has been extensively reviewed (see for example, Hoggett and Hambleton, 1987). Many of these initiatives have prioritised the decentralisation of repair and maintenance services to the estate level (Kendrick and Pilkington, 1987).

However, relatively few initiatives have specifically considered the implications of these new arrangements for levels of crime and insecurity at the local level. In the United Kingdom, the initiative which has most clearly aimed to demonstrate the importance of effective local housing management in the regeneration of run down estates is the Department of the Environment's Priority Estates Project (PEP). Power (1987a) describes in detail the beneficial effects which the existence of an estate office, together with associated initiatives, is claimed to have had in terms of reductions in crime and vandalism and feelings of security among tenants on 20 estates surveyed in 1984. Apart from PEP, most of the available literature in the United Kingdom refers to the work of the National Association for the Care and Resettlement of Offenders (NACRO), and in particular the Safe Neighbourhoods Unit (SNU). The overall approach adopted by PEP and NACRO in relation to crime reduction on estates is summarised by Rock (1988). The following sections review the available evidence relating to the impact of these initiatives with reference to specific examples.

Estate based management initiatives

The Priority Estates Project (PEP) was set up in 1979 as a joint DoE/local authority experiment in improving unpopular estates:

> The basic idea was not new or difficult: to establish a local management office, to carry out meticulously the landlords' responsibility for rent, repairs, letting the property and monitoring the environment of the estate; and to give tenants a chance to exercise maximum control over their homes and neighbourhood. (Power, 1984)

The PEP model has ten key elements which were considered to be essential to the success of an estate based management project: a local office; local repairs; localised lettings; local rent arrears control; an estate budget; resident caretaking; tenant participation; co-ordination and liaison with other services; monitoring of performance; training (Power, 1987b). The changing emphasis of the PEP approach during the past ten years, was outlined by Zipfel (1989).

Burbidge (1984) notes:

> The reduction of crime and vandalism, whilst an important goal of PEP, is by no means its sole or even main focus. The essence is getting dwellings let; getting repairs done; developing a good relationship with the tenants; keeping the estate clean and tidy; and last but not least, increasing actual and perceived security from crime and vandalism.

This clear focus on housing management tasks may help to explain the patchy nature of monitoring of levels of crime and vandalism on PEP estates.

During the same period, many other estate based management initiatives, initiated by individual local authorities, have also addressed themselves to problems of crime and vandalism, among other issues. However, as already noted, these tend to be less well documented.

The Department of the Environment's Housing Services Advisory Group notes the achievements of the Cowgate Project in Newcastle and the Springwell Project in Gateshead, as well as initiatives in Brighton and the London Boroughs of Lambeth, Islington and Brent (Department of Environment, 1981). Some of the earlier local housing management initiatives were reviewed in a Priority Estates Project survey carried out in 1982 (Power, 1984). The survey identified 42 estate based management projects in 19 local authorities in England. Of the 20 project estates subsequently assessed, 19 were considered to have high levels of crime and vandalism. Although crime records were available for only three projects, it was estimated that vandalism and levels of insecurity had declined on 15 estates following the introduction of estate based management.

On the basis of project staff assessments, feedback from residents and the police's own assessment, it was considered that local beat policing had played an important part in this improvement on thirteen of the estates:

> Thirteen of the 19 projects reported that beat policing had made a major impact in inspiring confidence and a sense of security in the community and reassuring workers and residents that the area was safe. (Power, 1984)

Overall improvements in security were also ascribed to 'improvements in door security, the existence of the estate office, a reduction in the number of empty dwellings, the role of resident caretakers in patrolling the estate grounds, the employment of guards, wardens and door porters and so on'.

Specific initiatives which were regarded as having had a beneficial effect on individual estates are described in Table 6:

Table 6 **Measures associated with reduced crime on PEP estates**

Estate	Initiative
Tulse Hill Estate, Lambeth Ragworth Estate, Stockton on Tees	Increased patrolling by caretakers
Goscote Estate, Walsall Tulse Hill, Lambeth	Security patrols by night watchmen
Goscote Estate, Walsall Milton Court, Lewisham	Reduced empty properties
Tulse Hill, Lambeth	Entry phones
Chalk Hill Estate, Brent Broadwater Farm, Haringey	Walkway closures
Milton Court, Lewisham Wenlock Barn, Hackney Tulse Hill, Lambeth Stockwell Park, Lambeth	Stronger front doors and frames
Ashfield Valley, Rochdale	Improved estate lighting

Source: Power (1984)

Improvements to security on a number of the estates were also considered to be related to increased tenant involvement and to the involvement of children on estates in improvements:

> Crime and fear of crime dominate the lives of many rundown estates. Communal social controls are often weakly exercised or have collapsed for a series of complex reasons. Residents must play the critical role in reversing this situation, and have laid great store in reasserting control on the estates we visited. (Power, 1984)

Clearly, this survey does not provide the quantitative data needed to establish the true impact of the various measures introduced, or the relative contribution of each element. However, the survey does serve a useful purpose in illustrating the difficulty of assessing how precisely local management initiatives can impact on crime rates.

Burbidge (1984) uses available data to summarise the effect of local management on burglary and vandalism rates in eight projects, although he stressed that monitoring of crime levels in the projects had been patchy. The six PEP estates included in the study were: Wenlock Barn, Hackney; Willows, Bolton; Tulse Hill, Lambeth; Broadwater Farm, Haringey; Afon, Wrexham and Penrhys, Rhondda. The non-PEP estates included in the study were Cunningham Road, Halton and Springwell, Gateshead. The results of the assessment are summarised in Table 7. In five of the eight estates, burglary rates were reported to have fallen during the project's duration, although only one of these assessments was based on a sample household survey. Vandalism was considered to have been reduced on all eight estates.

Table 7 **Effect on burglaries and vandalism of housing management projects**

Project	Burglaries/break-ins*	Vandalism**
Halton (NACRO) 1976-79	Down (17% - 8%)	Down
Bolton (PEP) 1979-83	Up (12% - 24%)	Down
Hackney (PEP) 1979-83	No change (10% - 10%). But fewer rated thefts and break-ins as a big problem (45% - 24%).	Down
Gateshead 1981-82	Reported crime and vandalism down by one third	Down
Lambeth (PEP)1980-81	Down (15 per week - 1 per week, reported to housing staff)	Down
Haringey (PEP)	Down	Down
Wrexham (PEP)	Down (1983/84, 13% reported in survey; 1984/85, 5% reported to police).	Down
Rhondda (PEP)	Little change in burglary or damage recorded by the police.	

* As reported in sample household survey, unless stated otherwise.
** Mostly impressions of project staff.
Source: Burbidge (1984)

Power (1987c) provides a useful summary of the way in which effective local management can impact on crime. At the same time, she points to the limitations placed on housing departments which are expected to deliver a comprehensive service to estates, yet which do not normally have direct responsibility for three of the main anxieties of residents: repairs; collecting refuse and preventing crime. However, she notes:

> ... a local housing management team provided a focus of effort which drew in other services. It was easier for these services to make a useful contribution when the basic job of running the housing was being tackled.

She underlines the importance of issues of crime and security on PEP estates:

Security overrode all other issues and was inextricably linked with the general decline and unpopularity, the level of poverty and unemployment, and the transience and instability of an area. It dominated all the estates and constantly dampened residents' confidence and staff morale. Not surprisingly, security measures were the most widespread and popular of improvements.

Beat policing had been introduced on all nine of the estates surveyed, and was considered to have been a failure on only one. Resident caretakers were introduced on a further seven estates, while physical security measures, such as locks, entryphones and laminated glass, were undertaken on six. Other initiatives included Neighbourhood Watch, lighting improvements and caretaking patrols.

Crime levels were considered to have been reduced on eight of the nine project estates, although crime statistics were available for only two estates. Similarly, vandalism was considered to have been reduced on five of the nine estates, on the basis of repairs reporting and levels of reporting to the police.

Rock (1988) also reports successes on PEP estates:

> Tricia Zipfel, one of its consultants, asserted that there is evidence of burglary rates decreasing on all but one of the Project estates. The most conspicuous change was observed on the Broadwater Farm Estate in Haringey; between 1982 and 1984, the burglary rate had dropped by 62 percent.

Hope and Dowds (1987) describe a current study which aims to evaluate PEP's impact on crime:

> Though measures to improve security of dwellings, and to create defensible spaces, have been implemented within PEP and the reduction of crime has been achieved as a benefit of this approach, little attention has been given to *how* PEP might reduce crime nor is this acknowledged as a specific goal.

As a basis for the evaluation study, Hope presents a preliminary model (see Figure 1) which aims to link the 'treatment' (PEP) with the outcome (crime and incivility):

> The core assumption of this model is that crime and incivility are affected by residents' ability to exert informal control over behaviour on their estate. Their collective ability to do so depends upon confidence acquired through greater commitment to the estate, and greater concern with conditions and standards of conduct within it. This greater concern (involvement) derives from their 'coding' of the estate - a summation of evaluative judgements about conditions on the estate. PEP may affect these conditions.

The following examples of estate-based projects illustrate the approach.

Broadwater Farm Estate, Haringey

The Broadwater Farm Estate in the London Borough of Haringey is a large system built estate with 1063 properties and a population of around 3,500. Most of the estate is contained in 12 blocks built on concrete stilts and linked at first floor level by long overhead walkways and internal corridors. Completed in 1973, the estate was initially popular with tenants, but within three years had become increasingly difficult to let.

During the late 1970s and early 1980s the estate had serious problems:

> *'The combination of a high proportion of elderly people, single parent families, young people, mostly unemployed, and a significant number of social services referrals created many tensions and resulted in a rapid turnover of tenants, as those who could moved off the estate.' (Priority Estates Project, 1988)*

The standard of management and maintenance services to the estate was poor, and this resulted in a high number of empty properties, an inadequate repairs service and a generally run down environment. The situation was made worse

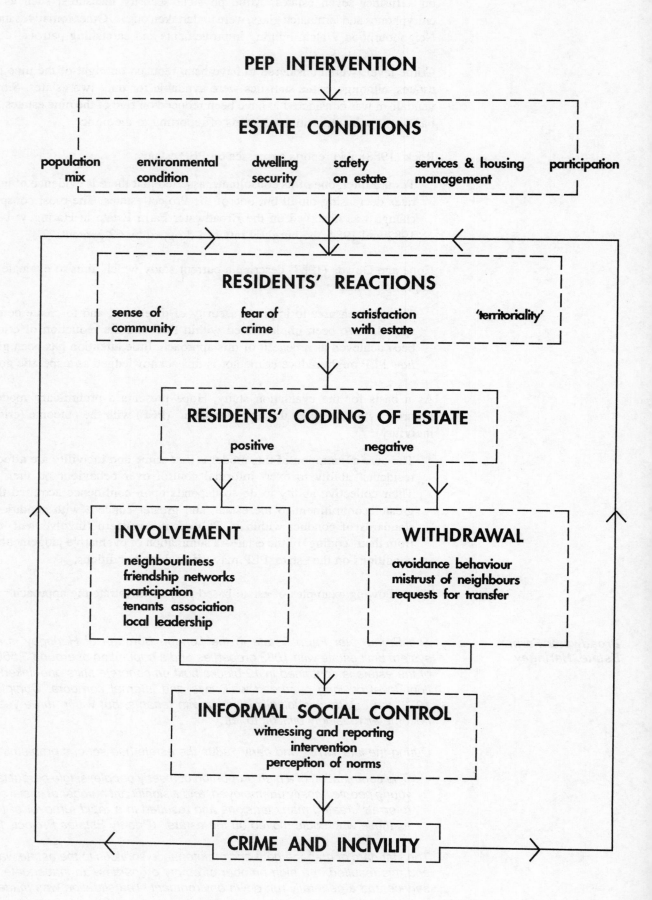

Figure 1 Model of Priority Estates Project Effect on Crime

PEP INTERVENTION

ESTATE CONDITIONS

| population mix | environmental condition | dwelling security | safety on estate | services & housing management | participation |

RESIDENTS' REACTIONS

sense of community   fear of crime   satisfaction with estate   'territoriality'

RESIDENTS' CODING OF ESTATE

positive   negative

INVOLVEMENT

neighbourliness
friendship networks
participation
tenants association
local leadership

WITHDRAWAL

avoidance behaviour
mistrust of neighbours
requests for transfer

INFORMAL SOCIAL CONTROL
witnessing and reporting
intervention
perception of norms

CRIME AND INCIVILITY

by the shortage of facilities for young people, tension between young people and the police and high levels of crime. In 1983 the ratio of burglaries to dwellings was 1:4, for vehicle crimes 1:4 and for major crimes 1:11.

In 1981 and 1982 there were clashes between young people on the estate and the police. In 1982 the number of beat officers on the estate was increased from one to eight. However, in spite of the increased presence of local officers and a continuing dialogue between the police and community leaders, there was little improvement in relations. In 1985, the estate was the scene of a five hour battle between young people and the police, and a police officer was killed.

As a result of pressure from a well-organised local community group, a programme of physical and social improvements had been initiated in 1983. A Neighbourhood Office was opened on the estate to provide an on-site housing management service. The office had responsibility for repairs, caretaking, cleaning and roadsweeping. The Neighbourhood Office Manager worked to the Broadwater Farm Panel which included tenants and council member representatives and had a remit to co-ordinate all council services to the estate.

'The opening of the Neighbourhood Office brought immediate and dramatic improvements to the estate. Management workers began dealing with over 800 queries a month. A small waiting list of people willing to move onto the estate was established. Repairs were being done faster than in the rest of the Borough. The average level of empty flats dropped from around 60 to 15. Resident caretakers and cleaners ensured that the estate was kept clean with very little graffiti or vandalism.' (Priority Estates Project, 1988)

In addition, block interiors have been refurbished and provided with new lighting; roads and footpaths have been improved; phone entry systems have been successfully introduced into blocks; all communal glass has been replaced with diamond glazed vandal-proof glass and residents' front doors strengthened.

The community on the estate has also contributed a great deal to the improvements. The Broadwater Farm Youth Association has set up a day centre for the under-fives, a meals service for the elderly, community workshops and a wide range of recreational activities for young people and adults. A range of job initiatives were also developed (see p.88).

Between 1983 and 1985, recorded crime on the estate fell by over 60%. Burglary rates fell by 78%, vehicle crime by 61% and major crime by 49%.

Despite the disturbances in 1985, crime has continued to fall on the estate. In 1987 the estate was described by one senior police officer as 'probably the safest place in Tottenham'. The estate accounted for 1% of the area's crime despite having 3.5% of its population.

Source: Priority Estates Project, 1988
          Osborn, 1989

Springwell Joint Project, Gateshead

The Springwell Estate is a cottage estate of 1,000 properties built in the late 1940s and early 1950s on the outskirts of Gateshead. Prior to the establishment of the project in February 1980, houses on the estate were unmodernised and inadequately heated; a high proportion of tenants were single parents, unemployed or on low incomes; houses were hard to let, with a high tenancy turnover and the estate suffered from extremely high levels of crime and vandalism.

The Springwell Joint Project was an Inner City Partnership-funded initiative involving intensive housing management and community development by a joint housing/social services team which operated largely independently of central *housing management in Gateshead. An MSC project also undertook gardening and decorating for pensioners, valeting of empty housing and cleaning.*

Local lettings aimed to ensure that priority was given to applicants with links with the estate and that neighbour disputes were avoided wherever possible. The time taken to re-let houses was reported to have declined due to quicker repairs and the letting of undecorated properties.

More frequent road and pavement sweeping and improved bulky rubbish collection led to an improvement in the estate's environment. Capital works to the estate included a new community centre and environmental improvements. The community workers encouraged and supported a whole range of tenants' activities in the new community centre which is managed by local residents.

A community policing initiative, operating from the estate office, was introduced in June 1981. Between 1981 and 1982 reported crimes fell by 33%. In addition:

> *'Trouble with youths has virtually disappeared. Tenants' morale has risen sharply.'*

No information is provided on specific crimes, nor is any indication given of the likely contribution of the various elements of the initiative to reduced crime levels.

Source: Power, 1984

Ragworth Estate, Stockton-on-Tees

The Ragworth Estate is a cottage estate of 393 houses situated on the outskirts of Stockton-on-Tees. In 1980 the estate was characterised by high numbers of low income families, a high child population (600) and 30% unemployment among heads of household. Houses were inadequately heated and damp, the estate was poorly maintained with high levels of tenant dissatisfaction about repairs, vandalism and lack of security.

In 1981 an estate office was opened on the estate with funding from Urban Aid. The office was responsible for general management, welfare advice, rent collection and arrears, voids inspection and the supervision of the modernisation programme.

All the houses on the estate were included in a modernisation programme, and open spaces were created through the selective demolition of 39 houses. As well as modernisation to individual dwellings, improvements included: a new community centre, tree and shrub planting, communal play facilities, the clearing of gardens and the renewal of walls.

An active residents' association was developed and was consulted about the capital programme.

In August 1980 two night watchmen were employed to patrol the estate at night on weekdays and at weekends. Costs associated with empty property maintenance and repairing vandalism was almost halved in the following year. Local beat policing was also introduced and it was reported that tenants were more willing to challenge young people causing damage.

Unfortunately, no information was provided on recorded crime rates or the costs involved in maintaining empty properties and repairing vandalism.

As a result, it is impossible to assess whether the initiative had any significant impact on crime levels on the estate.

Source: Power, 1984

**Co-ordinated Estate
Improvement
Programmes**

The Safe Neighbourhoods Unit (SNU) was established by NACRO and the GLC in 1980 'to carry out in-depth tenant consultations and contribute to comprehensive improvement projects on disadvantaged housing estates' (Bright and Pettersson, 1984). Between 1980 and 1986, SNU undertook 21 estate improvement projects, each lasting between two and three years, on GLC and ex-GLC estates. Progress achieved on these estates is summarised in two reports: *The Safe Neighbourhoods Unit: Community Based Improvement Programmes on Twelve Inner London Housing Estates* (Safe Neighbourhoods Unit, 1984) and *The Safe Neighbourhoods Unit Report 1981-86* (Safe Neighbourhoods Unit, 1986c).

Although less specifically concerned with the development of estate based management than PEP, SNU has consistently stressed the importance of the links which exist between the poor management of estates and problems of crime and fear of crime. In particular, SNU stresses the need for inter-agency co-operation in the resolution of crime problems:

> No one agency acting alone is likely to make a lasting impact on an estate with a serious security problem. Combating tenant insecurity and fear of crime should not be confined to installing phone-entry systems or introducing home beat policing, valuable though these are. Security should not be perceived as a separate issue or tackled in isolation from other problems of estate management. Estates with a serious security problem are often those whose management and maintenance services are unresponsive. Constantly inadequate services cause tenant dissatisfaction and high levels of applications to transfer elsewhere. An atmosphere of insecurity is created as a result of this neglect, leading to a lack of any real community organisation and the general observation that no one really seems to care. The combined absence of formal management control and informal community controls provides opportunities for disruptive behaviour and those crimes commonly associated with housing estates, such as burglary, auto-crime, racial harassment and vandalism. The responsibility for developing a climate of security on an estate therefore lies with the local authority in partnership with the tenants and the police. (Bright and Pettersson, 1984)

Several of SNU's projects have resulted in the establishment of estate based housing management offices and local repairs depots, although improved housing management has not necessarily emerged as residents' major concern on each estate (Safe Neighbourhoods Unit, 1986c). Other measures implemented on project estates have included: physical improvements and modifications to housing; environmental improvements; the development of youth and community facilities; improved beat policing; the introduction of resident caretaking; the establishment and support of tenants associations.

As with PEP projects, few SNU projects have been systematically monitored. Rock (1988) offers a possible explanation for this:

> . . . the initiatives were manned by a few people who were engaged in daily negotiatio₁ ₅ with diverse and difficult groups who had strong moral commitments and who were too busy to continuously record and assess what was happening about them.

Much of SNU's intervention on project estates was concerned with assuring that agreed improvements were actually implemented by the relevant agencies:

> As an independent, non statutory organisation, we can have a great deal of influence and exert pressure but we have no financial or political leverage

with councils, the police, the youth service or any other agency to make them respond. As a result, progress on a small number of estates has been unacceptably slow. (Safe Neighbourhoods Unit, 1984)

In spite of these constraints, SNU has claimed significant improvements, both in terms of crime reduction and general estate conditions, on a number of project estates.

On the Haggerston Estate in the London Borough of Hackney, a range of measures was implemented between 1981 and 1985. These included: the formation of an active tenants association and the opening of a tenants clubroom; the involvement of tenants in the planning of environmental improvements; the improvement of play and youth provision; improved beat policing and improved estate lighting. SNU claimed that:

> . . . the level of street crime around the estate fell during this period and the police have also reported a drop in the number of burglaries. (Safe Neighbourhoods Unit, 1986c)

Following the production of an Action Plan on the Teviot Street Estate in 1984, a detached youth work project was developed, employing a locally recruited youth organiser (Safe Neighbourhoods Unit, 1984). This, it was claimed, led to further reductions in crime and anti-social behaviour, although no evidence was put forward to support the claim:

> Starting in very difficult circumstances, with very limited resources and no building, the project has been remarkably successful. In particular, there has been a reduction in crime and social tension and a reduction in referrals to the police, social services and juvenile court. (NACRO, 1988a)

The following project descriptions illustrate the approach.

Pepys Estate, Deptford, Lewisham

Pepys Estate was built between 1966 and 1973 and has a population of around 4,500. The estate consists of ten interconnected eight-storey blocks, three 24-storey tower blocks and a small number of houses and flats.

A Safe Neighbourhoods Unit project was established on the estate in 1981 because of the high level of burglary, autocrime and vandalism and because it was considered that action was needed to arrest the gradual deterioration of the estate observed by tenants and the Council.

Following extensive tenant consultations, an Action Plan was prepared for the estate, recommending action on four complementary fronts:

- *Physical improvements and extensive modifications to the blocks, incorporating a zone locking system;*

- *The replacement of mobile caretakers with resident caretaking staff and the establishment of a local estate management office and repairs team on the estate;*

- *A substantial community development input;*

- *A strengthening of the tenants' and community associations.*

Between 1983 and 1986, a two phase improvement programme was implemented by the GLC and Lewisham Council. This included the following improvements:

Medium rise blocks

Double phone entry systems were installed in each block, together with a zone locking system to restrict access between inter-connected blocks. All internal public spaces were decorated and upgraded. Individual flats were programmed for a security package, including strong front doors.

Tower blocks

The three tower blocks were scheduled for improvement in phase two of the improvements package. This included extensive structural work, a double phone entry system at each entrance and corridor. In addition:

- *A new Neighbourhood Office was opened in one of the tower blocks to provide an intensive housing management service for the estate;*

- *12 resident caretakers were employed;*

- *Five home beat police officers were deployed on the estate, and foot patrols increased;*

- *A committee was established to examine and develop provision for children and young people;*

- *A new family clubroom was opened, and this became the main focus for community activities on the estate.*

According to police figures, there was a considerable reduction in crime on the estate between 1983 and 1985. Autocrime fell by 60%, burglary by 54%, beat crime by 18% and street crime by 48%. The crime rate continued to fall, albeit more gradually, over the next three years. (Safe Neighbourhoods Unit, 1986c)

The report suggested there were a number of factors associated with a fall in crime, including:

- *The GLC flat security package;*

- *Lewisham Council's resident caretaking and intensive housing management;*

- *Metropolitan Police's intensive neighbourhood policing;*

- *More community activity; and,*

- *The 'surveillance effect' of the large number of workmen who have been on the estate since September 1983.*

Hyder (1988) notes that this improvement had been sustained until 1988, with autocrime down 51%, burglary down 52%, street crime down 48% and other crimes down 27% between 1984 and 1988.

There was a generally held, but unsupported, view that the improved estate management systems introduced by the local authority and the police contributed to maintaining lower crime levels once initial reductions were achieved.

●Source: Safe Neighbourhoods Unit, 1985
Safe Neighbourhoods Unit, 1986c
Hyder, 1988

Apart from PEP and SNU projects, the impact which estate based management initiatives have had upon crime and fear of crime have been poorly documented. Even fewer have been independently evaluated. The following case study represents a rare example of a recent assessment.

61

**Possil Park
Tenants Co-operative,
Glasgow**

384 houses which are being improved by the Possil Park Housing Co-operative are a small part of a large 1930s housing estate managed by Glasgow City Council. The estate comprises long, three and four-storey terraces of staircase access dwellings. The terraces face onto the estate road, with grassed areas fenced off by metal railings. To the rear are dilapidated communal back courts and outbuildings.

The estate as a whole suffers from a high level of crime and vandalism, a high level of unemployment, a poor reputation and high numbers of empty properties. During 1987, there were 426 reported crimes on the estate, including 13 serious assaults, 10 robberies and 117 burglaries. Autocrime is also a serious problem. Many crimes are said to be related to drug and alcohol abuse.

In 1981, 49% of economically active residents were unemployed. The area also has an unusually high proportion of children and young people (64% of the area's population was under 25 in 1981, compared with 39% for Glasgow as a whole).

The Possil Park Housing co-operative was established in 1987 following several years of lobbying by local people. The co-operative initiated the first phase of estate improvements in 1987. This involved external improvements to 48 dwellings, together with environmental improvements. The co-operative owns the properties and the tenants have responsibility for managing the properties and the improvements.

The Institute of Housing and RIBA report, from which this case study is drawn, describes the impact which the initiative has had on crime in the area. Following the establishment of the housing co-operative in 1987, the overall crime rate had reduced by 28% (although the precise period to which this reduction applies is not specified). All types of crime had reduced, apart from vehicular crime, with burglaries down by 64%. Vehicular crime is still considered to be a serious problem. The police considered that the Co-operative and other local initiatives, such as the community business area liaison committee and the Saracen crime prevention panel, had played an important role in the reduction.

> *'The principal prevention measure is the existence and activity of the Co-op, although only a small proportion of the houses have been improved. It is acknowledged by the police already to have affected the crime rate in the area. Resident attitudes toward their homes have changed. We were told that former housebreakers (now turned to theft on a larger scale from commercial premises) were firm supporters of the Co-op. They did not want their own children to be brought up in an area where crime was rife.'*

The report concludes:

> *'The lesson here is that when there is a strong community commitment to improve an area, crime can be reduced rapidly. The resources and support that the local authority and others have provided are essential, but only the community itself could have involved the local criminal fraternity to the extent that they desist from their activities within the community area.'*

Basic security measures introduced as part of the improvement scheme include: secure window catches; fenced back courts; new entryphones, new controlled entrance doors to each staircase and new external light fittings.

●Source: Institute of Housing and Royal Institute of British Architects (1989)

**Multi-storey block
management and
security initiatives**

The close relationship which exists between housing management and problems of crime and fear of crime is particularly evident in relation to tower blocks and medium rise, linear blocks. The particular problems faced by residents living in multi-storey blocks, and by local authorities attempting to manage them, have been well documented in the publications of the National Tower Blocks Campaign and in the report of the Hulme Conference on deck access estates, *Deck Access Disaster,* held in 1985 (Manchester City Council, 1985).

Reviews of alternative approaches to managing multi-storey blocks are contained in *Tower Blocks* (Polytechnic of South Bank, 1985) and *Trends in High Places* (Institute of Housing, 1983). However, the report *After Entryphones* (Safe Neighbourhoods Unit, 1985) concentrated on highlighting the relationship between improved security in high-rise blocks and the need for some form of intensive management presence. In particular, the report highlighted the ineffectiveness of phone entry systems and other physical security measures in improving the safety and security of council tenants on many large multi-storey blocks. The report included a review of 15 phone entry, controlled access systems installed by the former GLC's multi-storey block improvement scheme. Only four of the fifteen schemes were considered to have been a success in terms of their objectives, which were: 'to provide tenants with a higher standard of security than hitherto and, thus, reduce vandalism to the property with an anticipated saving in maintenance and repair costs'. The report concluded that:

> Technological solutions were useful but only if linked to a system of intensive management that includes the deployment of door porters or concierges and a prompt maintenance system. (Safe Neighbourhoods Unit, 1985)

Realising the limits of control access technology, particularly for large blocks or blocks with a high proportion of children, a growing number of authorities are now either operating or developing block receptionist or concierge services. There is a continuing debate about the main purpose of these schemes. Some are clearly security schemes, where block receptionists, often in uniform and usually men, act as security guards with clearly defined surveillance, patrolling and door control duties. Schemes following this type of approach can be found in Bradford, Middlesbrough, Salford and Waltham Forest. Others use block receptionists as block managers with localised responsibility for elements of the housing management service, such as assisted viewing of dwellings for prospective tenants, repair processing and housing enquiries. Examples of this type of approach can be found in Brent, Hammersmith and Fulham, Preston and Swansea. Some also focus on the community development possibilities, where block receptionists help to service residents' groups and activities and provide support for vulnerable residents, such as the elderly. A good example of this type of scheme is the Barbot Estate concierge scheme in Enfield.

Other local authorities see their schemes as being developmental, changing their function over time, taking on different functions in response to changes in local circumstances and residents' priorities. For instance, Glasgow City Council's block receptionist programme, which will eventually cover over 80 blocks, has begun as essentially a security programme. The Housing Department perceived that the main resident priority was initially for improved security. However, as schemes take root and begin to address the problems of crime, there is an expectation that block receptionists will develop a management and community support role. The City is currently discussing modifications to job descriptions with the staff concerned.

A similar debate about the purpose of concierges on housing estates is under way in France (where they are called guards not concierges), although the main argument is over whether they should be withdrawn for cost saving purposes, rather than introduced.

In the Netherlands, a major programme of block receptionist schemes is under way. The evaluation of 150 block receptionists for high rise blocks is being part-funded, on a taper for three years, by the Ministry of Justice, with the expectation that local authorities wholly fund the schemes thereafter. In the Netherlands, the schemes are conceived of as being principally concerned with crime reduction and are widely thought to have reduced levels of vandalism and break-ins (see van Dijk, 1989). However, a full evaluation of the programme has not yet been completed.

After Entryphones reviews the development of some of the earlier concierge schemes, drawing on the findings of previous research carried out by Polytechnic of South Bank (1985) and Poyner (1982), whose findings suggested that:

> Burglars appear to avoid the risk of personal confrontation, as it has been found that unmanned alternatives to doormen or security guards are much less effective. (Safe Neighbourhoods Unit, 1985)

The report argues that a complex series of inter-related events that can arise from residents' experience and fear of crime on estates, including increased social segregation, the undermining of the public sphere, increased isolation and reduced levels of informal social control. A housing management response to those problems is advocated:

> The introduction of intensive policing, assault proof front doors and phone entry systems are not, in themselves, the answer to the problems . . . it is housing management, closely co-ordinated with an input from other agencies and council departments which is responsible for formulating an effective long term response to these problems.

The importance of involving the residents of blocks in monitoring this management input into blocks and estates is also emphasised in the report:

> The key to the deployment of staff on some estates is the creation of an estate or block committee which cleaners, caretakers, estate managers, hall porters etc are required to attend by the terms of their employment and which is attended by tenant representatives and area management and maintenance officers.

A range of initiatives developed by both local authorities and housing associations are described in the report. However, the assessments of the success of these initiatives in reducing problems of crime, vandalism and anti-social behaviour are largely based on the authors' own observation and limited published evidence, rather than on any systematic quantitative evaluation.

The report describes these successes in the context of the constraints which can restrict the ability of local authorities to respond to the problems of multi-storey blocks. For example, while multi-storey blocks, by their very nature, demand a greater degree of commitment on the part of residents: they increasingly have to be allocated to people who may be less capable of adapting to these conditions.

A range of possible solutions based on selective allocations policies are described, although, once again, no detailed evaluation of their effectiveness is attempted. Approaches described include: the stratification of blocks by household type; the upgrading of multi-storey blocks to attract tenants from council houses and other low-rise accommodation; upgrading selected multi-storey blocks for shared ownership schemes; sale to individuals or let for high rent and the use of capital receipts to purchase or build more appropriate council accommodation.

Skilton (1986) attempts to assess the cost effectiveness and service delivery benefits of a pilot block receptionist scheme introduced in Gloucester House, a 17-storey tower block on the South Kilburn estate in Brent in 1984. The assessment was carried out in order to inform the extension of the receptionist system to a further five tower blocks on the estate. The report also made the case for further broadening the service provided by receptionist staff to include a repair service, a void control service and an accompanied viewing service.

The report compared the estimated costs incurred on Gloucester House across a series of headings with those for a neighbouring block, Hereford House. Estimates were then made for potential savings in terms of reductions in the numbers of empty dwellings and squattings, consequent savings on bed and breakfast charges, graffiti removal and lift repairs. Potential savings were estimated at £27,741 as against the additional cost of £19,300 for running the block receptionist service.

Some of the assumptions underlying these calculations are questioned by the Safe Neighbourhoods Unit (1987). For example, in relation to assumed reductions in the use of bed and breakfast accommodation, the report questions whether a marginal increase of properties available for letting is unlikely to affect the authorities' block use of bed and breakfast accommodation. In relation to the proposed concierge scheme for Trellick Tower in the Borough of Kensington and Chelsea, the report notes:

> . . . it seems unlikely that the security aspect of a receptionist scheme in Trellick Tower would prevent the general problem of squatting and unauthorised occupation. Much of this is due to outgoing tenants passing the keys to others without the Council's permission.

The report questions the automatic assumption that reception schemes will result in financial savings in the management of the block due to increased security which will offset the high revenue cost of additional staff:

> . . . while a receptionist scheme will certainly improve the management of the block and the quality of life for many residents, potential savings are very difficult to assess and quantify and may only be achieved in specific circumstances.

Skilton (1988) provides an updated review of the development of concierge schemes throughout Britain and further develops the view that a broad management based approach offers a more promising way forward than narrowly focused security based and technological approaches. In a review of 61 schemes operating in 22 authorities, 90% were identified as being *security based* and 10% as reception based.

Although, once again, no detailed quantitative information was available, it was noted that:

> . . . all authorities contacted appear satisfied that their schemes have produced significant improvements to security. Misuse of blocks has been brought under control and increased resident satisfaction is noticeable. This seems equally true whether a security based or reception based approach has been taken, which raises questions about the advantages of using security surveillance equipment in quantity.

Unfortunately, the absence of quantitative data on crime rates, levels of resident satisfaction and various management variables prevents any objective verification of this conclusion or any detailed explanation of the advantages and disadvantages of alternative approaches. The report also describes further developments in the London Borough of Brent's concierge programme following the publication of *Making an Entrance*. This approach has been based on a recognition of some of the inherent disadvantages of the security based approach, which may partially outweigh their success in reducing crime and misuse of blocks. In particular, the report notes that:

> Security guards and cameras do not necessarily improve the 'feel' of the block. In some ways they can make matters worse, or their presence emphasises the need for them.

Most importantly, according to Skilton, the approach adopted by Brent recognised the importance of tackling the whole range of problems faced by residents in multi-storey blocks, in addition to those of crime and vandalism:

> Tackling these complex problems is not only a matter of security. Tower blocks can become places where people are happy to live and initiatives are needed to achieve this objective.

The report advocates the need for receptionist staff to meet wider objectives than security provision so that they come to represent an extension of the housing management service.

The most recent review of developments in managing multi-storey blocks is contained within *Securing a Future for High Rise Living,* a manual designed for use by housing practitioners (Safe Neighbourhoods Unit, Birmingham City Council, 1990). Although the manual provides case studies of only six schemes, it also provides detailed chapters describing: alternative responses to multi-storey housing problems; guidance on assessment and option appraisal; implementation, in the context of Birmingham City Council's experience; training options for concierge staff, managers and other agencies; available technology for access control.

The manual further extends the concept of concierge as outlined in *A Better Reception* and describes in detail a range of types of receptionist or concierge schemes, including: security schemes; reception schemes; dispersed concierge schemes and integrated concierge schemes.

Although the review provides a largely descriptive outline of each approach, it stresses the need to tailor systems to the particular needs of individual blocks. It asserted that systems which place a heavy reliance on technology, such as the *dispersed* concierge scheme currently being implemented by Birmingham City Council, can provide only a limited response to the problems of multi-storey blocks:

> An alternative to providing an individual concierge in each block is to group blocks around a central concierge point, using technology to extend the personalised reception concept to the individual satellite blocks. However, it must be stressed that, in such cases, technology cannot be a complete substitute for human presence and it is important to consider how problems in satellite blocks will be effectively responded to.

The following project descriptions illustrate the approach

Elizabeth Street, Moor Lane, Preston

Before 1987, the Moor Lane area of Preston had one of the highest crime rates in the Borough. At the core of the area are three multi-storey blocks, each containing 96 flats. As well as experiencing high levels of burglary and vandalism, the blocks were also characterised by: high numbers of empty flats; high arrears; low demand for tenancies and high demand for transfers.

Resident consultation also revealed high levels of insecurity among tenants, particularly fear of being burgled or assaulted. Residents feared going out alone at night and using the lifts, and also complained about the amount of vandalism in the blocks.

In August 1988 a local office was opened in a converted ground floor flat in one of the blocks. The office provides the full range of housing management services, including: door to door rent collection and arrears control; allocation of flats; repairs and all estate management enquiries.

Security and access control to all three blocks is provided from an office linked to the housing office in Cumberland House. This provides a reception counter to the tenants in the block and also controls all three blocks via television monitors and video recorders linked to seven cameras in each of the blocks.

The block reception scheme is operated on a 24 hour, seven day a week basis by a team of residential staff who also provide a comprehensive caretaking service.

On the basis of recorded crime figures, the scheme has already had an impact on burglary in the blocks. During the 18 month period up to and including September 1988, the three blocks were experiencing an average of nine burglaries per month: a ratio of one burglary to 2.7 dwellings per annum. In the three months following the introduction of the partially completed scheme, the three blocks experienced a ratio of one burglary per 23.8 dwellings per annum. This represents an 89% reduction in recorded burglary rates. (Clearly, burglary rates will have to be monitored over a much longer period before any firm conclusions can be drawn.)

There is an increased demand for flats on the estate - a waiting list has been established and flats are generally accepted after one offer. There has also been a reduction in the number of requests to move from the estate and a reduced turnover of tenancies.

Source: Osborn, 1989
Safe Neighbourhoods Unit/Birmingham City Council, 1990

Barbot Street Estate, London Borough of Enfield

The Barbot Street Estate in Lower Edmonton consists of four 22-storey tower blocks, each containing 130 dwellings. The development of a concierge scheme on the estate was prompted by tenants' concerns about high levels of vandalism in the four blocks. Vandalism in the blocks took the form of broken phone entry systems, frequent lift breakdowns, broken communal doors, arson, widespread graffiti and smashed windows and lighting.

A survey carried out by the Safe Neighbourhoods Unit in 1988 highlighted residents' concerns:

> *'The survey demonstrates the feelings expressed strongly at the block meetings concerning the problems of vandalism, fires in the block and the general anxiety felt travelling through the block in close proximity to people who may be strangers and who may be intoxicated. Over 81% of women in Camelot and Tintagel Houses expressed a fear of being attacked inside their block. 65% of attacks and threats of attack took place within the blocks. Vandalism is not only unsightly and costly, it increases the likelihood of lift*

breakdowns. Vandalism to the dry riser inlets is a particularly serious problem given the continuing risk of fire in the blocks.' (Safe Neighbourhoods Unit, 1989c)

Clearly, some of the people who caused fear and anxiety were residents in the block, so simply excluding strangers by the use of entry phones would not be sufficient. This finding supports Adams' assertion that residents in public housing may victimise their own neighbourhood or block (Adams, 1973). A second problem of nuisance such as litter and noise was also mainly caused by residents.

The survey report also stressed the importance of promoting a high level of tenant involvement in the development of the concierge team. A tenant/officer steering group was therefore set up to develop the initiative.

In 1989 a team of twelve full-time and three part-time concierge staff was employed to provide a receptionist service in all four blocks between 8.00am and 11.30pm, seven days a week. As well as providing a welcoming reception service and controlling access to the blocks, the receptionists also provide advice on Council services and take repair requests. Concierge staff are also helping to develop a range of community facilities in the ground floor areas of the blocks.

'The atmosphere in all the blocks has changed for the better. People visiting elderly parents in the blocks have commented how they no longer feel anxious about calling in on Barbot Street. While previously small incidents could generate widespread anxiety and unease, the presence of the concierge is a source of considerable reassurance.' (Safe Neighbourhoods Unit/ Birmingham City Council, 1990)

As yet, no evaluation of the scheme has been carried out.

Source: Safe Neighbourhoods Unit, 1989c
          Safe Neighbourhoods Unit/Birmingham City Council, 1990.

Gloucester House, South Kilburn Estate, London Borough of Brent

Gloucester House, a tower block with 169 units, was selected for the development of the London Borough of Brent's first pilot concierge scheme in 1984.

The block was selected as it was considered to represent a typical system built tower block which suffered from all the problems associated with such buildings. 'Misuse of communal areas was a frequent occurrence and poor security was a major concern for all residents' (Skilton, 1988).

In 1984, following consultation with the block's residents, a receptionist service was introduced to the block. This was staffed by two receptionists between 8am and 11pm, Monday to Friday. The main aspects of the receptionists' initial job description were:

- To maintain block security by controlling access through the inner main door;

- To act as a receptionist and receive callers;

- To offer assistance to residents wherever possible.

The receptionist scheme was assessed in 1986, and the results summarised in a report, **Making an Entrance**, which compared running costs and management issues at Gloucester House and five similar blocks in the area. The following findings emerged from the report:

- *Reported crime* - Levels of reported crime were substantially lower than in similar neighbouring blocks.

- *High number of visitors* - During 1985, there were 13,800 visitors calling at the Gloucester House reception desk.

- *Communal repairs* - During 1985 five repairs carried out to communal areas cost £309, compared with a corresponding figure of 131 repairs, costing £6,056 in neighbouring Hereford House.

- *Lift breakdowns* - During 1985 there were 28 lift breakdowns in Gloucester House, costing £840 compared with 75, costing £2,250 in Hereford House.

- *Graffiti* - During 1985 there was no expenditure necessary for graffiti removal in Gloucester House, compared with an average annual expenditure of £1,365 in five similar neighbouring blocks.

- *Voids* - During 1985/86 £5,791 in rental income was lost due to voids, compared to £11,898 at Hereford House.

- *Squatting* - During the twelve months of research, 6% of voids at Gloucester House were squatted, compared to 29% in Hereford House.

- *Caretaking and management* - It was estimated that caretaking and management costs were reduced by around £1,250 (due to fewer repairs, transfer applications and nuisance complaints).

- *Costs and savings* - It was estimated that the direct savings in costs for 1985/86, as a result of introducing the receptionist scheme, were in excess of £17,000. This excludes an estimated saving in bed and breakfast charges of £10,062.

Following the production of **Making an Entrance** it was decided to reproduce the Gloucester House scheme in other blocks in Brent. The approach adopted in the more recent schemes is described in the report: **A Better Reception** (Skilton, 1988).

Source: Skilton, 1986
           Skilton, 1988

Mitchellhill Concierge Service, Glasgow

The Mitchellhill concierge service was introduced to five 19-storey blocks in July 1989.

The aim of the service was to provide improved on-site management in the blocks by increasing the level of security, improving standards of care and cleanliness and ensuring the availability of staff at all times. Improvements to the blocks included:

- Uniformed concierge team providing 24 hour service;

- Controlled entry, video cameras and monitors in the concierge station;

- Improved foyers and landings;

- Secure hardwood entrance doors to each flat;

- Housing staff and an office on site;

- Tenants involved in management including allocations;

- Close working with community police officer.

The City Council Housing Department monitored a number of key variables, including crime rates over a two year period from the beginning of 1988 to May 1989. The results of the monitoring exercise are summarised below.

Crime

There was a notable reduction in recorded crime on the blocks, from a high of 23 per quarter in 1988 to a low of six in the most recent quarter (see Figure 2). It was reported that burglaries and attempted burglaries had 'almost been eliminated'. Other crime, including autocrime and reported vandalism, had also been reduced.

> 'Perhaps more important, the fear of crime has reduced. Residents now tell us they feel much safer and secure in the knowledge that they can leave their homes and they won't be broken into.'

Figure 2 **Mitchellhill Development - total number of crimes**

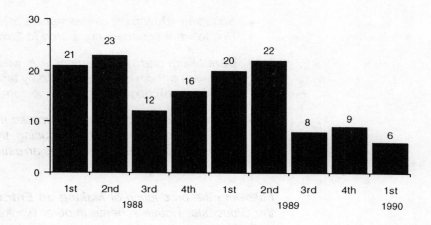

Voids

Following the introduction of the scheme, accompanied by positive marketing both to existing residents and potential new applicants, voids declined sharply from 125 in the first quarter of 1990 to 97 in the third quarter.

Turnover

The turnover rate declined from 27% in 1988 to 13% during the last six months of 1989. It was considered that an increase in turnover during the most recent quarter could reflect less desirable tenants leaving because of increased security and more vigorous enforcement tenancy conditions.

Rental income

From a low of £79,073 in the last quarter of 1988, rental income had risen to £122,313 during the first quarter of 1990.

Conclusions

Although the above findings do not provide the basis for a thorough evaluation of the scheme, they suggest that the scheme is having a beneficial effect according to a range of objective criteria, including recorded crime rates.

●Source: Glasgow City Council, 1990

Trellick Tower, Kensington and Chelsea

Trellick Tower is a 30-storey tower block with 217 dwellings situated in the Royal Borough of Kensington and Chelsea. The Safe Neighbourhoods Unit undertook an assessment of the management and security needs of the block in 1986.

They concluded that the level of burglary in the block was average for an inner city area, but that there was a high level of fear of crime among tenants. The existing phone entry system was found to be inadequate and tenants prioritised the following improvements:

- Refurbishment of the phone entry system;

- Strengthening of front doors;

- Improved security for windows;

- A block receptionist system;

- Video cameras in lifts and on landings;

- A two-way intercom system in lifts.

The report noted that, 'the more security measures are introduced, the greater need there is for a local management presence'. CCTV is also more suited to identifying strangers who may cause trouble in the block than dealing with anti-social residents. Too much surveillance security can give a block a fortress like feel which may increase fear of crime. 'CCTV is only an effective deterrent where those committing some anti-social or criminal act feel they are likely to be caught. In practical terms, this means either that there must be someone at hand who will intervene or that it will be possible to positively identify the perpetrator.' Having a receptionist who gets to know people in the block is essential if s/he is to monitor possible trouble. The emphasis is on allaying fear as much as on stopping crime, and on the receptionist as a helpful and supportive block manager rather than a security guard. These ideas may not seem out of place alongside Newman's theories of creating safety by breaking down anonymity.

The report stressed the important role that allocations policies play in maintaining a proper balance of household types within a block, and the need for adequate play provision for children in the block. The need for careful monitoring and evaluation of the new security measures before any further changes or additions are made was also stressed. Other proposals related to the need for properly paid and trained block receptionists, resident involvement in management and efficient service back-up.

Source: Safe Neighbourhoods Unit, 1986b
          Safe Neighbourhoods Unit, 1987

The available research suggests that although physical security measures appear to offer a tangible and flexible approach to problems of crime, particularly acquisitive crime such as theft and burglary, it is important not to overstate their potential outside the context of wider and supporting policy measures. Physical security is often applied with little reference to the social situation. There is a tendency to assume that physical measures are somehow unproblematic and generalisable to quite different social situations.

Discussion of the social dimension of physical crime prevention measures has generally been limited to the problem of displacement. Displacement occurs when a measure causes crime to shift to other neighbourhoods, to different times of the day, to other offence types or to different groups in the same neighbourhood. There is some uncertainty about displacement evident in the literature. Situational factors, such as cover from surveillance and occupancy, do appear to be important in influencing what Bennett calls 'the final decision' to commit crime (Bennett, 1986). Bennett's study is based on *rational choice* theory and draws its evidence from interviews with former burglars. West (1982) argues that most offences committed by young people (a substantial proportion of total indictable offences) are 'disorganised, impulsive and generally unprofitable'. To the Parliamentary All-Party Penal Affairs Group this underlines the essentially opportunistic nature of much crime: 'exactly the sort of crimes most likely to be prevented by situational measures' (Parliamentary All-Party Penal Affairs Group, 1983). This seems at odds with the more calculating opportunism of Bennet's more mature subjects. However, it is argued, although displacement may occur, it is not inevitable. Only a proportion of the initial potential offenders will pursue their intent to commit crime. It is argued that, if situational measures are used widely enough, there must be spatial and temporal limits to displacement. Heal and Laycock (1986) conclude:

> . . . where the basic needs are weak and the costs and risks of committing a crime high, displacement is unlikely; however where the situation is reversed displacement may well occur.

This begs the question of how one decides in any particular context whether such an approach has failed because the motivation to commit crime is high or the measures insufficiently comprehensive (see also Barr and Pease, 1990).

These problems of definition and uncertainty may be traced through the typical approaches employed in situational crime prevention. Situational crime prevention is referred to by some as *primary prevention* or *opportunity reduction* (Bennett, 1986). Atkins (1989) suggests a more comprehensive definition which goes beyond the *locks and bolts* approach: situational crime prevention 'aims to reduce the opportunities for crime by changing the environment or context in which criminal activity takes place'. Hough et al. (1980) emphasise that situational crime prevention is 'directed at highly specific forms of crime', but there are differences in opinion between those who feel situational crime prevention is limited to reducing acquisitive offending, such as burglary, autocrime and, possibly, robbery and those who believe it may also be helpful in respect of *expressive* crimes such as those involving violence, for example, murder, rape and racial harassment.

Target hardening or removal

In the context of housing estates, target hardening has often taken the form of initiatives aimed at individuals, for example, the potential victims of burglary. Households are encouraged to make their home more secure. Initiatives may take the form of publicity campaigns which aim to persuade people to lock up their property or to fit additional security locks. Publicity campaigns continue to be a popular response to crime, and large sums of money are allocated to national campaigns by central government, despite the evidence that they have no, or at most a short term, effect on crime levels (Riley and Mayhew, 1980). The police employ crime prevention officers able to undertake free security surveys for households, although Laycock (1989) suggests that demand for such surveys is low and largely confined to higher socio-economic groups.

At the local authority level, target hardening on housing estates has often taken the form of upgrading inferior fixtures and fittings, installing stronger front doors and frames - anything from providing mortice locks to steel multiple locking doors. These programmes may be very costly, tend to be limited in scope and may create problems of displacement. Allatt (1984a) points to the difficulties of providing complete security to dwellings:

> Installation of security, therefore, cannot be assumed to be complete, even following a rigorous installation policy. Security must be maintained and factors influencing the maintenance of security need careful consideration.

Moreover, doors of sufficient strength to delay intrusion (for no-one claims a burglar proof entrance) increase the risks to residents of multi-storey blocks in the event of a fire (Crouch S, 1990; DoE, 1991). This is a particularly serious risk given the vulnerability of *dry risers* to vandalism. Within blocks of flats there is a dilemma between increasing security to reduce the risk of arson and facilitating unrestricted movement in the event of a fire.

The importance of the social context to target hardening may be illustrated by examining the widespread use of phone-entry systems to improve the physical security of many different types of flatted block. There is now considerable experience of their relative effectiveness. The Safe Neighbourhood Unit's report *After Entryphones* (Safe Neighbourhoods Unit, 1985) described the failure of many costly schemes, which were characterised by:

- Lack of consultation with residents;

- Inadequate maintenance arrangements;

- Inadequate assessment of the level of abuse and misuse, and volume of traffic which the technology will have to withstand.

After Entryphones and other research undertaken into the management and security of multi-storey blocks (see, for example, Safe Neighbourhoods Unit, 1986b; Safe Neighbourhoods Unit, 1989c) has indicated the possibility that fear of crime (particularly fear of incivilities) may be caused, often unwittingly, by *strangers* who may live in the block or whose access is authorised, for example, visitors and tradespersons. A common assumption of target hardening measures is that crime and fear of crime is generated by people living outside the secured area.

Target removal may refer to the removal of vulnerable items such as cars, gas and electricity meters and communal or street furniture which is vulnerable to vandalism. Targets may also include people. As with target hardening, target removal measures may have contradictory effects.

The replacement of communal windows with steel panels and the removal of all but the most durable street furniture may produce a bleak and forbidding environment, further weakening residents' commitment to the estate. Such an environment may increase residents' concerns about crime. It may invite anti-social behaviour. It may simply displace such behaviour elsewhere. Hope and Dowds (1987) draw attention to the role of environmental coding in increasing the problems of crime, fear of crime and anti social behaviour.

For many local authorities, however, target removal may be the only short term option available to cope with unacceptably high maintenance and replacement costs.

Target removal also describes the kind of precautionary advice offered mainly to women by the police. Surveys, such as the Islington Crime Survey, appear to show that such advice is scarcely necessary. Lynch and Atkins (1988) enumerate the precautionary tactics taken by many women, particularly those living on high density housing estates. These include: not going out alone; not going out after dark; not walking at night; trying to travel with other people; avoiding using buses in the evening; not waiting at bus stops at night; using cars as often as possible; travelling with car doors locked; avoiding particular areas; taking self defence classes; trying to find a job near home; being more cautious. Clearly, for many, particularly those who work anti-social hours for relatively low wages, self removal as a potential target is not a practical option. For those who can afford it, self removal may mean moving away altogether from the estate.

To date, very few systematic evaluations of residential security measures have been attempted, and most studies have used police data rather than victim surveys. However, a number of in-depth studies have been carried out in Britain during the last ten years. These include: a study of victims and non-victims of burglary in Kent (Winchester and Jackson, 1982); an evaluation of a target hardening exercise on a difficult to let estate in Newcastle (Allatt, 1984a); and an evaluation of a burglary prevention project on the Kirkholt Estate in Rochdale (Forrester, Chatterton and Pease, 1988). An interesting, if limited, study of the impact of phone entry systems in Ealing (Osborn, 1986) was also carried out. A small scale evaluation of a pilot scheme of security improvements to multi-occupied homes in Handsworth, Birmingham, was also carried out in 1987 (NACRO, 1987) but was too soon after the improvements were implemented to draw meaningful conclusions.

Study of burglary victims in Kent

Winchester and Jackson compared the characteristics of a general household sample with a group of households in the study area who had all been recent victims of burglary. The study concentrated on four factors which were already thought to be important in determining the vulnerability of particular households to burglary: security, reward value, levels of occupancy and environmental risk (the characteristics of the site and location of the house). The study found that the most important factors differentiating victim and non-victim households were environmental risk, followed by occupancy rates and reward. Relative security levels did not contribute to the differentiation.

However, the study area was characterised as being typical of stockbroker or commuter areas. It was noted that those local authority houses which were burgled tended to be of low reward and low environmental risk. Although the number of such households in the sample was small, Winchester and Jackson tentatively concluded that basic security measures might be important in determining burglary risk in these cases:

'Those households which appear to be most likely to benefit from installing and using the recommended security hardware are householders whose homes are easily visible from public areas as is frequently the case with local authority housing.'

On the basis of these findings Allatt (1984a) also concludes: *'target hardening may have greater scope for success in public as opposed to private housing especially, perhaps, in those areas of high deprivation with high burglary rates'.* No further evidence is presented to substantiate this view.

Source: Winchester and Jackson, 1982
              Allatt, 1984a

Scotswood Estate,
Newcastle

Allatt's Newcastle study involved the installation of ground floor security devices on the Scotswood Estate in the West End of Newcastle. The evaluation investigated effects on the rate of burglary on the estate and the displacement of burglary to adjacent areas and other types of property crime within the estate, as well as on residents' anxiety about crime (Allatt, 1984a). The study concluded that the upgrading of security on the estate *'had a positive effect for residents, especially in the first year. Whereas on the control estate and in the police subdivision encompassing the target estate burglary increased, on the target estate it steadied.'*

However, the study also identified some displacement of burglaries to two adjacent residential areas and to other properties within the estate. There was also a clearer displacement effect to other property crimes within the estate. It was also found that the burglary rate began to climb once again after around a year. This was attributed to the effectiveness of the security devices being overridden *'either by more astute or a greater number of burglars, or by carelessness on the part of the householder'.*

Source: Allatt, 1984a

Kirkholt Estate,
Rochdale - burglary
prevention project

The Kirkholt Estate is a large council estate with 2,280 dwellings located two miles south of Rochdale town centre. In 1985 the estate was selected as the site for a burglary prevention demonstration project funded by the Home Office and staff from the Greater Manchester Probation Service and Greater Manchester Police Force.

During the first five months of 1985, recorded domestic burglaries on the estate were equivalent to an annual rate of 24.6% - over double the average rate of all burglaries, both reported and unreported, for high risk areas in the 1984 British Crime Survey.

Interviews were held with 76 convicted burglars from the Rochdale area, and with 237 burglary victims and 136 neighbours of victims on the estate. Through these interviews, and interviews with a range of local agencies, a detailed picture was built up of the circumstances under which burglaries were carried out on the estate. Key features which emerged included:

- The majority of burglaries were committed in the vicinity of the burglar's home (63% of most recent burglaries were committed within a mile of the burglar's home);

- Only 16 of the burglars gained access because the premises were insecure;

- 70% of points of entry were visible to neighbours, compared with 35% visible to passers-by;

- 49% of burglaries involved the loss of meter cash.

In analysing those characteristics of victim households which distinguished them from neighbouring houses, the main distinguishing features proved to be the lack of a dog and the absence of signs of occupancy, rather that the absence of window locks. Analysis of 1986 domestic burglary figures also revealed that the chance of a second or subsequent burglary was over four times as high as the chance of the first burglary.

On the basis of the above factors, together with a general belief in the need for a series of measures, the following package of measures was adopted and targeted on prior burglary victims:

- Upgrading of household security;

- Property postcoding;

- Removal of gas and electric cash pre-payment meters;

- Mini Neighbourhood Watch schemes, targeted on burglary victims;

- Setting up a computerised monitoring and evaluation system.

An initial evaluation of the success of the crime prevention package was carried out in 1987. Recorded burglary on the estate fell from 316 in 1986 to 147 in 1987, compared with a slight increase in the rest of the police sub-division. Unlike the Newcastle study (Allatt, 1984a) there was no evidence of displacement to adjoining areas. Other forms of acquisitive crime also showed a reduction in comparison with neighbouring areas, suggesting that there had been no significant displacement to other offences on the estate. Repeat burglary victimisation was found to have declined by 80% during the seven month post-implementation period in comparison with the seven month pre-implementation period.

A postscript to the initial evaluation report suggests that these reductions were being sustained some eleven months after the implementation of the initiative.

The initial results of the initiative appear to demonstrate the potential for reducing burglary rates on high crime estates through the application of well resourced and well co-ordinated packages of crime prevention measures and approach basing strategies on the prevention of repeat burglaries.

However, it is important to bear in mind that a large proportion of the reduction in burglary rates could be attributed to the removal of coin meters from the estate, a measure which is clearly not replicable in many areas (although the researchers would argue that the overall approach could be). In addition, the researchers did not describe the substantial programme of environmental improvements undertaken by the Housing Department at the same time and the effects that this programme may have had on the estate's crime problems.

Source: Forrester, Chatterton and Pease, 1988

South Acton Estate, Ealing

The estate has about 2000 homes, mainly built in the 1960s and 1970s. It is a mixture of tower blocks, medium size and small blocks of flats and maisonettes and some terraced houses. The Council began a gradual programme of physical improvements on the estate in 1981.

Police figures showed that burglaries on the estate increased in 1986 and were 39% higher in the first six months of 1986 than in the same period of 1985. The largest blocks (tower blocks of 75+ dwellings) had the biggest rate of increase over 1985: 46%.

The larger blocks on the estate had higher burglary rates. Blocks with 41 or more dwellings had the equivalent of one burglary to 11 dwellings per annum in 1986; smaller blocks had the equivalent of one burglary to 19 dwellings.

However, size of block was not the only relevant factor. 18 of 37 blocks had phone entry systems installed. The three tower blocks with reasonably effective phone entry systems had very low burglary rates in 1986, working out at about one burglary to 56 dwellings per annum. This was 67% less than in 1985. In contrast, the six tower blocks without phone entry systems or with largely ineffective systems had high burglary rates in 1986; about one burglary to nine dwellings per annum. This was an 83% increase since 1985.

Closer inspection of the two tower blocks with phone entry systems which were mostly inoperative showed that one system was out of order for all but 19 days in the first six months of 1986. The other block suffered 85% of its burglaries (in 1986) during a continuous period of 55 days when the front door was out of action.

The same was true for medium size blocks. Blocks without phone entry systems had a very high burglary rate in 1986: about one burglary to five dwellings per annum. This was 56% up on 1985. The blocks with phone entry systems had very low burglary rates in 1986: about one burglary to every 34 dwellings per annum. This was a decrease of 50% since 1985.

The small blocks on the other hand were completely unaffected by phone entry systems. Those with and those without phone entry systems had uniformly low burglary rates.

To sum up:

- *Burglary rates were higher in the larger blocks.*

- *Where phone entry systems worked reasonably well most of the time, burglary rates went down dramatically. Unfortunately it was impossible to guarantee that they would work reasonably well most of the time because of maintenance problems.*

The study provides an interesting perspective on the apparent failure of many phone entry systems to reduce crime: namely, that there was little guarantee that systems once installed ever worked properly. The analysis was based on recorded crime rates only and other supporting data would have been useful. Furthermore, the focus on burglary, and neglect of violent incidents in particular, presents only a partial picture of the local crime problems. Also, no attempt was made in this study to assess the impact of other improvements introduced at the same time such as block refurbishment and landscaping changes on defensible space principles.

Source: Osborn, 1987

Reducing the pay off

A second approach is to try and find ways of reducing the profit or pay off from crime through, for example, property marking or the removal of coin operated meters for electricity and gas. Implied here is the rational decision making model for the intending criminal. A calculation is made in weighing up the pay off with the anticipated risks.

Property marking initiatives may be of value, although little research is available. There is no evidence that property marking significantly increases the chances of goods being returned to owners and there is only one example of a scheme which substantially reduced crime levels. This exception (Laycock, 1985) used intensive publicity and was carried out in an isolated and close-knit community in South Wales. Laycock concluded that the apparent success of the scheme in reducing burglary was not in the marking of property but:

> ... in the message to potential burglars that the risk of breaking into this home is greater than that associated with another 'unmarked' home: the residents here, so the message reads, are concerned about burglary and the risk of capture is therefore greater. (Laycock, 1986)

There is evidence that the removal of pre-payment coin meters has an impact on burglary levels (Hill, 1986). It seems clear that their removal was a major element of the previously mentioned Kirkholt project. Pre-payment coin meters are becoming a rare housing feature.

If the risks of detection are considered to be negligible, then the pay off, particularly for opportunist break-ins or snatches, may be freely gambled on. This point is made in respect of target hardening and levels of security by the Parliamentary All-Party Penal Affairs Group (1983). They state:

> ... research studies have found that the level of security is less important than factors such as ease of access, surveillability and the presence or absence of potential witnesses in determining a house's likelihood of being burgled.

Increasing risk of detection

This introduces a third approach - namely taking measures to make detection or intervention more likely. Target hardening may, of course, serve this purpose, in that it increases the length of time to effect a break-in. That said, residents of multi-storey blocks have reported ignoring what sounded like sledge-hammer attacks on neighbours' doors because of fear of reprisals (Safe Neighbourhoods Unit, 1985). Opportunities for surveillance will often be ignored by potential witnesses because of such fears.

Burglar alarms are a widely canvassed means, not of actually stopping access, but of altering the potential offender's perception of the probability of being caught. Although research has indicated that the presence of an alarm may figure in the potential burglar's decision making process, the main effect is probably displacement (Bennett, 1986). A proliferation of alarms in a residential area, with the associated problems of accidental release, may devalue their deterrent effect. The main measures used in this approach may be described as those which seek to improve *formal* and *informal* surveillance (Atkins, 1989). Formal surveillance measures include increasing the frequency of patrols by police or security staff, possibly assisted by closed circuit television. Informal or natural surveillance implies observation by other people not necessarily those in positions of authority or responsibility. Informal surveillance is said to be facilitated by careful attention to the design and layout of estates to minimise isolated *dead areas* where there is little pedestrian movement and which are not overlooked by dwellings. It may be enhanced by Neighbourhood Watch (discussed in Section 5) and improved lighting. The issue of environmental design and management, particularly in respect of lighting, will be returned to below.

The mushrooming of security patrols has been a major feature of the last decade. There are said to be over 1,000 security patrol teams in the UK and that half of these are employed directly or indirectly by local authorities (see PSLG, May 1989, *Privatised Protection*). Although initially focused on non-residential areas such as industrial estates, private patrols are increasingly being used for public housing estates. For instance, the London Borough of Bromley has used a private security company to patrol six estates; Livingston New Town Corporation employs 42 staff to provide a mobile patrol of all council estates; Wolverhampton Borough Council has experimented with security patrols on one of its least popular high rise estates, Blakenhall Gardens; and Middlesbrough Borough Council employs *Community Security,* a community-based security co-operative for a number of estates.

There is little evidence of the effectiveness of security patrols and concern has been expressed by the police and others about a range of issues from traditionally low rates of pay for patrol staff, their precise duties and responsibilities, and about their potential for exacerbating existing tensions on estates. The only scheme which has been partially assessed is the Barrowfield Estate community based scheme in Glasgow. This is described in the section on Social Measures for Residential Areas and it is noteworthy that, whilst the scheme is said to have dramatically reduced some crime problems, it replaced a private security scheme which was singularly unsuccessful. The success of the community based scheme appears to have been related to the form of organisation (a community co-operative with widespread community support) rather than to its functions.

Little meaningful research has been undertaken on the effectiveness of closed circuit television (CCTV) in residential areas. Aside from concerns about civil liberties, there are diverging views about the effectiveness of CCTV. There is no evidence that CCTV on its own, without other complementary measures, has any effect on residential buildings (Mayhew, 1984). Most CCTV schemes in multi-storey blocks depend on a high level of staff presence in the block itself. Birmingham Council's dispersed concierge scheme on the Highgate Estate, which monitors five blocks from one monitoring point, emphasises the importance of resident contact with the concierge, the high quality of service delivery and the 24 hour presence (Safe Neighbourhoods Unit and Birmingham City Council, 1990). It is not considered to be an invincible security system, although levels of break-ins and vandalism have apparently decreased. The scheme was introduced to blocks with *middle range* management and security problems. The cameras and residents' positive perceptions about their effectiveness, together with other important management changes, have seemingly contributed to a much more positive relationship between residents and their local authority landlord.

Although CCTV may have a role to play, it may be at its most useful in non-residential settings or in smaller residential schemes where it is useful in identifying intruders in restricted areas (see, for example, Burrows, 1980). CCTV has, however, proved an attractive option to many local authorities seeking to provide additional security in the context of cuts in expenditure, particularly with respect to staff. This includes reductions in residential caretaking staff whose informal role in surveillance and in reassuring residents can be very important. In relation to the use of CCTV on public transport, Atkins (1989) notes: 'cameras alone do not provide much reassurance to passengers, who need to be convinced that such systems are an extension of staff presence and not a substitute for it'. But even the presence of staff may be problematic and far from reassuring. Retaining high quality staff in situations alternately boring and stressful is difficult. The alternative may be lower paid staff working long hours, often poorly motivated and poorly supervised.

Other means of extending the influence of staff include communication and alarm systems. There are theoretically no technical limits. It is ironic that in many blocks access to a telephone is often restricted for many residents. Dispersed alarm systems introduced initially for the vulnerable elderly have been extended to other vulnerable groups. The Leicester scheme to combat racial harassment employs a package of target hardening measures, alarms and cameras to focus surveillance on vulnerable households. The strength of these systems is that they have the staff resources to make them effective.

Staffing resources impose limits on the wide applicability of all the measures discussed here. As a result, improving informal surveillance may be the only practical option. Cost considerations may also prevent even limited remodelling of estate layouts and social and community development initiatives to improve activity levels. These factors may help to explain the present interest in limited technical improvements such as lighting schemes.

Lighting

Until recently, there has been relatively little research in this country about the relationship between lighting and crime. It has been suggested that, in certain circumstances, improved lighting may reduce crime and is highly likely to reduce fear of crime. What previous research exists has been extensively reviewed in recent years (see, for example, Fleming, 1987a; Fleming, 1987b; and Fleming and Burrows, 1987). The key features of this review are summarised below.

A major American study by Hartley (1974; cited in Fleming, 1987a) examined the impact of high intensity street lighting installed in four high-crime areas of the Columbia District, Washington. Hartley reported a 30% reduction in crime during the subsequent year. Fleming (1987a) describes the results of a comprehensive evaluation of the use of lighting to deter crime undertaken by Wright et al. (1974) in Kansas City. Following a major relighting programme carried out between 1970 and 1973, the study showed that robberies and assaults were significantly reduced by the new lighting. Wright also concluded that just under a quarter of this crime had been displaced to blocks not affected by the relighting programme.

However, Fleming (1987b) also summarised the results of a major evaluation undertaken by Tien et al. (1979) which concluded that nearly all the studies evaluated were based on inadequate understanding of the effects of different types of lighting and moreover employed poor analytical techniques. However, the review also suggested that there is 'a strong indication that increased lighting - perhaps lighting uniformity - decreases the fear of crime'.

Research undertaken by Mariner (1974) concludes that: '40% of night-time street crime occurs where lighting levels are at 5 lux or lower . . . 32% between lux levels of 5 to 10 and . . . 19% where lux levels are between 10 and 15'.

During 1988, the Safe Neighbourhoods Unit undertook research into current lighting provision, and its relationship with the incidence and fear of crime, on three priority estates in the London Borough of Brent (Safe Neighbourhoods Unit, 1988c). The research focused on the needs of residents and pedestrians on the three estates, as opposed to the needs of vehicular traffic. The study indicated that poor lighting has a pronounced effect on residents' sense of security and daily behaviour. There was a close relationship between levels of fear of crime and lighting levels. Poorly lit areas on all three estates were regularly avoided. A majority of victims of crime felt that lighting had been a contributing factor to the crime taking place, both inside and outside blocks. Most respondents also believed that lighting improvements would help greatly in making people feel safer. Priorities for lighting improvements included improved systems of maintenance and checks, brighter lighting, vandal resistant fittings, extra lights and better locations. It should be noted that the study is based on residents' perceptions, rather than on a controlled study of incidents. The suggested links between lighting levels and the occurrence of crime should be considered in this context.

Situational lighting measures have been used to combat crime which is known to occur in particular areas, such as in public offices, telephone boxes, shops etc. When combined with *social* crime prevention methods, Painter (1988) asserts that situational lighting improvements can physically alter and improve an area and the incidence of crime in that setting. She says, 'A bright uniformly lit environment is more attractive, encourages people to use the streets at night, enhances public safety and decreases fears which centre around the possibility of violent interpersonal crime.'

Lighting may have an impact on some forms of crime rather than others. A criticism of lighting as a crime prevention measure is that it will simply displace crime. But as Cornish and Clarke (1986) point out, there is little systematic evidence to test the hypothesis.

Lighting may have a particular impact for women and elderly people, many of whom are living under a *self-imposed curfew* because of fear of crime. Much area or estate based research has claimed widespread support for improved lighting as a crime prevention measure, as illustrated by the following project descriptions.

The Edmonton Project, Enfield	*The research by Painter (1988) comprised a before and after study of one street which was provided with improved lighting. The period covered was 12 weeks, arguably an insufficient time span for adequate monitoring and evaluation. Crime appeared to decline. On the basis of survey data Painter claimed that incidents of assault, autocrime and threats fell by 75% in the six week period after the lighting improvements were installed.*

The overwhelming majority of women expressed fear of crime when walking alone along the street at night. After the installation of improved lighting, most people interviewed thought that crime had reduced. Lighting appears to have a strong psychological impact. In particular, Painter claimed that improved lighting had the following effects:

- *It encourages people to use the streets;*

- *It consolidates and regenerates the public sphere and brings public areas back into use;*

- *It encourages informal natural surveillance by pedestrians;*

- *It increases the likelihood of the victim or a witness identifying offenders.*

There is, however, no independent evidence to support these ideas about the way improved lighting may affect the behaviour of individuals using an area.

Source: Painter, 1988

Landor Walk, Hammersmith and Fulham	*In 1989, the London Borough of Hammersmith and Fulham commissioned a study into the impact of street-lighting on crime, fear of crime and community safety in a small, poorly lit area. The study aimed to examine: the nature and extent of victimisation among elderly residents and pedestrians; the influence of physical setting and lifestyle on householders and pedestrians; the effects of the*

quality of street lighting on lifestyle and the scope of street lighting as a crime preventive measure within the study area.

The study area, a small side road called Landor Walk, was selected for the following reasons:

- *It has inadequate public lighting.*

- *It was a short, clearly demarcated route.*

- *It was an essential pedestrian through route from residential housing to high street shopping, leisure and transport facilities.*

- *It contained residential housing.*

The study area also contained a large proportion of sheltered/warden assisted accommodation, which meant that the researchers were able to examine the impact of street lighting on a largely elderly population. The surrounding demography (including a public house, shops and restaurants) meant that the road was well used, and it was considered that the mixture of householders, pedestrians and surrounding shops and public houses, together with the inadequate lighting, would lend itself to opportunist offending.

The study methodology comprised a household survey, a pedestrian survey, pedestrian traffic flow counts and detailed crime mapping six weeks before and six weeks after the relighting improvements.

43 people were interviewed in both the before and after household surveys and 400 pedestrian survey interviews were conducted - 200 before the lighting improvements and 200 after.

The household survey revealed a total of eleven incidents of crime (burglary, threatening behaviour, property damage, vehicle crime) occurring after dark before the lighting improvements were carried out. This figure was reduced to nought after the improvements. Whereas 20 respondents had witnessed men urinating in the road or against their homes during the six weeks before re-lighting, only one incident of this kind was recorded after re-lighting.

As the pedestrian survey revealed only two incidents of crime to pedestrians in the road during the six week period before re-lighting, it was not possible to conclude that re-lighting had had any effect on reducing or preventing crime to pedestrians in the road itself. However, it was found that the number of incidents occurring in the two adjacent roads had reduced from 19 in the period before lighting to four in the period after. It was considered that this might be due to the increase in the number of pedestrians using the road after dark.

Both the household and pedestrian surveys revealed that fear of crime had been reduced by the improved lighting. Pedestrians were less concerned about physical attack and threatening behaviour following the improvements. Respondents living in Landor Walk were said to worry 'slightly less' about being burgled.

It was also concluded that improved street lighting had a positive effect on respondents' assessment of crime problems in the area. 'Before relighting, the majority of respondents thought that burglary, street robbery, vandalism, threatening behaviour and sexual assaults had become more common in the previous five years . . . After re-lighting 70% of respondents on the street survey thought that street robbery/physical assault had decreased; 60% thought that sexual assault had decreased; 80% thought that incidents of threatening/pestering behaviour had decreased.'

The study clearly shows that improved lighting can have an immediate impact upon pedestrians and residents' experience and perceptions of crime, particularly in relation to incidents of threatening, pestering and insulting behaviour and property crime. However, the relatively short monitoring period means that it is not possible to draw any conclusions about long term effects of the lighting improvements on crime levels. Similar reservations must be expressed in relation to respondents' improved perceptions of crime problems, which may have represented a positive reaction to improvements to the area, as much as to the enhanced lighting levels. The small sample size for the household survey, together with the small number of crime incidents picked up in the pedestrian survey, also limits the usefulness of some of the evaluation findings.

Source: Painter, 1989.

Watney Street, Tower Hamlets

This study by Painter (1989b) assessed the impact of lighting improvements to the Watney Street area of Tower Hamlets through before and after surveys. Interviews were carried out with 143 pedestrians in January 1988 prior to improvements and with the same number in March 1988 after improvements.

A total of 18 incidents were reported in the six weeks prior to improvements and only four incidents in the six weeks following improvements. This was a substantial reduction in reported incidents (mainly threatening/insulting behaviour). Fear of crime was also reduced. Fear of physical attack fell by 45% and fear of rape and sexual assault (against women) by 22%.

The same reservations about the results can be made as in the case of the two previously described Painter studies: 12 weeks is arguably too short a monitoring period and there are too few incidents to properly analyse trends.

Source: Painter, 1989b

Easton/Ashley, Bristol

In 1987 Bristol City Council upgraded the lighting in the Easton and Ashley wards of Bristol as a crime prevention measure. £250,000 was spent on the improvements through the Inner Area Programme. Recorded crime figures for the eight month period prior to improvements were compared with the same eight month period in 1988. These showed a 17% reduction in robberies, a 33% reduction in theft from cars and a 21% reduction in vandalism (but no reduction in burglary). The total number of recorded incidents fell from 3,245 to 2,507.

No assessment was made of the possible impact of any external factors on the crime rate and no supporting data was presented. Some reservations about the scheme were reported, in particular the harsh floodlighting used.

Source: Bristol City Council, 1989

Erdington Hall Area, Birmingham

In 1987, Birmingham City Council introduced lighting improvements to the Erdington Hall area as a crime prevention measure. Recorded crime figures for the year prior to relighting were compared with figures for the year after relighting. These showed 50% reductions in auto crimes and criminal damage and a reduction in the total of crimes recorded from 260 to 145.

No other data was provided in the case study report on the nature of the lighting scheme nor was there any description of the implementation.

Source: Institute of Lighting Engineers, 1990

Social measures to prevent crime are typically aimed at tackling the causes of crime and the motivations of individuals to offend. It could be argued that all areas of social policy have a bearing on crime but most often cited are housing, education, employment, youth, health and family policy.

An investigation of social measures taken at the estate or neighbourhood level presents a number of difficulties. Firstly, social measures are usually conceived of in broad programme terms rather than in relation to specific geographical locations and a good deal of the literature ignores the community dimension. In fact, it is difficult to see how some kinds of social measure could be introduced locally in isolation from or in conflict with national or regional policy developments. Secondly, social measures which have an impact on crime are not necessarily introduced with crime prevention in mind and may be considered in these terms only in retrospect or not at all. Consequently, there is little relevant material in the crime prevention literature. Thirdly, social measures tend to be conceived of as long-term in their effects with obvious implications for measuring their effectiveness. Finally, there have been specific objections to the use of community-level social measures. Clarke and Cornish (1983) claim 'there is little evidence to date that youth work, voluntary welfare, school liaison work by the police, community self-help groups and tenants associations have any effects on levels of crime'.

In this section of the report we have attempted to summarise the main themes which underpin community-based social measures and to locate, where possible, practical examples of the different kinds of measures which have been implemented. It is worth highlighting at this stage that not all the measures we describe as *social* are concerned with the *causes* of crime. Some, like the American inspired *citizen involvement* programmes are clearly defensive measures which aim to protect the individual rather than affect the behaviour of potential offenders. The material available has been organised into a number of categories which aim to describe the major focus. This is a somewhat subjective exercise and there are, at times, overlaps between categories and it would have been possible to locate some examples under more than one category.

Community development schemes

Concern about the social condition of residential areas prone to crime has its roots in the work of Shaw and McKay in the 1920s and 1930s in Chicago and other American cities. They noted that the areas of the cities which were heavily victimised were physically run down and had residents with low economic, social and political status. The Chicago Area Project set up in 1934 used the *neighbourhood* as the basic unit of operation, involved residents in planning and management, employed local residents as staff and attempted to co-ordinate and make the best use of community resources (see Shaw and McKay, 1942). The aim was to assist demoralised residents to improve their community organisation through co-operative self-help, to encourage intelligent use of local talents and leadership and, through a wide variety of activities, to change the community situations which mould the values of young people.

The themes developed by Shaw and McKay emerge in many of the later community development programmes. In particular, ideas of *socialisation, community integration, informal social control* and *self-help* or *empowerment* recur with some regularity.

In the United States in the 1950s and 1960s, the work of Cloward and Ohlin (1960) was the justification for extensive community development programmes for specific urban areas, with a focus on job creation (for example, War on Poverty programme). In Britain the Community Development Programmes (CDP) of the early 1970s aimed to meet the needs of people living in areas of high social deprivation by influencing local social and economic conditions. These large scale programmes are widely regarded as having failed, although it is now difficult to locate evaluations or even descriptions of the initiatives themselves.

Up to the present, the focus on employment and training has been a feature of American community development initiatives in crime prevention. The Eisenhower Neighbourhood Programme which began in 1983 in ten urban neighbourhoods had a strong employment and training focus. For example, the programme in the Adams-Morgan neighbourhood in Washington DC involved the setting up of a dwelling rehabilitation and *weatherisation* business to employ local youth and a *teen parent self-sufficiency centre* which employs local single parents. The Programme as a whole has been described as producing inconclusive results (see Lavrakas and Bennett, 1988).

Subsequent initiatives by the Eisenhower Foundation have been less ambitious. Their programme for the 1990s is being developed with 12 cities and involves employment and social support measures (particularly for young people) and the development of self-financing programme through the introduction of non-profit businesses. The new programme is based on the apparent success of a number of model programmes, two of which are described here by way of illustration.

Centre for Orientation and Services (El Centro)

Established by a Catholic nun in the La Playa community of Ponce in Puerto Rico, El Centro employs local residents to run more than 30 programmes for local young people at risk of or actually in trouble with the law. El Centro is primarily a day time programme, although it also provides some temporary housing for runaways. The programmes it runs include an alternative school for dropouts, vocational training in a wide range of subjects (including computer technology and horticulture), family counselling and a number of local enterprises (including small companies producing agricultural products, ceramics and bookbinding).

Curtis (1987), reports that the number of adjudicated delinquents fell by 85% over a 15 year period and the delinquency rate by half, despite an increase in the overall at risk youth population. Silberman (1978) described it as 'the best example of community regeneration I found anywhere in the United States'. However, Graham (1990) says that 'the results appear impressive, but the evaluation was designed in such a way that it is not possible to say with any degree of certainty whether these reductions can be attributed to El Centro or other forces which may have been operating in the community over the same time span'.

Source: Curtis, 1987

Fairview Homes, Charlotte, North Carolina

The Fairview Homes Crime Prevention Programme was initiated by Charlotte Public Housing in 1979. With grants from the national Urban Initiative Anti-Crime Programme, adult residents and high-risk youth were employed to work alongside professionals to deliver job training and work opportunity in many management, employment, health and anti-drug services for residents of Fairview. During the course of the two year demonstration period, crime rates as measured by police reports and interviews with residents declined, whilst crime rates in the city rose. The programme has continued, with alternative funding, throughout *the 1980s, and has been extended to other housing estates in Charlotte. The wider initiative is called the Safe Neighbourhood Awareness Programme and is costing about $100,000 a year. An analysis of police statistics in 1987 showed that crime rates in SNAP estates had declined by between 2% and 18% since 1985, whilst crime rates in the same size developments outside the programme increased by 32% and 64%.*

Curtis (1990), reports that the evaluation confirmed the original assumption that public housing residents were the most able to deal with their own problems: 'In those areas in which the commitment to involving residents as working partners in the programme development and implementation was achieved, the greatest amount of success was experienced.'

Source: Curtis, 1990

In Britain in the late 1970s and early 1980s, NACRO developed what was essentially a community development approach to problems of crime on run down public housing estates in England and Wales. Following the NACRO model, SACRO (Scottish Association for the Care and Resettlement of Offenders) and the Strathclyde Safe Neighbourhoods Unit developed similar initiatives in Scotland, as did EXTERN for Northern Ireland. NACRO's approach was characterised, at least up until the mid 1980s, as principally concerned with the involvement and participation of residents in the affairs of their communities and with the reinforcement of informal social control over delinquent and antisocial behaviour. Rock (1988) describes NACRO's earlier work in the following terms:

It is the main contention of the National Association for the Care and Resettlement of Offenders that crime reduction flows from the structure and communality that are injected into run-down housing estates; on a well-managed estate with a stable population, there is likely to be a degree of neighbourliness conducive to good neighbour relations. It is argued by many that the gradual development of neighbourly behaviour and informal networks of support among tenants is the most effective deterrent of anti-social behaviour.

Earlier NACRO projects certainly emphasised the importance of the process of consultation. The aims of NACRO's first estate based crime prevention project on the Cunningham Road Estate in Widnes, Halton were described in the following terms (Hedges et al., 1980):

What we were trying to do was to test out the theory that only if people have a sense of belonging and responsibility for the place in which they live will they want to look after it and improve it. We set out to see whether people's attitudes might change if improvements were made to the estate and to the services provided by the authorities based on the wishes and priorities of the residents; and if so, whether there would be less vandalism on the estate.

Very little of NACRO's work, or for that matter the work of its counterparts in Scotland and Northern Ireland, has been properly evaluated. The evaluations which have been carried out have tended to be *in-house*. Three such evaluations are briefly described below.

Cunningham Road Improvement Scheme, Widnes

*An **anti-vandalism** project on the Cunningham Road Estate began in 1976, with funding from Urban Aid. The estate has 250 houses built in the 1950s and 200 houses and flats built in the 1970s.*

Important elements of the project included: a programme of detailed resident consultations facilitated by an independent agency (NACRO with SCPR), the establishment of an inter-agency project steering committee and the setting up of a residents' association. Following the implementation of a programme of estate improvements the project was evaluated in a follow up survey conducted in 1979. Although police crime statistics for the estate remained fairly constant between 1976 and 1979, the follow up survey revealed a decline in the burglary rate from 17% of the households affected in 1976 to 8% in 1979. Survey respondents also considered that vandalism had declined. According to the evaluation report: 'The main symbol of this improvement is the residents' association, which arose out of common purpose engendered by the consultative group meetings.'

Source: Hedges et al., 1980

Bushbury Triangle Project, Wolverhampton

The Bushbury Triangle area of Low Hill in Wolverhampton has about 400 houses built in the 1920s and 1930s. Following consultations with residents in 1981 a series of improvements were implemented over a period of three years. These included a comprehensive modernisation programme, home security improvements, new fencing for gardens and the development of a range of community activities managed by the residents themselves from a new community house.

The modernisation programme in Low Hills had been under way for some time but the local authority was concerned that some parts of the area were reverting to pre-modernisation conditions not long after completion of the works. The impetus for the initiative in the Triangle area was the belief that improvement schemes were likely to be more successful if there was thorough resident consultation and community ownership of the improvements. As part of the process of developing a feeling of ownership, the area which became known as the Triangle was redesignated as a separate estate within Low Hill and pedestrian routes were created within the area to encourage circulation within the area.

In 1985 an evaluation was carried out on the impact of the project:

- Analysis of police statistics showed that there had been an overall reduction in crime of more than one third (and 50% reduction in both domestic burglary and meter thefts), compared with an increase of over a third in the rest of the beat area (most of which had been modernised). Rates for other crime categories remained stable.

- Comparisons between victim surveys carried out in 1981 and 1985 confirmed the police statistics. In addition, vandalism to homes (mostly unreported to the police) had dropped by 50% and there had been substantial reductions in burglary and vandalism to local shops. Worry about crime also appeared to have dropped. For example, nearly half of the residents had been worried about going out after dark in 1981 but only a quarter in 1985.

- Follow up small group meetings with residents in 1985 provided qualitative confirmation of the survey findings (as well as highlighting some new issues).

- Unstructured interviews with officials from key local agencies confirmed that the area was presenting fewer problems in terms of case loads and attested to the area's increased popularity with residents.

It was interesting to note that these apparent improvements came about at a time of dramatically increased local unemployment; 70% of the heads of household were unemployed and seeking paid work in 1985.

Source: NACRO/SOLACE, 1986

Thirlmere Estate Project, Preston

The Thirlmere Estate Improvement Project was established on an inter-war estate of 134 homes in 1983. Following a programme of resident consultations, a residents' association was formed and an action plan produced. The plan recommended the modernisation of homes and a refurbishment of the estate's general environment; the construction of new play areas; the erection of fences and walls; investment in community activities; and 'a systematic programme of positive publicity for the estate' (NACRO, 1983).

In 1987, progress on the estate was reviewed and the following changes described (Osborn and Bright, 1989):

- *An increase in the level of community involvement through the local residents' association and the development of community co-operatives.*

- *A reduction in estate stigma which resulted in a waiting list for people wanting to move onto the estate.*

- *A reduction in crime according to police statistics and little evidence of vandalism and graffiti. The recorded crime level was described as being **negligible**.*

Source: Osborn and Bright, 1989

More recently, NACRO's work on housing estates, and most significantly the work of the Safe Neighbourhoods Unit, became concerned with a much broader range of issues including physical security, design and housing management. This work was described more fully in Section 2 of this chapter.

The other major recent initiative in British public housing is the Department of the Environment's Priority Estates Project. PEP adopted similar community development approaches to NACRO, but with a housing management focus. In retrospect, PEP projects are said to have had an impact on crime levels. PEP's work is also covered in Section 2 of this chapter, but one case study is reproduced here (see Osborn and Bright, 1989) as an example of community-based employment generation. Although it is difficult to attribute the remarkable drop in crime rates on the Broadwater Farm Estate (see p.57) to any one of the several initiatives taken on the estate in the 1980s, the job creation scheme has been a major element of the estate improvement programme.

Job Initiatives on the Broadwater Farm Estate, Haringey

The Broadwater Farm Estate in Tottenham has had a long-standing problem of high unemployment, particularly among young people. The Broadwater Farm Youth Association set up in 1981 made job creation one of its top priorities and has both created employment opportunities itself and persuaded the local authority to employ residents in its estate-based office. Haringey Council's neighbourhood office, opened in 1983, employed 19 residents out of a total of 42 housing management, maintenance and cleaning staff. Furthermore, private contractors were persuaded to recruit residents (to work on the £1m improvements scheme undertaken on the estate from 1985) as well as the Council's direct labour organisation; 44 residents were employed in this way.

During 1986, the community co-operative won the contract to carry out a number of environmental improvements for the estate, including murals, anti-graffiti painting and the creation of two community gardens. The youth association also provides training and helps small groups to develop enterprises, with some help from the European Social Fund.

In all, some 120 jobs were created on the estate by 1989, with further plans to develop enterprise workshops in under-used parking bays under the blocks.

Source: Osborn and Bright, 1989

Examples of employment based community initiatives in Britain which have been initiated with crime prevention as even one of the subsidiary goals are rare. However, Strathclyde Community Business has helped to develop a number of crime- related community enterprises; one of these, on the Barrowfield Estate in Glasgow, was reputed to have had a demonstrable effect on levels of criminal damage.

Barrowfield Estate, Glasgow

The Barrowfield Estate is an inner city housing estate suffering from high unemployment, high levels of crime, poor housing and lack of amenities. Strathclyde Community Business helped local residents to set up a community enterprise including a building, a landscaping and environmental maintenance business, a social work project (established to make social work delivery more appropriate to the needs of the area), a family flat, a repairs co-operative (to offer an alternative service to that provided by the local authority) and a workspace scheme for small businesses.

Another activity involved the setting up of a security company. The estate had a reputation as a high crime area. Companies refused to deliver goods there and doctors and other professionals refused to visit for fear of being victimised. Vandalism to flats was a particular problem. As flats fell vacant, they were stripped of their contents and the fabric damaged. Such vandalism was costing the local authority in excess of £250,000 a year, plus a further £100,000 for a contracted security firm.

The community enterprise approached the local authority to take over the security contract at a cost of £80,000 a year. Subsequently, the cost of vandalism to the local authority was reduced to £25,000 a year.

Source: Ball, Knight and Plant, 1990

Citizen involvement schemes

During the 1970s and 1980s new rationales emerged for community involvement in crime prevention. As described by DuBow and Emmons (1981), the approach says that residents can be mobilised to participate in collective crime prevention projects, and that these activities create stronger community ties which in turn lead to more effective social control.

This approach can be distinguished from that put forward by Shaw and McKay and others following in the same tradition in that it has adopted what has been described as the 'victimisation perspective' (Lewis and Salem, 1981). This perspective, although sharing Shaw and McKay's belief in the mobilisation of informal social controls, sees these as being directed towards the 'defence of communities against a perceived predatory threat from outside' (Hope and Shaw, 1988). This is in sharp contrast to the stance taken by the Chicagoans and many others that crime is a problem which originates from within particular kinds of community.

The most popular form of citizen involvement scheme has been *Neighbourhood Watch*. Neighbourhood Watch, or Block Watch as it is more commonly termed in the United States, involves residents in particular neighbourhoods coming together to share information about local crime problems, exchange ideas on prevention and make plans for mutual surveillance and crime-reporting activity. Schemes are invariably initiated and serviced by local police officers.

Neighbourhood Watch Schemes are expected to have an opportunity reducing role by encouraging collective surveillance to deter would be offenders and are also expected, through increased social interaction between residents, to strengthen informal social control over offending behaviour. In practice, Schemes spend a great deal of time on encouraging residents to protect their homes and property through home security measures and property marking.

American research into the effectiveness of Neighbourhood Watch has been fairly extensive and has produced mixed results, although there are questions over the quality of the evaluations carried out (see Greenberg, Rohe and Williams, 1985 - in particular, the use of unreliable outcome measures and lack of consideration of external factors which could have explained the results.

Two types of question have been asked of Neighbourhood Watch: does it prevent crime? and is it possible to set up in areas with high crime rates?

The most thorough evaluation of Neighbourhood Watch was an assessment of schemes in the Chicago Neighbourhoods (Lewis, Grant and Rosenbaum, 1985). This used a quasi-experimental research design involving pre- and post-test surveys (including a panel element) and control groups. The study found generally negative results, with no overall crime reduction and some increases in the fear of crime. However, some American research has found evidence for crime reduction in Neighbourhood Watch areas, but these have generally been in more affluent residential areas (see for example Silloway and McPherson, 1985).

A national survey of Neighbourhood Watch Schemes in the United States revealed that the residents living in scheme areas were generally white, more affluent and home owners (Garafalo and McLeod, 1985). Attempts to persuade residents of less affluent areas to participate have generally been unsuccessful. For example, an examination of Neighbourhood Watch in Minneapolis (Silloway and McPherson, 1985) found that organisers tried far harder to set up schemes in areas with lower socio-economic status but with far less success.

Similar findings are evident from the more limited research carried out in Britain and Canada. Neighbourhood Watch has been largely an Anglo-Saxon initiative, with little interest, and some antagonism, evident in other parts of Europe, except in the Netherlands where schemes have been introduced on an experimental basis (see Lohman and Van Dijk, 1988). In Britain, some 14% of households report being members of a scheme, but schemes are less in evidence in poorer areas with the highest crime rates (Mayhew, Elliot and Dowds, 1989). In Britain, as in the United States, considerable doubts have been expressed over whether schemes can be set up in areas which have high crime rates. Husain (1988) found substantial over-representation of schemes in more affluent low crime areas and lower than one would expect in the poorest council estates and multi-racial areas. And little evidence has been found of crime reduction. Bennett (1988), in his study of two schemes in London, found no improvements in recorded or survey crime rates (although there were reductions in the control areas). Bennett concluded that programme failure was the explanation for lack of success - in other words, the schemes were not properly implemented.

Social and recreational needs of young people

Measures to address the social and recreational needs of young people in Britain have tended to ignore the community dimension, focusing instead on improvements to the education service, access to training and employment, and general measures to support families and reduce drug abuse amongst young people (see Parliamentary All-Party Penal Affairs Group, 1983). The same has been the case in the United States and in other parts of Europe. The much vaunted French national crime prevention programme (see King, 1988), which appears to have had considerable success in reducing levels of juvenile crime in the participating cities, has tended to focus on city wide initiatives or on particular categories of young people rather than on specific neighbourhoods (although see below).

That is not say that there are not many locally based social and recreational schemes for young people, which of course there are, but the vast majority are not conceived of as crime prevention schemes nor monitored for the effect on crime. Consequently, there is little written on the topic, few examples of initiatives at the estate or neighbourhood level and little systematic evaluation. The research that has been carried out does not generally support the view that such initiatives have an impact on crime. Baldwin and Bottoms (1976) found that inadequate youth club provision on public housing estates did not contribute to high rates of juvenile offending; although earlier research by Bagley (1965) found that juvenile crime rates were inversely related to the level of expenditure on youth services in English towns and cities. However, both studies relied on cross-sectional evaluation, the limitations of which are described in Chapter Two.

Nevertheless, there are examples of initiatives which appear to have had some impact on local crime levels.

The *ete-jeune* programme in France involves summer holiday camps for those under 18 in the *quartier chauds* (problem areas of the inner cities) and a wide variety of activities for those who stay behind. The example given here, by way of illustration, is taken from King (1988).

Ete-jeune, Clichy

*Clichy is a densely populated suburb of Paris with a large immigrant population where anyone under 25 can purchase a **passport** for 10 francs. This enables the person to take part in any of the summer activities, ranging from tennis to mechanics. These are held every day of the summer holidays excepting Sundays. The **passport** also serves as insurance cover and helps organisers to monitor take-up. Organisers (**animateurs**) also help groups of young people to plan their own camping holidays with equipment supplied free. There is also a sports and recreational centre with overnight accommodation 40 miles outside Paris open to anyone with a **passport**. The programme also recruits youth leaders (**fixateurs de bande**), often from the North African communities, to encourage others, younger and less enthusiastic, to become involved. Often they go on to become professional organisers and some qualified social workers. The programme has not been evaluated but is said to have contributed to general reductions in crime throughout the city. There are no figures to support this however.*

Source: King, 1988

In Britain there has been particular concern about the level of provision for young people and the child density levels on public housing estates. Reviews commissioned by the Department of the Environment in the 1970s and 1980s drew attention to the paucity of play provision on many housing estates (see Department of the Environment, 1973 and Department of the Environment, 1981). A NACRO (1988a) report on the play and recreational needs of young people highlighted the situation on many public housing estates: 'The level of social and recreational provision for children and young people on public housing estates in most areas is minimal. Many estates have no facilities at all. Others have limited facilities for perhaps one age group.'

High child densities have been linked with high levels if crime, and vandalism in particular. Wilson (1981) found that this applied to estates of houses as well as flatted estates. The need to reduce child densities and remove children from some types of accommodation has often been stressed (for example, Coleman, 1985). Much less is said about the need for play and youth facilities on estates.

In Britain, the only current programme directed towards the social and recreational needs of young people on individual public housing estates with an explicit crime prevention goal is that organised by NACRO's Youth Activities Unit. The programme has involved projects on more than a dozen estates in England and Wales and one example where crime rates have apparently fallen is described below.

Golf Links Youth Project, Ealing

In 1984 a youth project was established on the Golf Links Estate, a public housing estate in Southall. An Advisory Group involving youth workers, voluntary bodies and the police co-ordinated the project. A youth organiser, employed by NACRO, was appointed to work on the estate for three years to help develop social and recreational activities. In the event, a large number of adults and older teenagers were recruited from the local community to help plan and run activities, a range of adventure activities was organised for local teenagers, regular outings were arranged, clubs were set up for different age groups and residential camps organised.

The project was generally regarded as being successful. As well as providing a better level of overall provision for young people, local youth workers believed that racial conflict had been reduced and the total number of recorded crimes in the police beat area roughly coterminous with the project areas fell by three quarters between 1983 and 1987. However, the reduction in crime needs to be put in the context of other initiatives on the estate at the same time, including improved dwelling security, the introduction of a neighbourhood office on the estate and increased police collaboration with residents and the local authority.

Source: Osborn, 1989
NACRO, 1988b

Most recently, Crime Concern published a report highlighting the crime prevention outcomes of a number of youth projects in the United Kingdom (Findlay, Bright and Gill, 1990). For two projects recorded crime statistics were obtained which purported to show that crimes associated with young people had been reduced. These projects are described below.

Hamilton Information Project for Youth (HIPY)

The project was established in 1988 as part of the Youth Enquiry Service (YES) by the Youth Information Resource Unit, which is funded by the Scottish Community Education Council (SCEC). A network of YES projects is being established in areas with high crime rates, poor youth facilities or high unemployment. Local projects provide free information, advice and support for young people aged 16-25 years.

The Hamilton Information Project for Youth (HIPY) is based in a converted shop on a housing estate with a large, poorly served youth population. The project has three full-time and three part-time staff, as well as 20 young volunteers. HIPY provides information, counselling and activities for local young people, and encourages them to set up their own initiatives.

Although the local YES projects are not set up specifically to reduce crime, this is considered to be an important indirect effect. Reductions in several types of crime in the area surrounding the HIPY project were reported between 1988 and

92

1989: house breaking, 44% reduction; vandalism, 16% reduction; serious assault with weapon, 45% reduction. However, no information is provided on other crimes, such as street crime and autocrime, which, presumably, did not show a corresponding reduction. As a result, it is not possible to make an assessment of the impact of the initiative on overall crime levels.

Source: Findlay, Bright and Gill, 1990

Top End Youth Action Group, Ferguslie Park, Paisley

Ferguslie Park Estate is characterised by high unemployment (40%); a declining population and large numbers of empty properties, many of which are vandalised and derelict. The estate has a reputation for crime and social problems, much of this attributed to local young people. Many of these problems were concentrated in one area of the estate, known as the 'top end'. Young people from this area were generally excluded from using youth facilities in the centre of the estate.

Concern about these problems peaked in 1986 as a result of disturbances and the increasing occurrence of solvent, drug and alcohol abuse.

Following a special meeting of the Ferguslie Park Youth Development Team, an inter-agency group of voluntary and statutory organisations and local people, a social action initiative was launched to involve local young people in developing solutions.

Following initial development work by the initiative's three youth workers, the Top End Youth Action Group was established. In April 1987, the group obtained Urban Programme funding for the conversion of local shop premises into a Youth Action Centre and the employment of two workers. The group is now responsible for the management of the centre and the day to day management of the youth workers.

Although the initiative's most important achievement is considered to have been the development of the Action Group itself, a great deal of emphasis is placed on its impact on crime reduction.

Although the overall crime rate in the Ferguslie Park area showed a fairly modest decline of 5% between 1985 and 1988, an assessment carried out in 1989 highlighted reductions in four selected crimes 'which often involve young people' - vandalism and malicious damage, 22% reduction; petty assault, 32% reduction; reckless/wilful fire raising, 55% reduction; supply/possession of drugs, 100% reduction. The reduction in all the selected crimes was 30%.

Since the 'selected crimes' do not include burglary, autocrime or serious assault it is not possible to make a full assessment of the impact of the initiative (or any other factors) on crime in the area. The presentation of a handful of selected crimes, with no reference to these other crime categories, seriously detracts from the assessment presented.

Source: Findlay, Bright and Gill, 1990

This section deals with the policing of residential areas, particularly council housing estates, and focuses on the contribution of neighbourhood or home beat policing to crime prevention initiatives. A major police preoccupation during the 1980s was the introduction of Neighbourhood Watch schemes (and variations on the same theme). There are now said to be in the region of 80,000 Neighbourhood Watch schemes in England and Wales (Home Office, 1989). A review of the initiative is included in the previous section. Also much in evidence during the 1980s was the involvement of police officers in the initiation and organisation of social and recreational activities for young people. However, little has been written about initiatives at the estate or neighbourhood level, notwithstanding the considerable attention given to county schemes such as the Staffordshire Police Activity and Community Enterprise Programme (see Home Office, 1990). This section of the report concentrates, therefore, on aspects of police work which have been described and, sometimes, evaluated.

There is considerable public support for increased police patrolling of residential areas on the assumption that formal surveillance deters potential offenders by providing a constant threat of apprehension. However, there is little evidence that either foot patrols or car patrols have any effect on levels of crime. Bright (1969) looked at variations in foot patrol strengths in three British cities and concluded that, provided there was some police presence, the precise number of patrols made little difference to levels of reported crime. Similar results were found from research carried out in a number of American cities. For example, an evaluation of foot patrol activity in Newark, New Jersey found no relationship between levels of crime in particular areas and the presence or absence of foot patrols, although awareness of foot patrols did decrease residents' fear of crime (Police Foundation, 1981). Clarke and Hough (1984) believe that these results are to be expected because 'given present burglary rates and evenly distributed patrol coverage, a patrolling policeman in London could expect to pass within 100 yards of a burglary in progress roughly once every eight years - but not necessarily to catch the burglar or even realise that the crime was taking place'.

Research has also found little evidence of the efficacy of car patrols. The best known study, the Kansas City Preventive Patrol Experiment, showed that doubling or trebling the level of vehicle patrols in some parts of the city had no impact on crime (Kelling et al., 1974). However, the significance of the results can be challenged on the grounds that there could not be complete control over car patrol movements, not least because cars had to pass through areas that were not designated to patrol to reach the areas they were supposed to patrol.

Random foot or car patrolling is '. . . no longer seen as the most intelligent use of police resources. The emphasis now is on directed patrolling, to places and at times where crimes such as burglary are most likely to be committed; and on strengthening home beats' (Osborn & Bright, 1989).

The key to effective local policing is increasingly being seen in terms of greater police visibility and accessibility, improved liaison with the community and other organisations and longer term commitment to areas on the part of individual beat officers. There is little evidence that this *community policing* model (if it can be called a model, given the wide variety of activities described in this way) is any more effective in reducing crime. Weatheritt (1987) concludes that there is little or no sign that they have made any measurable difference: 'Whilst community policing ideas have been useful in stimulating debate and action, answers to policing problems cannot be found in community policing philosophy nor in the practice to which it has given rise.'

And yet questions remain over whether *community policing* has actually been tried. Most policing is still carried out by uniform reliefs and specialist units. Permanent beat officers are a small additional resource, amounting to perhaps only 5% of the establishment of the average police force (Smith, 1987).

Particular problems have been experienced with the policing of public housing estates and, more especially, the large high-density multi-storey developments. Concern has been expressed over the logistical difficulties of patrolling, in terms of the problems of access to *private* spaces (such as corridors) and design-induced lack of visibility, over conflict of responsibility between police and any estate security personnel, over the very high rate of turnover of beat officers and over the high profile and sometimes insensitive policing provided by mobile police units; there has also been concern over what precisely local beat officers should do on estates other than random and often invisible patrolling (see Osborn and Bright, 1988).

One response to the problems of policing high crime neighbourhoods has been to set up local police offices or mini police stations or, less ambitiously, local police surgery sessions. For example, Northumbria Police opened small *section stations* in Newcastle, serviced by Urban Programme funded civilian staff, as well as a *community initiatives office* jointly with other agencies on the Cowgate Estate in the 1980s. However, there is little evidence that these kinds of initiatives have any impact or that they are even sustainable over time. Police surgeries in particular have suffered from lack of attendance by the public. Evidence from other countries shows a similar picture (see Walker and Walker, 1989).

However, there are examples of police initiatives at the estate or neighbourhood level which appear to have had an effect on crime levels although, it seems clear, only as part of broader initiatives to prevent crime in the areas concerned.

Neighbourhood/ geographical policing

Policing is generally organised on a relief (shift) basis and through the deployment of specialist units. However, in the 1980s there was increasing interest in *geographical* policing strategies in which specific police officers were to be given responsibility for most of the policing in particular geographical areas. The idea behind this was to give officers better understanding of the areas they policed, to build up better links between the police and local communities and to provide the basis for a collaborative and proactive approach to dealing with local crime problems. The Neighbourhood Policing Project undertaken by the Metropolitan Police and Surrey Constabulary was the strategic realisation of this concept in this country. The Project which began in 1982 involved experiments in a number of police stations on the transfer of policing responsibility from a shift based system to one that was geographically based and a pilot estate policing project on a housing estate in southwest London involving the deployment of one sergeant and five police constables (Metropolitan Police, 1984; Metropolitan Police, 1985). The model for the estate policing project was the Koban/Chuzaisho schemes used in Japan, Singapore and Hong Kong, which give territorial responsibility for policing a local area to residentially-based teams or individual officers, and schemes in the United States such as the Neighbourhood Responsive Policing Joint Programme in Boston which introduced a system of geographical responsibility.

In the event, the Neighbourhood Policing Programme disappeared without the systematic evaluation promised having materialised, although Surrey Constabulary has continued to implement aspects of the programme. It appeared to have fallen prey to changes in policy direction at Commissioner level and to resistance to change within the police stations concerned.

However, within one Division of the Metropolitan Police an apparently successful estate policing initiative has been introduced on three estates, not directly linked to but undoubtedly influenced by the Neighbourhood Policing Programme. This initiative, and a similar project from the West Midlands, are described below.

Community Policing Initiative - Pepys Estate, Deptford

The Pepys Estate in Deptford was built in the late 1960s and early 1970s and consists of 10 interconnected eight-storey maisonette blocks, three tower blocks and a number of other smaller blocks. The estate has nearly 1,500 dwellings. In the early 1980s the estate had an exceptionally high crime rate: about 300 recorded burglaries a year and nearly 500 recorded incidents of autocrime.

Following the preparation of an action plan by the Safe Neighbourhoods Unit in 1982 a series of improvements was made over the following three years, including physical security improvements to dwellings, phone entry systems, improved lighting, improved community facilities and new resident caretakers and a local housing office. In addition to this, a Community Policing Unit was established comprising of a sergeant and five police constables. Initially, hours of duty covered a daily period from 7am to 2am but it became apparent that a more directed approach was needed and hours of duty were modified to cater for peak periods. In addition, officers were given responsibility for specific sections of the estate in order to concentrate their attention on more localised problems and to promote closer links between officers and residents. Each police officer was assigned the same section of the estate as an individual estate housing officer in order to facilitate close day to day working relationships and joint problem solving between the police and local authority.

The Community Policing Unit is also responsible for managing the police service for the estate as far as other police officers in Deptford are concerned. In practice this has meant that interventions by other police officers are minimal and when they have been required, for example, for drugs surveillance operations, they have been undertaken in close collaboration with the Community Policing Unit.

The improvements to the Pepys Estate were accompanied by substantial reductions in crime. The reported burglary rate fell by about 50% in 1985 and the autocrime rate by about 60% The rate of crimes per household had peaked at 49 per 100 households in 1982. The rate was 26 per 100 in 1985, greatly reduced although still higher than in most urban residential areas. Racial harassment was said by the police to be 'virtually non-existent' following the introduction of the scheme. The lower rate of reported crime continued throughout the 1980s. An examination of the work of the Community Policing Unit in 1988 testified to its continuing effectiveness and popularity (Hyder, 1988). It has not been possible to determine the weight of the contribution of the Community Policing Unit to the estate's crime reduction in relation to the many other physical, social and management improvements on the estate.

*Source: Osborn and Bright, 1988
            Hyder, 1988*

Gospel Estate Policing Project, Birmingham

The Gospel Estate (or Fox Hollies) at Acocks Green, Birmingham, is an estate of terraced and semi-detached houses built in the 1920s and 1930s. The estate had a long-standing reputation as a high crime area.

In 1980, following a survey of residents' views of crime and policing in the area, the police introduced increased foot patrols on the estate but with no apparent effect. The police then decided to establish a team for the estate, consisting of one sergeant and four police constables (later increased to six constables). The scheme ran for a trial period of two months, which was then extended indefinitely. The police team was expected to develop close working relationships with the community and local agencies, to take a victim orientated approach (for example, by helping victims to claim compensation), to improve the detection rate and to take responsibility for completing all jobs originating from the estate (referring work to special units only in extreme circumstances). The team was also expected to deal with domestic disputes, missing persons, road accidents and general nuisance. The most immediate effect was a dramatic increase in the clear up rate from virtually zero to about 38% and a 70% reduction in complaints from residents about children causing a nuisance. However, this has not been accompanied by reductions in recorded crime.

Other schemes were introduced on the estate following the police initiative, most notably the allocation of £6M for a leisure complex for young people in the area.

Source: Osborn and Bright, 1988

This chapter summarises the evidence of housing-related crime prevention. It focuses on the evidence from *before and after* studies, where some attempt has been made to measure changes over time, albeit retrospectively. Although studies carried out at one point in time, which try to identify crime generating or inhibiting factors through comparing high and low crime neighbourhoods, provide useful pointers to what could be done to prevent crime, there are strong arguments against their use in neighbourhood-based evaluation research on the grounds of their inability to separate cause from effect, as well for other methodological reasons (see p.19).

Before looking in more detail at the evidence, the chapter begins with some general observations about the quality of the evidence and what we might have expected to find.

Great expectations

In Chapter Two a set of criteria was put forward as a kind of yardstick against which evidence of success could be judged. It is fair to say that none of the initiatives described in Chapter Three completely satisfied those criteria. In fact, as a general rule, the *best* evaluated initiatives produced the *worst* results, and vice versa. This in itself was not surprising. The more thorough evaluations are often carried out by researchers who, as we have said, tend to err on the side of caution. The least thorough evaluations tend to be carried out by practitioners, who may not have the time or the inclination to search for further evidence and for whom least is often best.

Were we expecting too much of the evaluations? Yin (1986) gave the thumbs up to American community crime prevention schemes on the basis of far less. Referring to his summary table of schemes in the United States (reproduced on p.24 of this report), he concluded that 'a study of the table suggests that the findings from the eleven evaluations were indeed positive, and that they were robust and credible methodologically'. He concluded this on the basis that crime reduction actually took place in six of the eight interventions where crime reduction was a goal and that outcomes were in a 'positive direction' in two of the remaining three interventions where crime reduction was not a goal. He believed that the results were methodologically sound because:

- each study examined at least two different types of outcome, typically both the incidence of crime and the perceptions of key participants;

- in most cases (six out of eight), the incidence of crime was measured through victimisation surveys and not just recorded crime statistics;

- in nearly every case results were confirmed by tests for statistical significance;

- a great deal of attention was paid to evaluation design and 'the ultimate approaches reflected truly potent designs . . . in some cases, the designs actually approximated true experiments . . . in other cases, compromises had to be made between generally acceptable quasi-experimental designs and the limitations imposed by the real-life constraints of the interventions, but these compromises appeared more than acceptable'.

But is Yin's confidence justified? In fact, he was rather more confident about the results than were most of the researchers who carried out the studies he was reviewing. There are a number of problems with the evidence Yin presents:

- His claim that two kinds of outcome measure were used in each case is not really justified. In some cases, evidence of crime reduction from victimisation surveys was only 'confirmed' by evidence of changes in residents' perceptions from the same surveys.

- He tends to present positive results (if there were any) and to ignore negative ones for the six interventions he judges to have successfully reduced crime. For example, in one case, commercial burglaries were reduced but other types of crime were not (Lavraskas and Kushmuk, 1986); in one case, there was no actual reduction in crime, only less of an increase than elsewhere and then only for a limited period (Fowler & Mangione, 1986); in one case, a reduction in overall crime rates disguised increases in burglary and robbery (Trojanowicz, 1986); and in one case, reductions in commercial burglary were not evident at all three sites (Tien and Cahn, 1986). In the two remaining cases (Schneider, 1986; Lindsay and McGillis, 1986), evidence of burglary reduction was not put in the context of changes in rates of other crimes or the overall crime rate. Of course, the initiatives were mainly concerned with burglary reduction but this should not have precluded investigation of other crimes, if only to test for offence displacement.

- Whilst accepting that burglary rates did go down in some cases (although only temporarily on occasion), we know very little about the circumstances in which this was achieved. As Yin himself concedes, even though surveys were carried out in most cases, very little information is provided on the demography or social characteristics of the areas concerned.

It seems apparent, therefore, that by just asking one or two additional and quite reasonable questions about the evidence presented by Yin, the overall results can be seen in a very different light - probably closer in many respects to what the original authors had intended.

A number of questions are asked of the housing-related crime prevention initiatives in this report. Not only do we want to know whether crime was reduced and became less of a problem, we also want to know whether the initiative was responsible and, if so, whether the effect lasted and could be replicated elsewhere. The assessment criteria provide a framework for asking those questions. We did not expect initiatives to provide all the information required to satisfy the assessment criteria (although we expected more than we got). We did believe, however, that it would have been practical for them to provide that kind of information given the right circumstances.

Conclusions about design led initiatives

Design-led solutions to the crime problems of residential areas have gained widespread acceptance amongst a broad range of professionals.

Crime Prevention through Environmental Design (CPTED) is promoted heavily by the Home Office Crime Prevention Centre at Stafford and through the work of police crime prevention and architectural liaison officers. The Centre's manual of guidance for police architectural officers leans heavily on the operational handbook produced nearly a decade earlier by the US National Institute of Justice (Wallis and Ford, 1980). Police forces in south-east England have also devised a *Secured by Design* campaign, whereby builders are awarded seals of approval for following certain design (and physical security) principles.

Design guides have been produced by local authorities in-house (for example, in Wandsworth and Southwark) or as joint exercises with the police (for example, in Leicestershire). And, in general, housing authorities have taken on board many of the ideas popularised by Oscar Newman - in particular, defensible space concepts were behind the 1980s trend to break up large expanses of open space to create semi-private and private gardens on many housing estates built in the 1960s and 1970s.

There are also numerous guide books produced by professional bodies, practitioners and academics promoting design solutions to crime problems in a variety of settings from housing estates to city centres to underground transport systems.

It is interesting to note that, in the midst of this widespread promotion of crime prevention through design, one professional body, the National House Building Council (NHBC, 1986), has emphasised the need to balance crime prevention against other desirable outcomes when new estates are being designed - in particular the appearance and amenity value of the site - and that these may conflict with, and even outweigh, any security requirements of the design.

A good deal of design practice and advocacy is based on research into the relationship between design and crime rather than on any lessons learnt from monitoring the introduction of particular measures. The recommendations made on the basis of comparative studies carried out by Oscar Newman and others are heavy with qualifications (either at the time or later when the researchers had second thoughts) but these tend to be overlooked by practitioners.

We were only able to locate eight British examples of evaluations of design-led crime prevention initiatives (see Table 8 overleaf), although it should be noted that our categorisation of initiatives was at times rather arbitrary and that some of the other initiatives we describe have strong design elements. Four of these initiatives were said to have reduced crime on the basis of **anecdotal evidence only**. Two others, where walkway removal had been linked with crime reduction, presented either disappointing early outcomes (Mozart Estate) or reasonably strong evidence that crime reduction was not associated with the measure (Lisson Green Estate). The evidence from the two remaining initiatives, involving expensive re-design on defensible space principles, showed in one case that early gains in terms of crime reduction were rapidly being lost (Woodchurch Estate); in the other case (Stockbridge Village), there was an element of selectivity in highlighting burglary reduction figures as evidence of success when, for instance, autocrime rates had remained high and, furthermore, the police cast doubt on the claimed source of burglary reduction by suggesting some link with their arrest of those responsible.

We cannot conclude from this, however, that all these initiatives failed to bring about reductions in crime problems. The absence of pre- and post-survey data, control group data and monitoring data does not allow for judgements one way or the other.

Table 8 **Design-led initiatives - summary of 8 evaluations**

Intervention site and period; author	Description of intervention and cost (if known)	Outcome measures examined	Nature of outcomes	Comments on outcome	Comments on method
Stockbridge Village, Knowsley (1983-91) *(IoH & RIBA, 1989)*	Selective demolition and extensive estate redesign on defensible space principles; change of landlord; physical security measures; concierges; neighbourhood watch; security guards for shopping precinct. Capital cost £45m by 1991.	Recorded crime 1984-88; subjective views gathered by external assessor.	50% reduction in recorded burglaries but no reduction in thefts from and of cars. Claims that muggings and shopping precinct crimes reduced but no figures presented.	Police claim some burglary reduction due to arrest of culprits. No breakdown available for crimes other than burglary. Concerns expressed over continued vandalism to empty properties.	Used recorded crime statistics selectively; no supportive data other than anecdotal; retrospective monitoring of implementation but no monitoring for outside influences.
Woodchurch Estate, Wirral (1983-late 1980s) *(IoH & RIBA, 1989)*	Selective demolition, *topping* & extensive estate redesign on defensible space principles; physical security measures; concierges; single generation lets. Capital cost £5m.	Recorded crime 1982-86 and police estimates for 1989; subjective views gathered by external assessor.	50% reduction in recorded burglaries 1983-86 but rate rising towards 1983 level by 1989; unspecified increase in thefts from cars 1989.	Early gains in burglary reduction being eroded. No data on trends for other categories of crime.	Used recorded crime statistics selectively; no supportive data other than anecdotal; retrospective monitoring of implementation; no control data or monitoring for outside influences.
Adswood Estate, Stockport (mid-late 1980s) *(Stollard et al, 1989)*	Securing garden enclosures; building car hardstands; creating culs-de-sac; improving surveillance.	Views of Director of Housing 1989.	Unspecified crime reduction.	No real evidence presented.	Anecdotal evidence only.
Brinnington Estate, Stockport (mid-late 1980s) *(Stollard et al, 1989)*	Creation of private gardens and semi-private areas through landscaping; home security measures; creation of children's play area.	Views of Director of Housing 1989.	Unspecified crime reduction.	No real evidence presented.	Anecdotal evidence only.
Mozart Estate, Westminster (1986) *(Safe Neighbourhoods Unit, 1988a)*	Removal of walkways affecting 4 blocks on estate.	Recorded crime statistics 1986; residents' perceptions.	50% reduction in burglary on whole estate 2 months after removal compared with 2 months prior to removal; but burglary rate increased in 4 blocks affected during 5 months after walkway removal. Assaults/robberies increased. Over 60% of residents of 4 blocks said removal made no difference to safety.	Initial results not encouraging.	Recorded crime statistics only and for inadequate follow-up period. No supportive or control data. Census survey undertaken after walkway removal but not before. Detailed monitoring of implementation but no monitoring for outside influences.
Lisson Green, Westminster (1982-83) *(Poyner, 1986)*	Removal of walkways; local housing office opened; phone entry systems.	Recorded crime statistics 1981-85. Views of housing officers.	Burglaries and robberies reduced.	Burglary reduction trends coincided with distribution of voids (ie unrelated to intervention); robbery reduction coincided with introduction of phone entry but preceded walkways removal.	Used recorded crime statistics only; no supportive data other than views of staff; retrospective monitoring of implementation but no monitoring for outside influences and no control data.
High Str Area, Pendleton, Salford (tower blocks only) (1983-mid 1980s) *DoE, forthcoming*	Security guard service; remodelling of access routes & CCTV; modified allocations.	Views of Council.	Unspecified crime reduction.	No real evidence presented.	Anecdotal evidence only.
Chalk Hill Estate, Brent (1986-) *(IoH & RIBA, 1989)*	Isolation of blocks by cutting off inter-connecting routes; new stairs, lifts, entrances; block receptionists; phone entries & CCTV.	Subjective views gathered by external assessor.	Unspecified crime reduction.	No real evidence presented.	Anecdotal evidence only.

It was disappointing to find so few published (or unpublished but available) examples of design-led initiatives where even minimal evaluations had been carried out. In the light of this, it is surprising that so many expensive redesign options have been taken on the grounds, at least partly, of expected crime reduction. It is to be hoped that the Department of the Environment's *Design Improvement Controlled Experiment* currently under way settles at least some of the arguments about the impact and cost effectiveness of design measures.

Conclusions about management led initiatives

Much of the discussion about the effect of management initiatives on crime was initiated by retrospective claims about the impact of estate-based management projects such as those developed by the Priority Estates Project. Many of these appeared to have reduced local crime problems. For example, a PEP survey of 20 estate based management projects in 1982 found that 15 claimed reductions in crime (see Table 9 overleaf).

More recently there has been considerable attention paid to the security aspects of block receptionist or concierge schemes. A great deal of this interest stemmed from general disillusionment with the performance of phone entry systems in the mid-1980s (see Safe Neighbourhoods Unit, 1985) and from the results of a single evaluation of a block receptionist scheme (Gloucester House on the South Kilburn Estate in Brent).

We were able to locate 14 *evaluations* of management initiatives (see Table 9). One of these, from the PEP survey of 20 estate based management projects in 1982 (Power, 1984), did not claim to be a thorough assessment but showed that project participants on 15 of the estates were confident that crime had been reduced. This was supported by recorded crime statistics for three estates, although only one estate (Springwell, Gateshead) was actually named in the survey report. A further estate (Ragworth Estate, Stockton-on-Tees) produced some evidence of reductions in the costs of vandalism to the housing authority. A summary of the specific initiatives on Springwell and Ragworth estates is given in the table.

Although PEP-type projects were not conceived of as crime prevention initiatives, they have proved a valuable source of information on housing-related crime prevention. The existence of PEP as a programme since 1979 has meant that projects have been consistently monitored over long periods of time and PEP's promotional role has meant that a good deal of case study material is available on individual projects. Most of the crime-related information has been gathered retrospectively and it is not always ideally presented but it nevertheless does provide a useful guide to the impact of estate based management initiatives.

Eight PEP or ICP funded estate-based management are summarised in Table 9. On three estates there was no evidence of crime reduction, although in one case (Wenlock Barn) residents' concerns about crime were reduced. On a further estate (Afon) claims of burglary reduction were based on a totally unsatisfactory comparison between recorded crime at the start of the project and survey crime rates one year later. On the remaining four estates there was some evidence of crime reduction on the basis of reductions in recorded crime (Springwell and Broadwater Farm), reductions in reports of burglary to the housing office (Tulse Hill) and reductions in costs of vandalism (Ragworth). The most interesting of these (Tulse Hill and Broadwater Farm) are worthy of further discussion.

Tulse Hill Estate in Lambeth experienced a remarkable drop in the number of burglaries reported to the housing office - down from 15 a week to less than one

Table 9 **Management led initiatives - summary of 14 evaluations**

Intervention site & period; author	Description of intervention	Outcome measures examined	Nature of outcomes	Comments on outcome	Comments on method
20 Estate based management projects (PEP Survey 1982) (Power, 1984)	Housing management initiatives involving local offices plus a range of other measures.	Recorded crime (undated) for 3 projects only; structured interviews with project staff and feedback from residents and police.	Unspecified and undated reductions in vandalism and crime on 15 estates.	Apart from effects of localised management, reductions were associated with increased police patrolling, reduced voids, phone entry systems, home security improvements, patrolling by caretakers/night watchmen &, in one case, walkway closure.	Evidence mainly based on views expressed in structured interviews with staff, except for 3 cases where recorded crime statistics were used. In general, no supporting, control or monitoring data.
Springwell, Gateshead (1979-83) (Power, 1984)	ICP funded PEP-type estate management package; community policing initiative; community centre.	Recorded crime 1981/82; anecdotal evidence from project staff and/or residents.	Recorded crime down by third; vandalism reduced.	No data on trends for individual categories of crime. Vandalism reduction anecdotal.	Used recorded crime statistics supported by anecdotal evidence only. No supportive or control data; implementation monitored but no monitoring for outside influences.
Ragworth Estate, Stockton on Tees (1981-83) (Power, 1984)	Opening of estate management office; opening of community hall; modernisation & environmental improvements; night watchmen. Urban aid funded: revenue costs £24,470 in 1982.	Costs of crime to housing authority; project staff assessments.	Cost of empty property maintenance & making good vandalism almost halved in one year (1981-82).	Project staff attribute reduction to night watchman patrols & increased informal social control.	Used costs of crime to housing authority only (no details of actual costs). No supportive data other than anecdotal. No control data. Project monitored closely.
Willows, Bolton (1979-83) (Burbidge, 1984)	PEP estate management package.	Survey burglary rates (undated); residents' perceptions.	Burglary rate increased from 12% to 24% of dwellings pa. No change in residents' perceptions of crime as a problem.	No evidence of reduced burglary & vandalism problems. No data on trends for other crime categories.	Used (undated) cross-sectional survey data only. No supporting, control or monitoring data.
Wenlock Barn, Hackney (1979-83) (Burbidge, 1984)	PEP estate management package.	Survey burglary rates (undated); perceptions; anecdotal evidence from project staff and/or residents.	Burglary rate unchanged; residents' concern about burglary and vandalism reduced.	No empirical evidence of reduced burglary & vandalism but problem reduced according to residents. No data on trends for other crime.	Used (undated) cross-sectional survey data and anecdotal evidence only. No supporting, control or monitoring data.
Tulse Hill, Lambeth (1980-82) (Burbidge, 1984)	PEP estate management package.	Reports of burglaries to housing staff; anecdotal evidence from project staff and/or residents.	Burglaries reduced from 15 to 1 per week 1981/82. Vandalism reduced.	No data on trends for other categories of crime; vandalism reduction anecdotal (estate reverted to previous condition after transfer from GLC to Lambeth in 1982).	Assessment only based on reports to housing staff and anecdotal evidence. No supporting, control or monitoring data.
Afon, Wrexham (1984-) (Burbidge, 1984)	PEP estate management package.	Recorded burglary 1984/85; survey burglary rates 1983/85; anecdotal evidence from project staff and/or residents.	Recorded burglary rate (5%) in 1984/85 was lower than survey burglary rate (13%) in 1983/84. Vandalism reduced.	Reduction in burglary rate may be explained by differential rates of reporting to police & to survey. Vandalism reduction anecdotal.	Unsatisfactory mixing of recorded crime statistics and survey data. No supporting evidence other than anecdotal. No control or monitoring data.
Penrhys, Rhondda (1984-) (Burbidge, 1984)	PEP estate management package.	Recorded burglary and vandalism (undated)	Little change in rates.	—	Used undated recorded crime statistics only. No supportive, control or monitoring data.

Table 9 **Management led initiatives - summary of 14 evaluations (continued)**

Intervention site & period; author	Description of intervention	Outcome measures examined	Nature of outcomes	Comments on outcome	Comments on method
Broadwater Farm, Haringey (1983-) (*PEP, 1988, & Osborn, 1989*)	Opening of local management office; refurbishment; improved lighting; phone entry systems; home security package; vandal proof glazing; employment initiatives & co-op development; youth initiatives.	Recorded crime 1983-85; police crime estimates 1987.	Recorded crime reduced 60%; burglary 78%; vehicle crime 61%; major crime 49%. Police estimate that estate accounted for only 1% of Tottenham's crime in 1987, against 3.5% of its population.	Large long-standing fall in crime rates across the board.	Used recorded crime statistics and detailed monitoring of implementation. No other supportive or control data.
Pepys Estate, Lewisham (1981-86) (*SNU, 1986c, & Hyder, 1988*)	Local management office; refurbishment; improved lighting; phone entry systems; home security; resident caretaking; youth & community facilities; neighbourhood policing project.	Recorded crime 1983-88; continuous monitoring of crime statistics.	Recorded crime reduced 60%; burglary 60%, autocrime 70%, beat crime 25%; street crime 55%.	Crime rates dropped sharply after introduction of home security measures & start of refurbishment programme when a large workforce was present on estate (surveillance effect?). Local authority & police management changes may have contributed to maintenance of crime levels at dramatically reduced levels.	Used recorded crime statistics and detailed monitoring of implementation. No other supportive or control data. Pre-survey only.
Possil Park, Glasgow (1987-) (*IoH & RIBA, 1989*)	Introduction of tenants' co-op to part of estate leading to management changes; home security; fencing; phone entry systems; lighting.	Recorded crime 1987-88; anecdotal evidence gathered by external assessor.	Recorded crime reduced 28%; burglary 64% over unspecified period since 1987. Autocrime still a serious problem.	No data on crime trends other than for burglary. Police attribute reductions to establishment of co-op.	Recorded crime statistics supported by anecdotal evidence only.
Elizabeth Street, Moor Lane, Preston (1988-) (*Osborn, 1989*)	Block receptionist scheme plus associated technology & localised management.	Recorded burglary 1987-88.	Recorded burglary rate reduced 90% in 3 months after scheme introduced.	Very large reduction in burglary but 3 month monitoring period too short. No data on other crimes.	Recorded crime statistics only. Follow-up period too short. No supporting, control or monitoring data.
Gloucester Hse, South Kilburn Estate, Brent (1984-85) (*Skilton, 1986, 1988*)	Concierge service & associated technology & localised management.	Recorded crime statistics 1985/86. Cost benefit assessment.	Recorded burglaries & criminal damage lower than rates for other blocks on same estate. Estimated savings of £17,000 in 1985/86 due to reduced expenditure on communal repairs, lift breakdowns, graffiti & caretaking/management & increased rental income.	No details of crimes other than burglary & criminal damage.	All evidence based on comparisons over 1 year between Gloucester Hse & control block(s) on same estate. Displacement not accounted for; implementation monitored.
Mitchellhill, Glasgow (1989-) (*Glasgow City Council, 1990*)	Concierge service plus associated technology & localised management; flat security package.	Recorded crime 1988-90. Monitoring of voids, turnover, lets & rental income by Housing Dept.	Recorded crime reduced 60% in 9 months after scheme introduced compared with 9 months prior to introduction; burglaries & attempted burglaries "almost eliminated". Reduction in voids turnover & increase in lets & rental income after introduction of scheme.	Short follow-up period, no details on specific crime categories but fuller evaluation planned for later in 1990, including follow-up household survey.	Quarterly recorded crime statistics only measure of crime changes; pre-survey carried out prior to introduction of scheme—post survey imminent.

a week during the course of the project - and noticeable although unquantified reductions in the numbers of 'muggings' (Power, 1982a). The situation changed dramatically when the estate was transferred from the GLC to Lambeth Council in April 1982. Many of the management improvements introduced prior to transfer were abandoned. A report to Lambeth Council in June 1982 (Power, 1982b) identified serious problems already emerging - a sharp increase in empty and squatted flats, delays in lettings, repair backlogs building up and increasing rubbish and litter problems. In a very short period of time, Tulse Hill reverted to pre-improvement conditions and the fact that this happened could be seen as powerful evidence of the effectiveness of the measures which had been lost. Questions remain, however, about the extent of the crime reduction on the estate in the absence of data from sources other than the Housing Department.

Broadwater Farm Estate in Haringey has experienced a sustained effort to improve conditions since 1983. This began with the launch of a PEP project and the opening of a local office and continued with a broad range of physical and social measures throughout the 1980s. The crime rate dropped very sharply during the first two years and then continued to decline more gradually. The fact that there was a major disturbance on the estate in 1985, involving the deaths of a resident and a police officer, did not affect the overall downward trend in recorded crime. The results appear quite impressive. The scale of the reduction in recorded crime is probably too great to be explained by reporting and recording artefacts. There were similar scale reductions for most offence categories. The effects appear to be long-lasting. The initiative has been well-documented and there is no indication of any demographic changes or external factors which might explain the crime reductions. The main issues which remain unresolved are which of the wide range of initiatives were responsible for the reduction - probably an impossible and maybe an irrelevant question - and whether the initiative is replicable. Replicability is a serious issue on two counts. Firstly, the resources for the initiative were consistently found over a period of several years, not least because the Leader of the Council chaired the Broadwater Farm Panel for many years until his election to Parliament; this sort of powerfully sustained focus is rarely achievable. Secondly, we do not know whether the youth and business initiatives on the estate were uniquely reliant on the drive and personality of one particular community leader.

A further initiative with some similarities to the approach adopted in PEP-type schemes was the co-ordinated estate improvement project on the Pepys Estate in Deptford. The project involved the introduction of a package of measures: physical improvements, security measures, housing management changes, youth and community initiatives, the initiation of a resourceful tenants association and a neighbourhood policing project. There were dramatic reductions in recorded crime and this applied to most categories of crime. The local estate office and the neighbourhood policing initiative were not introduced until after the initial crime reduction had occurred. However, these measures may have contributed to the sustaining of lower (and gradually decreasing) crime rates thereafter. The scheme was well-documented and no evidence emerged of any other external factors which may have accounted for the changes. Not all aspects of the scheme are necessarily replicable. The neighbourhood policing project involves a heavy commitment of police resources. Deptford police have been prepared to commit these kind of resources on three estates, but there has been consistent pressure to replace the project on the Pepys Estate with a Neighbourhood Watch Scheme now that the crime rate has stabilised.

We were only able to locate one *evaluated* example of an initiative where a change of ownership may have been a major factor. A part of the Possil Park Estate in Glasgow has been given over to a tenants' co-operative and the police have attributed crime reductions on the estate to this measure. There were claims that potential offenders had adopted a more 'protective' attitude towards co-op properties, but it may have been that the physical security and management measures introduced by the co-op had some deterrent effect. Details were only available from recorded crime statistics and these were rather unsatisfactory. The length of time over which crime reductions occurred is not specified and the reductions appear to be limited to burglary - autocrime in particular was apparently still a serious problem, although figures were not supplied. For these reasons, and because of the absence of any other (than anecdotal) information about crime, it is difficult to come to a conclusion about the results.

As we have noted, a major focus of recent management initiatives has been multi-storey blocks. The introduction of block receptionist or concierge schemes has been seen as the solution to the problems being experienced on many blocks, both in terms of better local management and, more specifically, as a way of reducing crime problems. Three examples are included in the table on Management Initiatives. The Elizabeth Street scheme in Preston has led to dramatic reductions in burglaries during the three months following implementation, but a longer follow-up period is clearly required.

The Gloucester House scheme in Brent was monitored intensively over a period of one year. During this time, attempts were made to compare the management costs for Gloucester House with other similar blocks on the same estate. It was concluded that the scheme had accrued substantial revenue savings due to reduced expenditure on repairs and breakdowns and increased rental income, even after taking account of the scheme's additional staffing costs. Recorded burglaries and incidents of criminal damage were also lower than for other similar blocks on the estate. Although the study's claim that the scheme resulted in net savings can be challenged on methodological grounds, it seems clear that substantial savings were made from reduced criminal damage. The evidence of reduced levels of recorded crime is less persuasive as comparisons were made with other blocks on the estate but no details were given of changes in Gloucester House over time. The absence of information on crimes other than burglary and criminal damage also presents a difficulty, particularly as violent and sexual offences within high density environments such as tower blocks can have particularly damaging effects on community life.

A similar approach to information collection has been taken by Glasgow City Council in respect of its block receptionist scheme for Mitchelhill and similar claims have been made about revenue savings. In this case, however, more details on recorded crime were available and the scale of reduction in overall crime rates is impressive. The follow-up period of only nine months may be too short a time to conclude that the scheme was effective but a further evaluation is due, at which time a post-survey will also be carried out.

A number of questions remain about the evaluation of block receptionist schemes. The areas where they are introduced are relatively small and, in most cases, the number of crimes committed are too small to provide a meaningful analysis of changes over time. There is a case for looking at the introduction of a programme of block receptionist schemes within a local authority rather than at individual schemes. There are plans to undertake this kind of evaluation in Glasgow in late 1990. Furthermore, it should not be assumed that the kind of revenue savings achieved by schemes such as Gloucester House could be achieved more generally. Gloucester House is a very large tower block (170 dwellings) and was selected for the scheme because of its very serious damage problems and high levels of voids. In these circumstances it was possible to achieve the kinds of savings needed to offset the expense of additional staff. This would not be so easy for smaller blocks with less problems and we do not yet have any data on the effectiveness of dispersed schemes which are able to operate on lower staff ratios.

In conclusion, although none of the management initiatives described in this section satisfy all the assessment criteria, a number provide both interesting and persuasive results. On balance, from the evidence presented here, estate-based local management initiatives appear to have an impact on crime problems where they are part of a broad programme of physical and social improvements. For individual blocks, localised management in the form of block receptionists may be an appropriate and cost-effective response; results from assessments are encouraging but further evidence is required.

Conclusions about security led initiatives

If the phenomenal growth in the security industry is anything to go by, the last decade has witnessed an explosion in residential security. Government literature, police guides, local authority handbooks, professional journals and popular magazines heavily promote do-it-yourself home security as an effective anti-burglary measure. Government programmes such as the Community Programme (now Employment Training), Urban Programme and the Inner City Task Forces have funded numerous security fitting schemes for residential areas.

For much of the early 1980s, security technology in the form of phone entry systems was seen as the answer to the particular problems of multi-storey blocks. More recently, more faith has been put in other innovations such as security cameras.

The security patrolling industry, which for many years was considered as only appropriate for commercial sites, has taken root in a wide range of other settings from hospitals, to schools and housing estates.

The beneficial effects of lighting, largely based on uncritical summaries of American research and the supposed benefits of pedestrian (as opposed to motor vehicle) orientated lighting schemes on the European continent, is a current preoccupation.

Despite the scale of this activity, little attention has been paid to the effectiveness of home security measures in residential areas. We could only locate two published evaluations, despite requests for examples from a number of sources, including the Home Office Crime Prevention Centre in Stafford. Both studies are well known. Allatt's study of a home security scheme on the Scotswood Estate in Newcastle was one of the best examples of an evaluation we found (see Table 10 opposite), but her conclusions were that there had been no reduction in burglary as a result of the scheme, although there had been some (unexplained) reduction in the fear of crime.

A second, more recent, study of home security measures was carried out by Forrester et al. on the Kirkholt Estate in Rochdale (see Table 10). The security measures introduced were a mixture of physical measures such as improved door security and opportunity reducing measures such as *cocoon watch,* essentially small area Neighbourhood Watch schemes based on and around burgled dwellings.

Table 10 Security led initiatives - summary of 9 evaluations

Intervention Site & Period; Author	Description of Intervention	Outcome Examined	Measures	Nature of Outcomes	Comments on Outcome	Comments on Method
Scotswood Estate, Newcastle (1980) (*Allatt, 1984a*)	Home security measures.	Recorded burglary 1977-82; survey burglary rates 1980-81; fear of crime.		No reduction in burglary; fear of crime reduced.	No explanation for reduced fear of crime despite no reduction in other crimes.	Used monthly crime statistics pre- and post- (panel) surveys; used control estate; monitored for outside influences; partial monitoring of implementation.
Kirkholt Estate, Rochdale (1985-86) (*Forrester et al, 1988*)	Home security; property postcoding; removal of cash pre-payment meters; cocoon neighbourhood watch.	Police crime reports 1986-87.		Burglary reduced 50%, repeat burglaries 80%, woundings 21%. Criminal damage increased 21%, minor damage 13%, acquisitive crimes 9%. Little or no displacement of burglary to other areas or other crime categories.	Only 7 month follow-up period and, if burglary excluded, overall crime rate increased by 10%. Issue of replicability raised by possible effect of removal of cash meters.	Used police crime reports only; used control data (control estate and sub-division figures); monitored implementation; may not have fully taken account of outside influences.
Edmonton Project, Enfield (one street) (1988) (*Painter, 1988*)	Street lighting improvements.	Survey crime rates 1988.		Assaults, autocrimes, threats down 75% in 6 weeks after implementation. Reduced fear of crime.	Only 6 weeks follow-up period; no data on crimes other than assaults, autocrime and threats.	Used cross-sectional survey data only; no supportive, control or monitoring data; inadequate follow-up period.
Erdington Hall, Birmingham (1987) (*ILE, 1990*)	Street lighting improvements.	Recorded crime 1986-88.		Crime down by 45% in year after introduction. Reductions for all crimes except burglary where no change.	Very little descriptive data on what was done.	Used recorded crime statistics only. No supporting, control or monitoring data.
Easton/Ashton wards, Bristol (1988-89) (*Bristol City Council, 1989*)	Street lighting improvements.	Recorded crime 1988-89.		Theft from cars reduced 33%, robberies 17%, criminal damage 21% in 12 months after implementation. Burglary rate unchanged.	Lack of effect on burglary rate to be expected.	Used recorded crime statistics only. No supportive, monitoring or control data.
South Acton Estate, Ealing (1980-85) (*Osborn, 1986*)	Physical improvements, phone entry systems and garage security measures for part of estate.	Recorded crime 1980-86.		Crime rate up 30% 1980-86. But no increase in improved part of estate: burglary down 50% in 1986 where phone entries operational, autocrime down 7% where garages secured; opposite trends where security not operational.	Evidence of displacement of burglary from areas secured to areas without security.	Used recorded crime statistics only. No supporting, control or monitoring data. Pre-survey but no post survey.
Westminster Road area, Handsworth, Birmingham (1986-87) (*NACRO, 1987*)	ICP funded pilot scheme of security improvements to houses in multiple occupation.	Survey crime rates 1987; fear of crime.		Greatly reduced fear of household crime, but no reduction in fear of street crime, after implementation.	Survey carried out too soon after security improvements and too few dwellings to assess impact on crime.	Essentially a post-completion survey. No supportive, monitoring or control data.

The study found dramatic reductions in recorded burglaries (and smaller reductions in recorded woundings) with, it was claimed, no evidence of displacement to other estates or other crimes. However, the study does not claim that the results were anything more than 'encouraging', and this is largely because crime rates were only analysed for seven months after the scheme was completed[1]. There are other issues. Firstly, the overall crime rate increased by about 10%, mainly accounted for by increases in levels of criminal damage and *acquisitive crimes*. This may not be an important issue for the researchers as the scheme was designed as a burglary-prevention project, but may be an issue for residents. Secondly, although the study described the implementation in some detail it discounted the possible influence of the local authority's environmental improvements programme for the estate. Finally, we do not know how dependent the initial impact of the scheme was on the removal of cash pre-payment meters - an issue which may cast doubt on its applicability to other estates.

The only other example of a study of home security improvements, for the Westminster Road area of Handsworth, was designed as a post-completion survey rather than an evaluation and was carried out too soon after the implementation to produce evidence of crime reduction.

As we have noted, phone entry systems were regarded as the ideal security measure for blocks of flats for much of the 1980s. However, a review of phone entry schemes in London in 1985 (see Safe Neighbourhoods Unit, 1985) found that over half of the schemes were not working properly or at all. The apparent lack of effectiveness of phone entry systems in reducing crime problems could be attributable to widespread implementation failure rather than *theory failure*. Some evidence for this is provided by an analysis of recorded burglaries on the South Acton Estate in Ealing. The introduction of phone entry systems did not appear to have any impact on the blocks where they were introduced. However, further investigation revealed that the blocks where systems had been fully operational experienced dramatic reductions in burglary, whilst those with mainly or wholly inoperative systems experienced dramatic increases. It seems clear that the effective phone entry systems had displaced burglaries to other blocks. The impact on other crimes was not analysed.

Most recently, an increasing number of claims are being made about the crime prevention effects of lighting. We were able to locate five examples of *evaluated* schemes, all of which were to some extent unsatisfactory. The best known of these, the Middlesex Polytechnic studies in Edmonton, Tower Hamlets and Hammersmith and Fulham, measured the effect of lighting improvements on crime for a few weeks after their introduction and, although the results from before and after surveys showed big reductions in street crimes and fear of crime, the monitoring periods were clearly too short for any valid conclusions. In all three cases, no supportive data was available; not surprisingly, given the small size of each study area, the numbers of recorded crimes were too few to make meaningful comparisons over time. There are also questions over each study's capacity to fully monitor for external factors.

The two other lighting schemes, in Erdington Hall in Birmingham and Easton/ Ashley in Bristol, showed reductions in recorded crime and more specifically reductions in car crime, robbery and criminal damage but, as one might expect,

---

[1]   A second evaluation report was published more recently (Forrester et al)., 1990) which showed a sustained reduction in recorded burglaries.

little effect on burglary rates. Both schemes monitored crime rates for one year after implementation but very little descriptive data was available. We do not know what the schemes involved or whether crime rates had changed in neighbouring areas. We do not know whether any other external factors could have accounted for the crime reductions.

We were unable to locate any evaluations of security patrols or security cameras. Overall, the evidence in support of security measures is poor although, it must be said, security measures are often incorporated in design-led and management initiatives (and for that matter in schemes which focus on social measures) which show more promising outcomes.

Conclusions about social development led initiatives

Many of the early schemes initiated by NACRO were described as community development initiatives, although they do bear considerable resemblance to PEP estate-based management schemes and subsequent schemes run by the Safe Neighbourhoods Unit which are more housing management focused. This is not surprising, given that the basic problem assessment method used was common to all and sprang from NACRO's first project on the Cunningham Road Estate in Widnes. What distinguished the earlier NACRO schemes, however, was a commitment to developing and sustaining a broad range of community initiatives as a central focus and the importance placed on reinforcing informal social control.

We have already noted that evaluation was not built into NACRO's community development programme and, apart from the planned evaluation of its first scheme in Widnes, NACRO only carried out two further evaluations. These three evaluations are summarised in Table 11 overleaf.

The best known, and often quoted, evaluation was carried out on NACRO's pilot scheme on the Cunningham Road Estate. The study design stands up well in comparison with most of the other evaluations in this report. Unfortunately, however, the evidence from recorded crime statistics and pre- and post-surveys did not match up. Whilst there was no reduction in recorded crime levels over the period of the project, burglary rates and vandalism were considerably reduced according to the surveys. Whilst the explanation for the lack of reduction in recorded crimes has been widely accepted, doubts must remain over whether differences in pre- and post-test survey samples could have accounted for reductions in victimisation.

NACRO carried out an in-house evaluation on its community development scheme on the Bushbury Triangle Estate in Wolverhampton. The evaluation methodology was similar to that carried out on the Cunningham Road scheme, although some additional measures of effect were taken: qualitative data on crime from before and after quota groups of residents and before and after surveys of local shopkeepers. All the outcome measures pointed to a reduction in crime problems. Evidence from the quota groups suggested that meter thefts would have been further reduced if it had not been for the mis-siting of new cash pre-payment meters. Remaining concerns about the validity of the results stem from the small size of the estate (about 400 houses) and the difficulties of interpreting trends on the basis of relatively small number of incidents and over the extent of displacement to neighbouring residential areas.

Concern about estate size is more of an issue for the evaluation of NACRO's community development scheme on the Thirlmere Estate in Preston. There are

Table 11 **Social development led initiatives - summary of 7 evaluations**

Intervention Site & Period; Author	Description of Intervention	Outcome Measures Examined	Nature of Outcomes	Comments on Outcome	Comments on Method
Cunningham Rd, Widnes, Halton (1976-79) (*Hedges et al, 1980*)	Community development scheme involving youth & community activities, enhanced beat policing, repair service improvements & formalised liaison between council & residents.	Recorded crime 1976-79; survey crime rates 1976-79; residents; perceptions	No change in recorded crime rates. Survey showed burglary rate reduced by 50%, reduced vandalism & concern about crime.	Study claimed lack of effect on recorded crime stats explained by increased reporting rates.	Used recorded crime statistics (for a control estate as well), pre and post (cross sectional) surveys, monitored for outside influences and monitored implementation.
Bushbury Triangle, Wolverhampton (1981-84) (*NACRO/ SOLACE, 1986*)	Community development scheme involving modernisation programme, home security improvements, fencing and community initiatives.	Recorded crime 1981-84; survey crime rates 1981-85; fear of crime; qualitative data from selected residents; groups & structured interviews with officials, 1985.	Crime reduced by about a third, burglary & meter thefts by about half according to police stats and survey data; vandalism to homes by 50%; shop burglaries & damaged reduced according to survey; fear of crime reduced.	No reduction in non-household crime, although relatively few offences in this category. Meter theft reduction would have been greater but for mistakes in re-siting of meters. May have been some displacement to neighbouring (modernised) estates.	Used data from recorded crime statistics and pre and post surveys (cross sectional), supported by qualitative data. Control data (recorded crime) obtained for neighbouring area. Implementation extensively monitored. Monitored for outside influences.
Thirlmere Estate, Preston (1983-86) (*Osborn & Bright, 1989*)	Community development scheme involving modernisation programme, home security improvements, community initiatives (including co-operative development), play areas.	Recorde crime 1984-86. Qualitative data from interviews with residents' association & officials in 1987.	Recorded burglary rate reduced 50%; no data on other crimes. Crime reduction according to interviews with police & residents. Estate won RIBA Living in City Award 1988.	Size of estate (134 houses) means too few crime incidents to be confident about outcome.	Used recorded crime statistics supported by qualitative data. Implementation extensively monitored but no monitoring or outside influences and no control data; pre-survey only.
Barrowfield Estate, Glasgow (1989) (*Ball et al, 1990*)	Community enterprise development: building, landscaping, environmental maintenance, building repairs businesses & workplace scheme. Community security company to manage void properties.	Costs of vandalism to housing authority 1988-89.	Cost of vandalism 1988 £250,000 + £100,000 for contract security firm. Cost of vandalism 1989 £25,000 + £80,000 for community security company.	Dramatic reduction in costs of vandalism to local authority, but no data on other crimes.	Used cost data from local authority only. No supporting, control, or monitoring data.
Golf Links Estate, Ealing (1984-87) (*Osborn, 1989*)	Youth activities organised by local volunteers; home security improvements; enhanced beat policing; opening of neighbourhood office	Recorded crime statistics for beat area 1983-87; qualitative data from interviews with officials in 1988.	Recorded crime reduced 77%; all crime categories reduced by similar proportion; supported by qualitative data.	Results need qualification as beat area crime stats cover wider area than estate. Key role of youth activities confirmed by local agencies—home security could not account for across the board crime reductions & neighbourhood office not opened until after dramatic reduction in crime.	Used recorded crime statistics only but supported by qualitative data. Implementation extensively monitored but no monitoring for outside influences and no control data; pre-survey only.
Hamilton Information Project for Youth (HIPY), Hamilton (late 1980s-ongoing) (*Findlay et al, 1990*)	Estate-based activities for local youth aged 16-25, initiated by Youth Enquiry Service (YES). Cost approximately £65,000 per annum.	Recorded crime statistics 1988-89 for beats covering HIPY.	Housebreaking reduced 44%, vandalism 16%, serious assaults/ carrying offensive weapons 45% in 1989.	No data on other relevant crimes such as autocrimes.	Used recorded crime statistics only, and no supporting, control or monitoring data. Some selectivity in use of statistics.
Ferguslie Park, Paisley (1986-ongoing) (*Findlay et al, 1990*)	Youth centre and activities run by young people	Recorded crime statistics 1985-88.	Vandalism reduced 22% by 1988, petty assault 32% & fire raising 55%, but no reduction in overall crime rate.	Claimed that crimes often involving young people reduced but no data supplied on burglary or autocrime.	Used recorded crime statistics only and no supporting, control or monitoring data. Selectivity in use of statistics.

only 134 houses on the estate and a relatively small number of recorded crimes accounted for a large percentage change. Although the scheme was clearly successful on many fronts - it won the 1988 RIBA *Living in the City Award* - it is difficult to draw meaningful conclusions about its effect on crime problems.

Recently greater attention has been paid to the role of community enterprises in housing-related crime prevention, and this is particularly the case in Scotland where Strathclyde Community Business has helped to develop a number of security focused community businesses. As we have seen, community enterprises have also been a central feature of some local management initiatives and community development schemes.

We were able to locate one example of an evaluated community enterprise scheme on the Barrowfield Estate in Glasgow. Community business development on the estate, and more specifically a community security business to manage void properties, has apparently led to an overall saving of over £200,000 in reduced criminal damage. The scale of this reduction is very impressive but there is no description of the nature of local problems and no data on crime. The initiative is certainly worthy of further investigation.

Three examples of youth initiatives on housing estates are summarised in Table 11. The most impressive in terms of the scale of crime reduction is the initiative on the Golf Links Estate in Ealing. All categories of crime were substantially reduced over the period of the project, according to police statistics. Although the youth project was only one element of an estate improvement programme, it appears to have been the major factor because other elements could not have accounted for the changes - it is difficult to see how home security improvements could have contributed to reductions in autocrime and street crime, for instance, and the neighbourhood office was not introduced until after the crime rate had stabilised at its reduced level. The police supported this view. However, questions remain over the nature of the police statistics. They were supplied for the beat areas covering the Golf Links Estate and included a neighbouring, but far smaller, estate. However, project staff did not consider this to be an important issue because the youth project ended up catering for youth on the neighbouring estate as well.

The evidence presented for the other two youth initiatives is disappointing. The Hamilton Information Project for Youth and the Ferguslie Park youth project in Paisley both claim reductions in crimes associated with young people. Leaving aside their exclusive reliance on recorded crime statistics, the evaluations are selective in their presentation of data. Neither study describes changes in autocrime rates and one also fails to mention changes in burglary rates. Autocrime and burglary are the most common offences recorded for young people and we are left to wonder whether the figures, if they had been presented, would have undermined claims of success.

Conclusions about policing led initiatives

We looked exclusively at initiatives involving changes to the way in which residential areas are policed. We did not include examples of police involvement in physical security schemes, design improvements or community involvement schemes (these were covered in other categories). Nor did we refer to police involvement in multi-agency initiatives - most schemes described in this report were multi-agency driven.

Notwithstanding the rhetoric about community or neighbourhood policing, there is very little data on its effectiveness in crime prevention terms. The only example we could locate was the intensive neighbourhood policing project on the Pepys Estate in Deptford, Lewisham. This formed part of a co-ordinated estate improvement scheme involving physical, management and social measures. The scheme is described in some detail earlier in this chapter (p.103) where we concluded that the policing initiative did not account for the dramatic crime reductions but did appear to have contributed to sustaining lower crime levels once the reductions had been achieved. Deptford Police have been sufficiently impressed with the results to set up similar initiatives on two neighbouring estates. However, the initiative is not well known (or promoted) in police circles, even within the Metropolitan Police. Recently, Cleveland Constabulary has begun to introduce similar schemes (Cleveland Constabulary, 1990) but had to rely on information collected by the Safe Neighbourhoods Unit in the absence of Metropolitan Police reports.

The successful schemes

We have described a large number of initiatives. In every case we have presented some reservations about the evidence of their success. This was inevitable. There are always going to be questions left unanswered and extra data which would have been useful to obtain. However, having sifted through the evidence, it is our view that a reasonably strong case was made for the following schemes to be considered successful:

- Broadwater Farm Estate, Haringey

- Pepys Estate, Lewisham

- Gloucester House, South Kilburn Estate, Brent

- Mitchellhill, Glasgow

- Cunningham Road Estate, Halton

- Bushbury Triangle, Wolverhampton

- Golf Links Estate, Ealing

Two other schemes showed promising initial results - Kirkholt Estate, Rochdale; Barrowfield Estate, Glasgow. For each of the initiatives, a fairly convincing case was put forward for reduced crime problems (large reductions in recorded crime, in most cases across all offence categories and confirmed by other outcome measures); in each case, comprehensive monitoring of the implementation gave good grounds for concluding that it was the scheme which caused the effect (in some cases confirmatory control data was also available); in most cases, the effects were sustained over several years and appeared to stand a good chance of being permanent; and in most cases, the characteristics of the scheme appeared to be largely replicable.

Part Two — Assessing costs and benefits

Part Two of the report is intended to provide practical guidance on the measurement of costs and benefits associated with the introduction of housing initiatives which have a crime reduction objective. It does not attempt to be a thorough review of cost benefit analysis models, although reference is made to major cost benefit exercises carried out in the past and their theoretical frameworks.

We are principally concerned with methods of assessing the outcome of particular projects rather than comparing the potential outcomes of a range of different options. However, we have drawn on material from the *option appraisal* or *investment appraisal* field and some of our recommendations are also applicable to that field. In addition, we have drawn on examples of cost effectiveness analysis, which is most appropriate as a methodology where the benefits expected from a project are already clearly defined, or where budgetary limits have been established and the optimum way of spending the money must be decided (in cost benefit analysis both sides of the cost benefit equation are variable).

Chapter 5   Cost benefit analysis in the public sector

This chapter looks at two central government publications which give an overall framework for appraising options for investment of public sector funds. The first, the so-called *Green Booklet,* produced by the Treasury (HM Treasury, 1984) gives technical advice applicable to any public sector project. The second, *The Handbook of Estate Improvement - Appraising Options* (Department of the Environment, 1989), goes on to apply some of those techniques to housing estate improvement projects.

Treasury guidelines for investment appraisal

This guide focuses on the effects of spending on the economy as a whole. Forms of investment appraisal are described as ranging from, in their most *sophisticated* form, cost benefit analysis to cost effectiveness analysis which compares the costs of different options which have the same or similar output. The guide suggests that cost benefit analysis can only be used where there are well developed methods of valuing non-market costs and benefits - for example, in road building schemes.

According to the guide, the value of cost benefit analysis is that it 'leads to better decisions' and 'encourages managers to question and justify what they are doing'. There is only a passing reference to the use of cost benefit analysis for retrospective appraisals.

The guide outlines a basic methodology for cost benefit analysis, involving the following steps:

Define the objectives

If this is not done, it is not clear what counts as a cost or benefit. Objectives must not be so narrow as to rule out important options.

Consider the options

List the main ways of meeting the objective. One option will usually be to do nothing - the *base case.*

Identify the costs, benefits, timing and uncertainty of each option

Monetary costs and benefits normally include capital costs, running costs, any significant costs and benefits which affect other parts of the public sector or the private sector and benefits in the form of revenues, cost savings and other outputs.

Opportunity costs should also be taken into account. This is normally represented by the best alternative use to which the resource could be put in the economy.

Costs and benefits which cannot be measured directly in money terms can often be given imputed money values on the basis of analysing people's actual behaviour and declared or revealed preferences (for example, through surveys) or by analysing the value which people place on using a service, ie how much will they pay?

Discount those costs and benefits which can be valued in money terms	Even when they are expressed in real terms, costs and benefits occurring at different times are not directly comparable. They should be set on a common footing by discounting, to give the *present value* of the costs and benefits.

Weigh up the uncertainties	Valuing costs and benefits always requires some assumptions about the future. Those assumptions may have to be corrected and this may affect the balance of advantage between options. Assumptions which are especially uncertain should be highlighted.

Assess other factors	Other factors which cannot be usefully valued in money terms may need to be taken into account. These may include political implications, general environmental factors and effects on other parts of the economy. These need to be quantified and, where possible, taken into account.

Present the results

In any final presentation of results, it is often useful to set out:

- The objectives;
- The options;
- The capital costs;
- Other large costs and benefits;
- Any marked pattern of timing of costs and benefits;
- The net present value (ie total discounted costs set against total discounted benefits);
- Important uncertainties;
- Each of the factors which cannot be valued in money terms;
- The option which is judged to give the best value for money;
- How this option compares with important alternatives.

The guide concludes that measuring benefits in the public sector is problematic, in that 'most public sector output is not sold and it is difficult to measure the benefits; this may mean that benefits are exaggerated or underestimated'.

DOE handbook of estate improvement - appraising options

The handbook was produced to provide guidance on the appraisal of Estate Action schemes and has the stated objective of promoting 'a variety of measures designed to help housing authorities improve the quality of life on run-down housing estates'.

The handbook deals with a combination of cost effectiveness analysis and cost benefit analysis and, to some extent, merges the two approaches. It draws on the Treasury's Green Booklet but it has extended the approach to cover the 'wider exercise of estate assessment and the development of strategic objectives'.

Cost benefit analysis is used to compare options for estate improvements. It is intended a tool for decision making rather than for testing whether decisions on improvements achieve their aim. It looks at future options rather than retrospective appraisal.

118

The handbook wrestles with the problem of placing a value on unquantifiable costs and benefits such as quality of life, fear of crime and aesthetic judgement but does not come to any firm conclusions. It suggests that local authorities can 'test the market' by surveying tenants about the level of rent increases they would be prepared to pay for favourable outcomes such as reduced burglaries.

The handbook recommends a methodology for economic assessment of options involving four main steps.

Step 1 - Compare quantifiable monetary costs and benefits	Tabulate quantifiable monetary costs and benefits showing their timing and distribution over the period of the evaluation, subtract yearly costs from benefits to arrive at a net benefit or cost, convert annual totals to present values by applying discount factors (as per the Treasury's Green Booklet) and add up the annual net discounted benefits/costs to arrive at a total net benefit/cost.
Step 2 - Compare quantifiable non-monetary costs and benefits	Set out those costs and benefits for each option which cannot be quantified in monetary terms and reach a judgement on their significance for each option. The handbook suggests that benefits such as reduced crime and improved repair performance can be allocated a value. For example, the expected proportional reductions in crime can be recorded for each option and these can be converted into indices by taking the most favourable outcome to represent 100%. The same procedure can be adopted for repair performance by, for instance, listing expected response times against each option. These indices can then be added together to produce a total score for each option, the highest score representing the most favourable outcome. Scores can be weighted if some outcomes are considered more important than others.
Step 3 - Compare costs and benefits not quantifiable in any way	Appraise costs and benefits which cannot be quantified at all (for example, disruption to estate) and reach judgement on their significance in relation to the outcomes of Steps 1 and 2.
Step 4 - Final judgement	Final judgement calls for a decision on which option offers best value for money based on:

- A comparison of discounted monetary (quantifiable) net benefits;

- A comparison of non-monetary (quantifiable) factors;

- An assessment of unquantifiable costs and benefits.

If the three sets of information conflict, then decisions on which option to take can be resolved by establishing a *trade off* between the non-monetary net quantifiables with the monetary net benefits. For example, it may be that, for an additional net monetary cost of 20%, it is possible to achieve a 28% increase in non-monetary benefits. Problems emerge, however, if the ranking of options based on unquantifiable factors conflicts with that derived from an appraisal of quantifiable factors. As the handbook states: '. . . is a reduction in fear of crime, for example, worth a sacrifice of net quantifiable benefits plus other quantifiable benefits? If so, what are the limits to this sacrifice?'

The handbook sets out a range of typical costs and benefits for estate improvement schemes (see Table 1 overleaf).

Table 1 **Typical Costs and Benefits**

Options	Costs quantifiable	Costs unquantifiable	Benefits quantifiable	Benefits unquantifiable
(1) No action	Day-to-day management costs Repair/maintenance costs	Assessment of existing conditions	Assessment of existing conditions	
(2) Any option Costs and benefits which may be common to options (3), (4) and (5) below	Professional fees/costs of staff time		Savings on use of bed-and-breakfast accommodation Savings in repair and maintenance costs Savings in cleansing costs Reduction in crime Reduction in damage to residents' property Rental income from property returned to use Increase in market value of dwellings	Increased resident satisfaction Increased stability of community Improved quality of life Improved health of residents Reduction in fear of crime Improved reputation of estate Better facilities for children/youths Better facilities for special groups Increased take-up of Right-to-Buy
(3) Change of ownership/tenure Sale or transfer	Reduction in rental income Capital cost of new build/improvement Continuing loan debt		Reduction in management and maintenance costs Income from sale of land/stock	Diversification of ownership
(4) Management changes Estate management changes arising from *PS 1.1 and PS 2.1*	Increased cost of service per dwelling		Reduced cost of service per dwelling Reduction in: Re-let times Rent loss on vacant units Cost of void protection Cost of dealing with transfer requests Rent arrears Cost of chasing arrears Cost of repairing vandalism Cost of removing graffiti	Reduction in management difficulty Increased resident satisfaction Increased staff satisfaction Increased resident involvement Improved cleanliness/tidiness
Repairs and maintenance service	Increased cost of service per dwelling		Reduced cost of service per dwelling Reduced response times Reduced repairs backlog Increased productivity per tradesman	Improved condition of dwellings Increased resident satisfaction Improved standard of workmanship in repairs Increased staff satisfaction
Community facilities and community development	Capital costs Revenue costs			Increased resident involvement Improved provision for children/youths Improved provision for special groups
(5) Physical changes Demolition of dwellings	Demolition costs Cost of decanting/rehousing Compensation to residents Market value (if any) of demolished units Void protection prior to demolition	Disruption to estate/surrounding areas Break-up of existing community Effect of loss of housing stock on waiting list	Market value of site Reduction in repair/maintenance costs (of demolished units) Reduction in site density	Removal of eyesore
New-build for rent	Capital costs Increased maintenance commitment from increase in stock	Disturbance to surrounding area during works	Market value of new dwellings	
Improvement to blocks/dwellings/common parts/external areas Replacement Upgrading Remodelling	Capital costs Temporary rehousing (incl removal expenses) Disturbance payments Future repair and maintenance (life-cycle) costs	Disruption and inconvenience to residents	Reduction in day-to-day repair and cyclical maintenance costs due to improved conditions Reduced fuel costs for residents	Improved security of dwellings and external areas Reduced fear of crime Increased comfort of dwellings Improved appearance of estate

Source: DoE Estate Action 'Handbook of Estate Improvement — Vol.1 Option Appraisal' (1990)

Chapter 6

Cost effectiveness analysis in the public sector

Cost effectiveness analysis is a second stage of analysis after cost benefit analysis has demonstrated that the project has an overall benefit. Cost effectiveness analysis seeks to meet a defined target in the best possible way. It can be used to ensure that improvements represent value for money as well as giving overall benefit. One aspect of cost effectiveness analysis must include a measure of consumer satisfaction.

This chapter will look at specific studies of cost effectiveness in housing, with a view to identifying information on unit analysis which can be incorporated into cost benefit studies of housing related crime prevention. In order to introduce this area, it is important to look at the Audit Commission (1986) report which introduced an economic approach to housing management.

Managing the crisis in housing management

The report examined housing management and supervision. It made the case that council housing management was in a state of crisis and backed up this assertion with diagrams charts and graphs. These it called 'exhibits', as if it were prosecuting the case in court.

The report is based on in-depth studies of 15 authorities and a survey questionnaire completed by 387 authorities in 1985 (referring to the financial year 1983-4). There is no survey or consultation with tenants, although their views are often cited.

The report contains useful unit costs at 1984 and 1985 figures. It examines housing management in terms of economy and effectiveness. It does not take into account any policy issues.

Economy

Excluding loan charges and maintenance, £1 billion per year was spent on the 'day-to-day process of providing a housing management service' to tenants. This gives an average of £200 per dwelling per year, although figures vary greatly between authorities.

The Audit Commission uses CIPFA definitions which differentiate between general supervision and management costs, applying to all tenants (for example, rent collection and accounting) and special costs - services which are for some rather than all tenants (for example, caretaking and cleaning).

The Audit Commission looks in particular at the central establishment charges because this is an area where it felt that costs were excessive due to bureaucracy and lack of local budget control. Central Establishment Charges can include:

- Insurance;

- Sales administration;

- Central heating;

- Caretaking/cleaning;

- Services for the elderly;

- Maintenance of open spaces;

- Provision for the homeless;

- Personnel;

- Legal;

- Payroll;

- Architectural services;

- Engineering;

- Debt charges;

- Office charges such as heating, lighting, telephones, etc.

Effectiveness

The Audit Commission made a case for moving away from the practice of 'minimum standards for minimum rent' in favour of a move to 'provide better services and be prepared to charge more realistic rents for them'. It felt that the present 'pricing signals' (rent levels) were incorrect and raised rents will be affordable for 'deprived families' because Housing Benefit would cover the cost.

Practical recommendations on design, re-let periods on voids and hard-to-let estates followed. There were benefits to be had from reducing voids or making an estate more letable - homeless families can be rehoused and this would reduce overall costs. The Audit Commission also recommended that estate improvements should also be funded by increased rents.

Another reason it gave for increasing rent levels was to 'establish the opportunity cost for tenants considering the purchase of their dwellings'. In this way tenants would be encouraged to buy. An economic rent should be based on the sum of the depreciation on the property plus the opportunity costs (the annual return an owner would expect if the dwelling was sold at its current capital value). The Audit Commission felt that local authorities were charging only half the economic rent.

Performance indicators relating to a range of management tasks were set. An *optimistic* forecast was made that in three years, at 1984 prices, benefits of £810 million could be achieved through reductions in administrative charges, central establishment charges, housing benefit administration costs, fewer voids, lower rent arrears and increased rental income from improvements to properties.

Comparative effectiveness of housing association and local authority housing management

A recent report on the nature and effectiveness of housing management in England and Wales (HMSO, 1989) was carried out by the Centre for Housing Research at Glasgow University. The report's aim was to compare the economy, efficiency and effectiveness of housing management by local authorities with housing associations. It criticised the previous research by the Audit Commission on the grounds that it had not really taken effectiveness into account, in part because it was so difficult to assess. Three particular problems in measuring effectiveness were highlighted:

- The lack of unit data on services.

- The differing values applied to evidence by different groups (for example, tenants, government, councillors).

- The difficulty of assessing the quality of public services which cannot be measured by a market price.

The study defined 'economy' as the resources or inputs going into a service compared with outputs produced. 'Efficiency' was concerned with throughputs, such as the value obtained from the money spent on providing services. Effectiveness looked at impact and levels of satisfaction with the output.

The study was a *snapshot* and is worth looking at to see the way in which individual housing costs were isolated and the way different service aspects inter-relate. Unfortunately the study does not cover the London area nor does it look at hard-to-let high rise accommodation. In order to compare housing associations and local authorities it was only possible to consider the type of accommodation that they held in common - low rise, terraced and semi-detached housing.

Data was collected through a self-completion survey of housing authorities and this was supplemented by six case studies which included in-depth interviews with tenants and staff, a tenant satisfaction survey and a housing condition survey.

The methodology used by the study was similar to cost benefit analysis in that management was split up into its constituent functions and costs where possible.

The study took some of the main service outputs such as allocation of empty dwellings, rent collection and repairs to compare costs and outcomes. To make comparisons the functions were broken down into unit costs, such as the number of lettings as a percentage of the total number of dwellings. A number of different factors might influence speedy or slow lettings. In order to identify the significant causes, regression analysis was used which tests the strength of the relationship between variables. This relationship would be complicated, however, if the explanatory variables (such as stock size or size of waiting list) were co-linear or related to each other.

The study identified a number of problems in assessing overall effectiveness through surveys:

- Tenants are asked to express their satisfaction or otherwise without any reference to costs. There may be a strong incentive to argue for more or better services when the costs of improvements are not translated into rent increases.

- Tenants are not a homogenous group and their levels of satisfaction are also influenced by their personal circumstances.

- Service interdependency means that it is difficult to separate out assessments of individual services.

Priority Estates Project cost effectiveness study

A four-year study to compare Priority Estate (PEP) estate based management with centralised housing management has been carried out by CAPITA. An interim report is available (CAPITA, 1990) and the final report is likely to be published in 1992. PEP has developed a model of local management based on three central concepts: management and services physically based on the estate, tenant participation in management and a self-contained and locally controlled budget for estate services. It is widely accepted that this model can be more costly than centralised management but it is argued that the additional benefits of these arrangements can warrant their higher costs.

The central aim of the evaluation was to assess the cost-effective of estate-based management in comparison with more traditional centralised management. There were two implicit subsidiary aims: to assess how effective estate-based management is in relation to an agreed set of measures and to determine the relevant costs of management.

Five priority estates were included in the study and, to make individual comparisons of cost-effectiveness, five *control* estates were selected.

There were two components to the assessment of effectiveness: management performance and tenant satisfaction. The performance indicators selected to measure management performance covered the spectrum of management activity:

- lettings
- repairs
- debt management
- management of empty (void) properties.

Within each area of activity, performance measures were grouped together to provide an overview of that activity and a further step involved bringing together the performance of various management features to produce a single measure of housing management performance. This process of aggregation took on board the views of both officers and residents in order to provide weightings for the various aspects of performance.

To complete the picture provided by the measures of management performance, indicators of the level of tenant satisfaction were derived from questionnaire surveys. The satisfaction measures related to areas such lettings performance, repairs performance, debt management and estate cleanliness.

Because the evaluation concentrated specifically on housing management rather than housing, CAPITA took the view that only revenue expenditure made a direct input into the assessment of effectiveness. The basic cost-effectiveness evaluation relied solely on such data, which include staff and non-staff costs, both directly attributable and apportioned from central departments as necessary. However, information was also collected on capital expenditure and programmed repairs expenditure in order to provide a broad indication of its effect on cost-effectiveness. This expenditure was spread over the *life-cycle* of the capital works and the apportionment over the years of each cycle calculated using the public sector discount factor.

CAPITA also collected contextual data to provide background to, and explanation of, their direct measures. The main items were local authority housing policy, housing department organisation and procedures, local services (health, education, shops and transport) and socio-economic information about residents.

The final evaluation of cost-effectiveness involved combining the various indicators, measures and costs in a formal framework which was built up on explicit assumptions about their inter-relationships and relative importance to one another. Two models were used to combine the data. The first showed the movement in performance over time and related this to the total costs incurred in achieving that change. Changes in average performance were divided by total housing management costs for both years to derive an index of cost-effectiveness. This model provided a picture of the direction of change on the priority and control estates and, by relating that change to costs, it was possible to determine which estate had the more cost-effective management to achieve change. The second model related the level of performance and costs on both estates at a given time to provide a *snapshot* of relative cost-effectiveness.

Chapter 7

Assessing the costs of crime

Ideally, cost benefit analysis should take account of information on the costs of crime. The benefits which may derive from fewer crimes, in terms of reduced costs for the criminal justice system, local authorities, local businesses and individuals, should be taken into account. This chapter describes recent research on the costs of crime.

Home Office Standing Conference on Crime Prevention

In 1988 the Home Office Standing Conference on Crime Prevention reported its findings on the cost of crime (Home Office, 1988). The report identified a range of cost areas, although it was not able to attach monetary or other quantifiable values to each area.

Costs borne by individual victims of crime

The report highlighted two categories of victimisation - victims of violence and victims of thefts.

From the 1982 British Crime Survey (Hough and Mayhew, 1983), the report identified that 31% of victims of violence saw a doctor and just under 4% were admitted to hospital; in 3% of cases the victim had to take two days or more off work to deal with the effect of a violent crime. The report also noted the monetary values placed by the Criminal Injuries Compensation Board on some injuries, ranging between £650 for an undisplaced nasal fracture up to £15,000 for the loss of vision in one eye (updated 1990 figures). The report did not attempt, however, to place a value on the emotional costs of violent crime.

In relation to thefts, and the costs incurred by victims in terms of the illegal transfer of resources, the report noted that the Association of British Insurers' annual figures for claims on domestic insurance policies amounted to £276 million in 1989. There are also opportunity costs for the victim, such as time spent seeing the police, claiming insurance, possible court appearances and purchasing replacements.

The impact of theft clearly differs according to the victim's income. For example, the lower a person's income the greater the impact the theft of a given sum is likely to have. In addition, the likelihood of the victim being insured reduces with reduced personal income. The report did not attempt to put a value on the social cost of increased fear of crime or anger and frustration after a crime.

Costs of crime to offenders

The report points out that there are also financial and opportunity costs for offenders as a result of crime. These costs include social stigma, fines, imprisonment and loss of jobs. These costs also fall on offenders' dependants.

Costs associated with the fear of crime

The report does not attempt to quantify fear of crime but recognises that it is a social cost which reduces people's ability to be involved in community life, especially after dark.

| Costs of crime to local government | The report highlighted the direct private financial costs to local authorities as a result of criminal damage. A report by LAMSAC (1987), which is examined in detail later in this section, estimated that the annual cost of criminal damage to local authorities amounted to about £500 million per year. This includes repairs, replacements, higher insurance premiums, site clearance, dislocation and relocation, prosecutions and loss of revenue (for example, rents). |

Quoting Harrison and Gretton (1986), the report estimated that local government bears about half the cost of crime, including the direct costs of the police and other crime related agencies, the private sector about 30% and central government about 20%.

The report also estimated that around £20 million was being spent by local authorities on crime prevention each year.

The cost of mitigating the effect of crime on victims

The report described a range of measures which serve to mitigate the effect of crime: insurance, compensation to victims of crime, general help to victims, the recovery of property, and reparation and compensation ordered by courts.

Premium payments for insurance cover, against losses arising from crime continue to rise. These costs, says the report, represent an opportunity cost to society. Thefts account for 5% of insurance claims paid on buildings and 40% of claims paid on contents insurance.

Between 1986-7 the total amount of compensation paid by the Criminal Injuries Compensation Board was £37.5 million which, the report states, represents a net transfer of resources from taxpayers to victims awarded compensation. The £15.4 million administration costs of the CICB also represent a net opportunity cost to society of providing that compensation.

Between 1987 and 1990 the National Association of Victim Support Schemes received £9 million from the Home Office; this represents an opportunity cost to society.

Recovery of stolen property obviously reduces the net financial loss to the victim. The 1982 British Crime Survey found that 70% of stolen cars were recovered, but that the recovery rate for other kinds of property was very low.

Losses, damages or injuries suffered as a result of a criminal offence can also be compensated through the courts. In 1987 magistrate's courts awarded a total of around £10 million in compensation orders.

The costs of dealing with offenders

The final aspect of the cost of crime dealt with by the report was the criminal justice system. Overall, £3,500 million was spent on the police in 1987, around £170 million on the Crown Prosecution Service in 1988/89, about £200 million on defence costs in 1986/7, around £320 million on the courts, around £215 million on the probation service, about £700 million on the prison service and unspecified sums on voluntary bodies.

Economic and financial costs of crime

Examples of assessing the economic and financial costs of crime are provided by studies in Leicester and Nottingham. The methodologies would be generally applicable to units of different sizes.

Economic impact of crime in Leicester

Research in Leicester carried out by Locke (1989) takes a city wide approach to the costs of crime. It attempts to devise a method of measuring the effect of crime on the local economy. The components of the methodology used are a risk assessment pilot study, a profile of the local area context and an auditing frame of the costs of crime to a business.

The report refers to the broad range of crime against businesses. Locke also makes a brief mention of the 'hidden economy' of illegal economic activities such as concealed fraud and tax evasion and unofficial work. All of these activities deprive society of income through tax revenues and consequently inflate the cost of policing and justice.

Spending on crime prevention measures represents a direct cost and an opportunity cost. Locke points out how businesses concentrate their energy on reducing the impact of major or serious crimes rather than small, petty and persistent crimes. Yet businesses are most likely to suffer from persistent petty crime.

Locke argues that, if businesses have accurate information about the risk of crime, they can take appropriate security measures to protect their profits. The most frequent crimes suffered by businesses are burglary and theft and a first step towards crime management is to collect accurate information on the incidence of crime through crime surveys. Additionally, information can be collected from surveys of offenders. Also, he argues that insurers can play a role by making certain crime prevention measures a condition of insurance. Businesses are made aware of the insurers' perceptions of levels of crime in their area by the level of premium that they have to pay. High premiums are an incentive to businesses to prevent crime in the same way as they are an incentive for owner occupiers to prevent domestic burglary. 'The insurance market provides a price mechanism for the supply of crime protection but this mechanism works most effectively where there is (as far as practicable) perfect knowledge of the risks and opportunities.' (Locke, 1990)

Locke also quotes the Field and Hope (1989) conclusion that, left to themselves people would individually provide less protection against crime than would be desirable for 'aggregate social welfare'. This means that there is a clear role for central and local government in preventing crime. He gives examples of local government targeting resources to encourage crime prevention, such as Leicester's Inner Area Programme grants to commercial premises to improve the 'quality' of shopping areas. Central government's role in the criminal justice system governs how offenders are deterred or punished. The criminal justice system is very expensive, prevention is cheaper. But whereas the criminal justice system is paid for by government, crime prevention measures are largely paid for by individuals or by local government. As already stated, individuals tend to under-provide in terms of crime prevention. Locke argues that 'Investment by local authorities in crime reduction strategies would, if successful, reduce the burden on the rates of policing, probation and the courts'.

Locke advocated a risk assessment methodology to target crime prevention resources effectively. The information gathered from a risk assessment survey is set out in an *auditing frame* which divides the costs of crime into direct and indirect costs.

- *Direct costs:*

   Value of goods or property lost or damaged through crime.

Cost of repair to property damaged as a result of crime.

The cost of replacing stolen goods (at replacement rather than market value).

These direct costs would then be set against compensation from insurance or other sources.

- *Indirect costs:*

Cost of insurance premiums.

Cost of security measures, hardware and personnel.

Loss of profits through lost income.

Loss of production revenue, where means of production are lost or damaged by crime.

Emotional and personal costs of crime to staff.

Cost of internal security measures such as tagging.

Opportunity cost of time away from production spent on dealing with impact of crime.

This auditing frame constitutes a very narrowly based cost benefit analysis and only includes one external cost - the emotional and personal cost of crime to employees.

The Nottingham Crime Audit

The Nottingham Crime Audit (KPMG Peat Marwick/Safe Neighbourhoods Unit, 1990) is also a city-wide approach to the costs of crime. It attempted to identify the costs of crime to the public, to the local authority and to the business community.

Costs of crime to victims

The audit used victim surveys to identify the costs to victims associated with three offences: domestic burglary, auto theft and assaults. From these it estimated an average gross loss for each burglary event of about £750 and, on this basis, an estimated total loss for the City's victims of £2.6 million in 1988/89. Although some 50% of these gross losses were being met from insurance payments, the audit concluded that the gross figure was significant because the community at large met the costs in the form of insurance premiums.

The audit found it much more difficult to assess costs associated with assault because of low reporting rates and the sensitivity surrounding some forms of assault. It did find, however, that 55% of assault victims had to take time off work as a result of their assault and that these people had lost an average of 15 days from work. On the basis of the New Earnings Survey, this amounted to some £600 in lost wages/production and the audit estimated a total economic cost to the City of £1.4 million.

Costs of crime to the local authority

The audit selected the City's housing department for a monitoring exercise on the costs of crime. This involved management and technical officers in district and neighbourhood offices completing monitoring forms on all crime-related incidents which they had to deal with over a one month period. From the monitoring exercise, the audit estimated that around £100,000 per annum was being spent by the housing department in staff time and resources on dealing with tenants' problems and repairs associated with domestic burglaries and criminal damage to dwellings. This was felt to be an unrealistically low cost figure because the officers concerned felt that the number of incidents recorded in the monitoring period was lower than normal. The monitoring exercise also picked up a range of violent offences - domestic assaults and inter-neighbour assaults. It proved difficult to assess the costs of these to the housing department, however, because of the complicated and individual nature of the department's response. These kinds of offences were likely to trigger a range of management responses from emergency rehousing to legal action.

The audit attempted to illustrate the complicated nature of the housing department's response through a flow chart (see Figure 1 overleaf).

Costs of crime to the city centre economy

The audit used survey data to identify the level of public avoidance of the city centre because of concern about crime - mainly concern about autocrime during the day and concern about violence after dark. The audit conservatively estimated, on the basis of survey indicators of people avoiding the centre, that £12 million in turnover each year was being lost within retailing and £12 million within the leisure sector.

The audit also estimated that losses from theft experienced by the retail sector amounted to between 1% and 2% of turnover - £5-£10 million per annum.

Costs of crime to the criminal justice system

The audit attempted to estimate the criminal justice system costs associated with three offences: domestic burglary, auto theft and assaults. For this purpose, the audit concluded that there was no such thing as an average criminal justice cost for each category of crime because of differences in reporting, detecting, prosecuting and sentencing processes. Instead a *benchmark* event was selected for each category of crime. For domestic burglary the *benchmark* was an event leading to a three month jail sentence after appearance at a magistrates court. The costs associated with this *benchmark* event amounted to £7,765 - of which about half related to costs of imprisonment - and, on this basis amounted to £2.8 million for the City as a whole. A similar exercise in relation to theft from and of motor vehicles, involving a *benchmark* of police intervention limited to recording but not detecting the events, produced a cost of £7.1 million for the City as a whole.

The audit pointed out, however, that these kinds of costs 'are not marginal costs - that is they cannot be taken as directly identifying savings that could result from reductions in particular types of crime'. In effect, reductions in crime would have to be very large, sustained over long periods of time and across regions rather than in small areas such as estates, before they could be translated into fewer police officers, courts and prisons.

Applying risk analysis to the impact of criminal damage to public property

A report produced by LAMSAC (1987) aimed to analyse the financial impact of criminal damage on local authority property and provide a framework for managing this category of crime. It also gave guidelines on *risk management*. Risk management is based on an American system which insurance companies have used since the 1960s - it explicitly addresses the issue of the economically acceptable level of crime that an organisation may wish to maintain. It concentrates on property and the past history of damage to or burglary of particular buildings.

Figure 1 **Costs of crime to housing service - generated from housing stock**

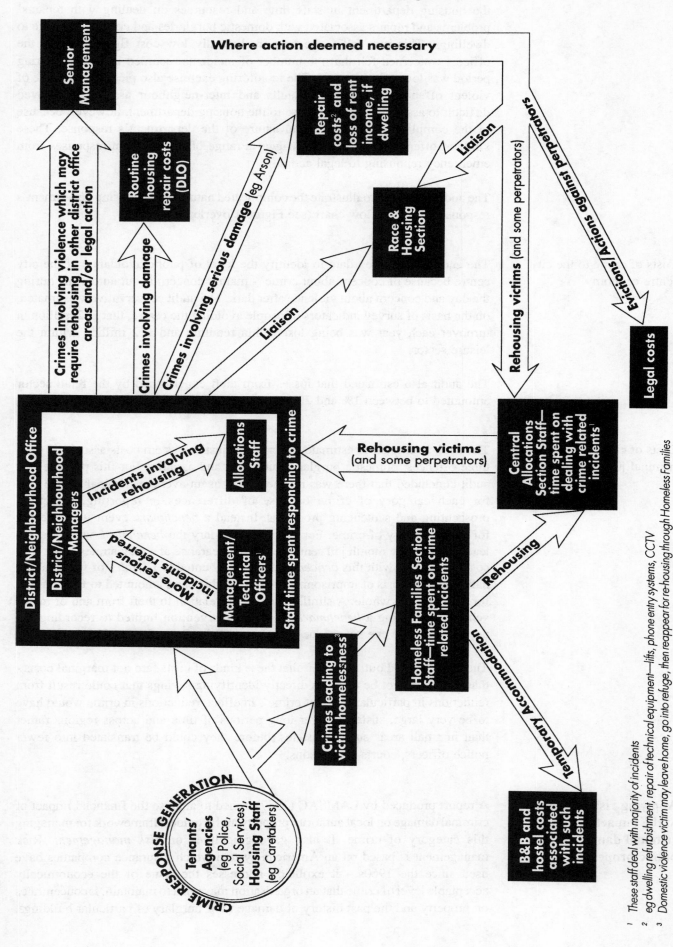

1 These staff deal with majority of incidents
2 eg dwelling refurbishment, repair of technical equipment—lifts, phone entry systems, CCTV
3 Domestic violence victim may leave home, go into refuge, then reappear for re-housing through Homeless Families

The report estimated that the cost of criminal damage to local authorities was over £500 million each year and rising. LAMSAC identified two main methodological problems. The first was the problem of distinguishing criminal from accidental damage. The second was the problem of getting authorities to code costs resulting from criminal damage; in practice, major damage such as arson was regularly recorded but the numerous minor, but cumulatively expensive, incidents such as broken windows were not routinely recorded.

The report stressed the need to identify the full range of costs resulting from criminal damage. For example, the cost coding by county councils for work done to rectify criminal damage to schools normally excludes many external and opportunity costs such as the cost of transporting children to another school when their school had been rendered unusable by arson. In addition, cost coding information tends to relate only to main buildings rather than other items such as parks, vehicles and road furniture.

Risk analysis and assessment is seen as a way of enabling an authority to make a planned response to crime. On the basis of risk assessment, a local authority can plan action to introduce physical measures to an area or building (for example, fencing, alarms and patrol systems) or address the possible financial losses from criminal damage (for example, by taking out insurance). LAMSAC stresses the need to carry out crime prevention measures, rather than depend on taking out insurance against losses, because the level of losses will increase over time and increase the overall cost to society.

The report details the methodology used by Cheshire County Council in the risk analysis of schools. The council assesses the size and level of use of the building, the cost of replacing it and the record of criminal damage suffered in the past. Against this is set the factors which deter crime in that building, such as security patrols, staff awareness and other crime prevention measures. Each negative and positive aspect is given a numerical value so that a final and comparable score can be set which signifies the overall level of risk. Resources are then prioritised to those schools most at risk.

The report concentrates on the relative effectiveness of different prevention measures. It points out that the effectiveness of a crime prevention measure does not rise in proportion to its cost - for instance, expensive occasional security patrols may not be the most effective way of combating crime. On the other hand cost effectiveness has to be tempered by the impact it has on service users, for example, cheap bars on windows my be cost effective but unacceptable to tenants. The report warns of the long term maintenance costs of electronic surveillance equipment but balances this with the great appeal of this type of equipment to tenants.

The step by step approach to risk management recommended includes:

- assessing risk;

- assessing alternative crime prevention measures;

- consulting the service users;

- investigating the experience of other authorities;

- preparing a clear brief and specification.

Risk management assessments are similar to the investment appraisals involved in cost benefit analysis. LAMSAC does acknowledge, however, that the risk management assessments carried out to date do not account for all the costs and benefits which flow from interventions.

The Northumbria Police Model

Bailey and Lynch (1988) analysed the individual components of the cost of crime at the *micro* (police force) level as opposed to the *macro* (national) level. In this way they hoped to identify a *starting line* against which future performance could be measured. Without a starting line, they argued, it was impossible to compare and measure alternative costings and resource uses. Local rather than national costings were used, and minimum rather than maximum costs were calculated.

The research concentrated on the two largest categories of crime: property crimes and violence (excluding homicide). No attempt was made to define the opportunity costs of police officer involvement in crime investigation because replacement activities were largely at the discretion of individual officers. The costs of the illegal transfer of goods were also ignored because of 'the extreme variables it attracts'. Victim costs such as the fear of crime and precautionary or evasive behaviour were also ignored because they were 'not quantifiable'.

The Northumbria Police model adopted a pricing approach based upon the minimum or average costs involved. The components costed ranged from a telephone call simply to report a crime, through the process of recording and investigation, to the cost of apprehending and administering justice to the offender, including the cost of various methods of dealing with the offender. Some of the costs to victims and others were also identified.

The costs identified ranged from notification by 999 system (£1.85) to a week in a secure prison (£502). Using this data, some typical examples of crime were costed:

- Theft from a motor vehicle (excluding the amount stolen or damaged, with the aggrieved person reporting the incident at a police station, and an officer visiting the scene and investigating it *on foot*) incurred a minimum cost of over £180. The subsequent detection of such an offence with the arrested offender simply receiving a caution increased that cost to £200.

- The detection of a burglary with similar policing resources involved in the investigation, the aggrieved person receiving advice from a victim support volunteer and the arrest of the offender who ultimately pleads guilty, obtains legal aid and is sentenced to a community service order of 240 hours would cost £1,390. If, however, a three month custodial sentence was imposed that cost would be over £3,200.

- A contested hearing in a magistrate's court for an assault, with the conviction of the offender who receives a 12 months probation order, would cost £7,690. A four months prison sentence would cost £9,600.

- A serious wounding involving a three day trial at the Crown Court which results in the offender being convicted and actually serving 11 months imprisonment, cost a minimum of £31,000. This figure included an average payment of £1,200 in compensation and over £1,500 for legal services. The largest proportion, comprising about two thirds of the costs, were consumed by the custodial sentence.

● The final example is an armed robbery in which two security officers receive injuries and two men are arrested, charged and plead not guilty during a Crown Court trial lasting two weeks. Both men received sentences of five years' imprisonment and these were served in a secure prison. The minimum cost of this case, and excluding the value of the stolen money, which was not recovered, was over £540,000. Nearly half of this cost was accounted for by the custodial sentence.

It should be noted that the Northumbria Police approach understates the true overall costs of an individual case. For instance, the cost of a police officer's time is given as the direct salary cost, without taking into consideration any organisational overheads.

Individual householders and economic decisions about crime

Home Office research by Field and Hope (1989) has made an appraisal of the costs and benefits to an individual householder of installing crime prevention measures. The research starts from the assumption that the householder has perfect knowledge of his or her risk of being a victim of crime. On this basis Field and Hope have looked at the costs and benefits of a householder doing nothing compared with doing something.

Firstly the research considered the diminishing returns from cumulative investment in crime prevention. Whereas the first year's investment of say £500 on a burglar alarm may reduce the risk of being burgled by half, a second year's investment of a further £500 does not halve the risk again but only (perhaps) reduces it by a further quarter. If a householder keeps on spending each year there will come a time when the £1 spent will yield less than £1 worth of risk reduction or prevented crime.

A second range of considerations for a householder contemplating the purchase of crime prevention measures relates to that person's income, their beliefs about the effectiveness of various measures, their *aversion* to the uncertainty and risk of crime and lastly the requirements made by insurance companies who may insist on the installation of crime prevention measures before agreeing to insure.

The report looks at the ways in which householders can be assisted or encouraged to make decisions about the purchase of crime prevention measures which will have the greatest overall benefit to society. There is a need for *market research* using crime surveys to identify risk. The information gathered in crime surveys can then be used to target publicity at relevant groups on measures that they should take.

The report argues that insurance does not tend to reduce the overall cost of crime to an individual because they may have to pay more in annual premiums than they claim for the occasional expensive loss. 'The function of insurance is not to reduce the direct cost of crime to victims; in fact it will tend to increase those costs.' But insurance reduces the impact of crime and spreads out the cost to the individual. The problem with insurance is what is called the 'moral hazard' - the insured person has no real incentive to install crime prevention measures. Lack of crime prevention measures may mean that crime is easier to commit and therefore more frequent, which in turn pushes up the cost of premiums resulting in the higher costs being spread across the community.

Time spent by householders on crime prevention has an opportunity cost. Field and Hope outline the possible incentives and sanctions which might encourage people to be involved in group crime prevention measures such as Neighbourhood Watch. They conclude that none is very effective.

A major factor in a householders' action on crime prevention is tenure. Owner-occupiers have an economic incentive because high crime rates in a area depresses property prices and reduces the value of their investment. But in the public sector, the main economic beneficiary of householders' crime prevention measures is the landlord.

The report concludes that there is underprovision of crime prevention at the household level because the economic incentives bearing on individuals are not large enough to achieve a level of crime prevention measures which society as a whole might benefit from.

Chapter 8

Cost benefits case studies

In this chapter we describe a number of studies which have attempted to determine costs and benefits for particular projects. The first two are studies of sheltered employment and home help services but provide useful illustrations of the issues involved in determining costs and benefits; the final four are housing and crime related.

Sheltered employment - Department of Employment

Morgan and Makeham (1978) carried out economic and financial analyses, assessing the costs and benefits of sheltered employment. The economic and financial analyses were intended to tackle different policy issues. Sheltered employment imposes a cost to the economy both in terms of resources (for example, labour, land and capital) and in terms of finance (for example, government expenditure on grants, administration costs and workers). Economic analysis considers the opportunity costs and social benefits of sheltered employment. Financial analysis compares the cost to public funding of providing sheltered workshops with the cost of other options (for example, funding social security or unemployment benefit); it considers the overall effect on the public sector borrowing requirement.

Economic analysis model

The Morgan and Makeham model placed a monetary value on resource costs but did not quantify the social benefits. The resource costs identified were:

- Cost of the labour of disabled people (shadow cost wages, national insurance and pension contributions).

- Capital costs (for example, the opportunity cost of the rent at full market value).

- Capital usage and depreciation at 12.5% per year.

- Materials (direct and indirect costs).

- Cost of Department of Employment staff (for example, workshop inspectors).

- Cost of marketing goods produced.

The resource benefits identified were:

- Value of the goods produced.

- Psychological benefit of employment for disabled people (unquantified).

- Benefit to society of having rehabilitative workshops (unquantified).

In relation to wages, a shadow cost is used when the opportunity cost is not equal to the cost which would be incurred in the market place. For example, the researchers argue that the opportunity cost of the labour of disabled people may be zero because a disabled person may not be able to find employment on the open market. So instead of calculating the opportunity cost of labour, the cost is based simply on wages, national insurance and pension contributions. Shadow costs are also used in relation to rents. For example, the rent paid by a sheltered workshop may be subsidised by grants but, for the purposes of economic analysis, the shadow price of the full market rent is included. If the sheltered workshop is in a prime site in the centre of town the shadow price resource cost may be very high indeed.

The model does not attempt to determine the views or experience of disabled workers and simply assumes that there is a psychological benefit.

Their economic analysis of Remploy, which ran most of the workshops the researchers investigated, showed an overall resource benefit. Over time the shadow price of labour did not rise as fast as other shadow prices such as rent and the market value of goods produced so, overall, benefits appeared to increase.

Financial analysis model

The financial analysis model compared the *present situation* (the existence of the sheltered workshop), with the *alternative situation* (the non-existence of the workshop).

The present situation was characterised by:

- Outflow of public funds:

- Grants by central and local government including capital grants.

- Training fees paid by central government.

- Regional employment premiums - paid by central government.

- Inflow to public funds:

- National Insurance contributions and tax payments by employees, both disabled and able-bodied.

- Indirect tax payments by employees spending their wages, both disabled and able-bodied.

- Interest charges on loans lent to workshops by local authorities.

The alternative situation was characterised by:

- Outflow of public funds:

- State benefits to unemployed disabled people.

- Inflow to public funds:

- National Insurance and tax payments of any able-bodied person in alternative employment.

- Indirect tax payments by able-bodied employees spending their wages.

- Indirect tax payments spending by disabled people on state benefits.

Financial analysis showed sheltered workshops to be a net financial cost to public funds. The study also showed that the assumptions made in order to quantify costs for financial and economic analyses have a differing impact on the outcome. Changes in assumptions have a greater impact on the outcome of financial analysis than on economic analysis. For example, the study assumed that the sheltered employment currently provided by Remploy would not have otherwise been provided by other firms. If this assumption was changed (ie if it had been assumed that other firms would have provided sheltered employment), there would have been no effect on the economic analysis because the output was evaluated in terms of the use which society derives as measured in terms of the price paid for output. In contrast, this change of assumption would have a dramatic effect on financial analysis because the output was evaluated in terms of criteria such as the outflow of public funds. It was concluded, therefore, that economic analysis was 'more robust'.

CIPFA - Cost benefit analysis of Coventry home helps

The Coventry Home Help Project attempted to show that it was better to keep frail elderly people in the community than to put them in residential homes. The project doubled home help resources in an area of Coventry for a five year period beginning in 1975 and then, using cost benefit analysis tried to assess whether there was a net financial and resources benefit to the community and to the Council's budget as a result.

The costs and benefits examined were:

- The cost of the extra home help resources.

- Costs and savings *accrued* in the provision of other services.

- Extra housing and living expenses incurred by clients staying in the community.

- Changes in the work status of clients, or relatives or friends who were thus freed to work.

The analysis had intended to examine changes in the general welfare of clients, relatives or friends as a result of the project. However, the view was that this could not be quantified, and it was dropped from the analysis. In the study's own words, this meant that it would 'fall short of being cost benefit analysis in the full sense'. The analysis concentrated instead on the wider impact of the project on the provision of other services.

Data was collected through a survey of the conditions of 65 new clients and compared with a control group of new clients outside the project area.

The study first assessed the difference between the project group's and control group's take-up of other services. The services considered were:

- Health visitors.

- District nursing and nursing auxiliaries.

- Mobile meals.

- Hairdresser.

- Social/luncheon clubs and day centres.

- Hospital outpatient services.

- Aids and adaptations.

Local knowledge about services had to be used to assess whether significant changes were due to a change in the service itself rather than as a result of the project. The research found that demand for residential services reduced as a result of the project but that there was an increase in demand for domiciliary services such as mobile meals and day centres. Because it was a small project, the change in demand could be easily accommodated. A city wide change would have been much more difficult to accommodate.

The costs of the services were translated into comparable unit costs on the same price base. It was decided that large changes in service levels should be measured in terms of average unit costs and small changes in terms of marginal costs. The researchers identified a major problem which they called 'lumpiness'. If there was spare capacity in a service, the costs of expansion to full capacity would be different than if there was no spare capacity. Where services were stretched to capacity, expansion was likely to mean major new investment in buildings, equipment or personnel. An example used in the study was the large-scale expansion of domiciliary care which, it was believed, could affect building programmes, admission criteria and management procedures in Part 3 residential accommodation. On this basis it was unrealistic to count only the marginal cost changes.

The study considered costs to the community and costs to the Council separately. The community costs, for the study's purposes, included costs to other organisations such as the Area Health Authority.

The results suggested that where a council had a choice between the provision of residential and domiciliary care, then it was cheaper to provide the latter. From the wider viewpoint of the community, the same general result emerged. The one important difference beween the Council and community viewpoints was that the Council perceived larger savings from domiciliary care being directed towards keeping people out of Council-run homes (because of direct savings on the Council budget) but the *community* perceived greater savings from domiciliary care being directed towards keeping people out of hospital.

Kirkholt burglary prevention project

The Kirkholt Estate in Rochdale has been the site of a Home Office sponsored burglary prevention demonstration project since 1986.

A recent evaluation of the project by the researchers (Forrester et al., 1990) involved a cost benefit analysis of the project which concluded that a net savings of around £1.2 million had been won from the intervention. A more detailed explanation of the methodology is contained in an unpublished report (O'Connell, 1990).

The costs of the project were estimated to be around £300,000. This was made up of Home Office grants, Housing Department budgets specifically dedicated to *safety and security* improvements on the estate and the cost of police and probation staff seconded to the project.

The savings from the project were calculated by putting a monetary value on the numbers of burglaries *saved* each year. Taking 1986 as the base year, estimates were produced for subsequent years of the numbers of burglaries which would have occurred if Kirkholt had followed the sub-division trend. The actual number of burglaries each year were then subtracted from these estimates to produce totals of burglaries *saved* each year. These *saved* burglaries each year were then multiplied by a series of cost items:

- Average electricity meter losses per burglary (using electricity board assessments);

- Average police costs per undetected burglary (using the Northumbria Police model);

- Average detection, sentencing and disposal costs per burglary (using the Northumbria police model);

- Average value of losses per burglary (using survey data);

- Average housing repair costs per burglary (using a combination of survey data and Housing Department estimates).

Our assessment identified a number of difficulties with the initial analysis, not least the omission of a considerable amount of additional expenditure on security related works by the Housing Department. The main question mark over the analysis, however, is the way in which *criminal justice system* costs associated with burglary are treated as wholly saveable. For costs to be translated into savings in this way, the reduced number of burglaries must be translated into reduced expenditure on the criminal justice system - fewer staff and fewer institutions, for example. A small local project is not going to have this effect.

Gloucester House concierge scheme

Skilton (1986) attempted to assess the costs and benefits associated with a pilot block receptionist scheme introduced in Gloucester House, a 17-storey tower block on the South Kilburn Estate in Brent. The study compared the estimated costs incurred on Gloucester House across a series of headings with those of a neighbouring block, Hereford House. Estimates were then made for potential savings in terms of reductions in numbers of empty dwellings and squats, consequent savings on bed and breakfast changes, graffiti removal and lift repairs. Potential savings were estimated at £27,000 as against the net cost of £19,000 for running the concierge service. However, no attempt was made to calculate the debt charge implications of the large programme of capital works.

Some of the assumptions underlying these calculations were questioned by the Safe Neighbourhoods Unit (1987). In particular, it was doubtful whether marginal increases in the number of properties available for letting would affect the Council's block use of bed and breakfast accommodation.

The study did not attempt to quantify increased tenant satisfaction and reduced concern about crime, nor any impact that the new service may have had on other agencies such as the police and social services.

It was interesting that, whilst the study identified substantial reductions in levels of rent arrears during the course of the project, these were dismissed from the final calculations because this area of savings had not been predicted and could not be confidently explained. One could argue, however, that reduced rent arrears may have been a function of either increased tenant satisfaction (and greater preparedness to avoid eviction for arrears) or enhanced on-site management (and greater pressure on non-payers).

Mitchellhill concierge scheme

Mitchellhill is a high rise development in Glasgow consisting of five 19-storey blocks. A concierge service was introduced in July 1989 as part of the Council's city wide programme.

An assessment of the impact of the scheme was carried out by the Housing Department on the basis of data collected prior to the introduction of the scheme and for between 12 and 18 months afterwards. A range of cost items were monitored: repairs to communal areas attributable to vandalism, void levels, tenancy turnover and rental income. Estimates of the net costs of introducing the scheme were based on the net cost of the concierge service (ie taking account of the costs of previous caretaker service) balanced against reduced costs of communal repairs and increased income from reduced voids. Estimates of reduced void levels were problematic, however, because it was apparent that the void level had been allowed to rise before the introduction of the scheme. In addition, no attempt was made to introduce debt charges on capital works into the analysis.

On balance, it seemed that the monetary savings did not cover the net monetary cost of the service. However, no attempt had been made to quantify any benefits accruing to tenants at this stage. This may emerge from a post-survey of residents due to be carried out in 1991.

Highgate Estate concierge scheme

The Highgate Estate in Birmingham is a mixed development of houses and multi-storey blocks. A dispersed concierge scheme was introduced for five of the blocks in 1989/90.

The City Housing Department produced an assessment of the costs and savings associated with the scheme in 1990. It was concluded that monetary savings had accrued from reduced lift breakdowns arising from vandalism and, mainly, from the reduction in caretaking staff which was made possible by fewer maintenance and cleaning problems. These savings, together with a supplement on rents of £3.50 per week, were roughly equivalent to the revenue costs of the concierge service. A survey was also carried out on completion of the works and this showed a high level of resident satisfaction with the scheme, but the absence of a pre-survey made it impossible to judge whether concern about crime or other problems had been reduced.

Interestingly, a previous evaluation of a concierge scheme on the Castle Vale Estate had concluded that the initiative was not worth pursuing in that form - concierges based in each block - on cost grounds. The Housing Department had monitored repairs attributable to vandalism in communal areas, lifts and voids, and rent losses arising from voids and concluded that the gap between the costs of the service and savings accrued was too large (equivalent to around £5 per flat per week) to cover it through increased rents.

No real attempt has been made in either evaluation to quantify benefits accruing to residents or to other agencies; nor to calculate the debt charge element of costs arising from the capital works.

Chapter 9

Costs and benefits and housing related crime prevention

In developing a framework for cost benefit assessment in the housing-related crime prevention field it is important to recognise, from the outset, that these kinds of assessments are bound to be rather imprecise. In abstract terms precision is possible, and even desirable, but is out of place with the practical reality of cost benefit analysis in much of the crime prevention field. Here much of the data on which assessments have to be made is bound to be questionable, incomplete or speculative. Recognising that there are bound to be data collection problems, the basic task is to get a sense of the costs and benefits involved rather than an accurate balance sheet.

A major difficulty we have had to confront in making judgements about the impact of housing-related crime prevention schemes is the multi-focused nature of many schemes. Crime prevention may have been just one of several objectives and may not even have been an objective at all - only emerging as an outcome in retrospect. In many cases, therefore, it is difficult to determine which elements of an initiative were designed to reduce crime or could have had that effect.

The easy way out of this predicament would be to count only those measures, such as physical security schemes, which have an *obvious* crime prevention purpose. However, apart from this being a rather narrow (and deterministic) approach to the issue, there is no real evidence that these so-called *obvious* measures lead to crime reduction, particularly if introduced in isolation from other less obvious measures.

To confuse matters further, the initiative under scrutiny need not be the only one taking place in the study area at that time. It is not likely that the effects of different initiatives can be confidently separated and, on this basis, there seems to be no real justification for excluding any coincidental initiatives from the cost benefit assessment. We have concluded that all additional inputs to the study area need to be listed, and if possible quantified, irrespective of their supposed potential for crime reduction or their relationship with the initiative being studied.

We have also come to the conclusion that the task is to find ways of incorporating the benefits of crime reduction into previously developed models for assessing initiatives (irrespective of their objectives) rather than to develop a model specifically for crime prevention projects. On balance, the most appropriate model for this purpose would appear to be that developed for the *Estate Action Handbook of Estate Improvement* (Department of the Environment, 1989). It is principally intended for option appraisal purposes rather than retrospective assessment of particular initiatives, but provides a useful basis for identifying costs and benefits in the housing related crime prevention field.

The methodological framework we describe below is a modification of the *Estate Action Handbook* framework *(Stage 3 - Option Appraisal),* taking into account our particular needs and incorporating specifically crime-related topic areas.

Methodological framework for housing related crime prevention

The *Estate Action Handbook* methodology involves four main steps which, for the purposes of this exercise, we describe as follows (with minor adjustments to the original text):

Step 1 - Establishing quantifiable monetary costs and benefits

Step 2 - Establishing quantifiable non-monetary costs and benefits

Step 3 - Establishing unquantifiable costs and benefits

Step 4 - Making a final judgement

Step 1 - Establishing quantifiable monetary costs and benefits

Overall, the framework provided by the *Estate Action Handbook* is a good guide to the types of quantifiable monetary costs and benefits which are likely to be associated with housing improvement schemes, particularly those which relate directly to housing authorities responsible for *producing* the schemes. However, and apart from the need to avoid spurious forms of over-precision which we highlighted earlier, we believe that the methodology employed needs some refinement in light of our focus, and that some additional measures of the benefits of crime reduction should be incorporated where appropriate. It should be noted that the *Estate Action Handbook* provides guidance rather than prescription and does not attempt to provide a comprehensive list of all relevant costs and benefits. Our refinements to the methodology make explicit factors which are implied but not explicit in the handbook.

Refinements to methodology
The costs of doing nothing - the minimum option

As the *Estate Action Handbook* points out, some account must be taken of costs which would have been incurred if the initiative had not gone ahead. Doing nothing, or what might be described as the 'minimum option', often means that a substantial input of resources would still have been committed to the site, if only to keep things as they were. To take account of this, all capital and revenue costs for the initiative need to be net of what would have been spent anyway. Whilst this is immediately apparent in relation to revenue costs - for example, the costs of new management arrangements are often described in terms of the additional costs on top of the previous arrangements - it is easy to overlook the need to offset the costs of capital schemes against the costs of repairs and maintenance which would have had to be met but were made unnecessary by the capital works.

However, and in addition to the explicit handbook guidance, it may not be satisfactory to assess the costs of the minimum option purely on the basis of costs incurred during the year prior to the implementation of the scheme. A longer period of monitoring is likely to be required to assess trends; for example, the costs of repairs may have been escalating over a number of years and it may be acceptable to conclude that this trend would have continued; or conversely, repair costs may have been decreasing because repairs were being neglected in anticipation of more radical measures.

Of course, benefits as well as costs may derive from the minimum option, although these are unlikely (almost by definition) to be particularly significant. And, in any case, these kinds of benefits (an example of which would be retaining existing numbers of dwellings rather than reducing numbers as part of the scheme) are likely to be taken into account as a *cost* element of the scheme itself.

Accounting for 'external' costs

When discussing monetary costs, the *Estate Action Handbook* tends to focus on the costs to the project *producer* - in this case the housing authority. Account

144

should also be taken of any monetary costs incurred by others, such as other departments or agencies (whether as part of or outwith the initiative under study) and residents.

Accounting for capital costs

Accounting for capital costs

The *Estate Action Handbook* allocates the total capital costs of schemes to the year(s) in which the monies are expended. This makes sense in terms of the handbook's focus on option appraisal, in that it is possible to assess *compensatory* benefits over a substantial period in the future. However, where a retrospective assessment is being made of an individual scheme, the evaluation period may only be a few years, by which time only a proportion of the capital debt is likely to have been paid. In these circumstances, it makes greater sense to translate capital costs into annually accruing loan charges.

It may not be satisfactory to calculate annual loan charges on the basis of the length of loan period (a traditional local authority approach to finance appraisal). The effective life of the improvements may be substantially shorter than the loan period. This may be particularly the case for expensive items of technical equipment such as phone entry systems and CCTV which, experience has shown, often need replacing or refurbishing after a short period because of technical advances or because of recurring faults. This may mean that loans continue to be serviced after the scheme is *finished* and has to be replaced with a further scheme - effectively meaning that two sets of loan charges will have to be serviced thereafter. The only real solution to this problem would appear to be to estimate the life expectancy of the scheme and, if that period is shorter than the loan repayment period, to use that period as the basis for estimating a more realistic annual capital costs figure.

Another issue to be addressed is the subsidised element of capital schemes. Local authorities have rarely had to meet the full costs of capital schemes because of government housing subsidy, although this situation has changed recently. Realistically, the full capital costs need to be assessed, irrespective of subsidy, although local authorities may wish to distinguish their own contribution (ie the *private* costs) from the contribution of central government (ie the *external* costs) in their presentation of outcomes.

Accounting for 'external' benefits

It is in the area of *external* benefits that the need for refinements to the *Estate Action Handbook* methodology appears most necessary, although we recognise that the handbook's list is not intended to be exhaustive. The handbook identifies some such benefits for residents (for example, the monetary value of reduced damage to tenants' property), but there are clearly other monetary benefits for residents from reduced crime (see *Savings for residents* below). No mention is made of any potential monetary benefits for other departments or agencies, where improvements may lead to reduced staff deployment for instance, or for other local players such as the business community, where improvements may very well have an impact on turnover. These kinds of benefits are often difficult to quantify in monetary terms, either because access to data is problematic or because they represent putative rather than actual savings (see below).

Accounting for putative costs and benefits

There will be a range of costs and benefits which can be described in monetary terms but where, in reality, the actual financial costs and benefits are unclear. For instance, the staff costs involved in mounting a project, including inputs to any project steering committee, can be allocated a monetary value on the basis of staff salaries (and on costs). Similarly, scheme improvements, such as a more efficient repair service, might release management staff time for more productive activity (reducing rent arrears for instance). However, whilst these costs and benefits can be given a monetary value on the basis of time costs and savings, it is difficult to arrive at a realistic assessment without some understanding of staff productivity or utilisation and, in practice, this kind of information is unlikely to be available. It may be, for instance, that improvements merely enable staff to take proper lunch breaks and finish work on time. It is really only where improvements lead to reductions in numbers of staff deployed that any putative savings can be readily translated into actual savings. An example of how this might work in practice was shown in our assessment of the Highgate Estate Concierge Scheme (described in *Cost Benefit Case Studies* section of this report), where the Housing Department claimed that reduced cleansing and maintenance problems had enabled it to reduce the numbers of caretakers.

Putative costs and benefits are a particular issue for housing related crime prevention, and feature prominently in the following section.

Measuring the monetary benefits of crime reduction

It may be possible to translate reductions in crime into additional measures of benefit which are quantifiable in monetary terms. The following are some potential areas for measurement.

Savings in staff time

For many staff involved in housing-related services, a proportion of their time will be taken up in responding to residential crime problems. This is likely to be particularly an issue for housing management staff who may have to respond to crimes such as domestic burglaries (often to process repairs), vandalism of dwellings and communal areas and violence associated with neighbour disputes, harassment and domestic assaults. For staff working on high-crime estates, crime-related work may account for a substantial part of their workload. As the *Nottingham Crime Audit* demonstrated (KPMG Peat Marwick McLintock/Safe Neighbourhoods Unit, 1990), property crimes are likely to have most impact on local staff but more serious incidents of violence can involve substantial staff inputs from centralised support services. For instance, incidents of domestic violence may necessitate re-housing and/or legal action.

Clearly, costings for these kinds of staff inputs are unlikely to be available (except perhaps for the labour costs associated with DLO repairs), and it may be necessary to undertake some form of monitoring exercise along the lines of the *Nottingham Crime Audit* to determine the extent and distribution of staff costs* (see p.130).

However, as pointed out previously, any financial *savings* from reduced staff time spent on crime-related incidents are likely to be putative or notional rather than real unless greater *productivity* can be quantified or staff reductions realised.

---

* Note - In many respects, the identification of these kinds of costs may be more important for considering the effectiveness or efficiency of management practices than for the purposes of cost benefit assessments. For instance, it may be felt inappropriate for housing staff to spend inordinate amounts of time on crime-related incidents, which they may not be best equipped to deal with, and that some other type of response is required. A study of a related topic, neighbour disputes, in Birmingham found that housing assistants were spending about 12% of their time on such incidents, with little effect, and concluded that neighbour disputes would be more effectively handled by an independent 'mediation scheme' (Tebay et al., 1986).

Savings on crime related repairs

The *Estate Action Handbook* identifies a full range of potential monetary benefits from reduced repairs and maintenance, some crime related and some not. However, as previously noted, the handbook does not identify the need to assess repair cost trends, over a number of years prior to implementation, to ensure that savings are not over or understated (see *The costs of doing nothing - the minimum option*).

Where appropriate cost centres are not in place, it may not be possible to distinguish crime-related repairs savings from other kinds. Even where they are in place, there is no guarantee that the system will be rigorously implemented and there will always be difficulties in attributing some repairs. Whilst overall (undiscriminated) repair savings figures do provide useful monitoring data, specifically crime-related savings figures can provide invaluable confirmation of any changes in rates of criminal damage.

Savings for the criminal justice system

As noted earlier (p.140), the kinds of monetary benefits from reduced crime claimed for the Kirkholt Burglary Prevention Project on the basis of reduced police, courts and sentence disposal costs were highly misleading because they did not represent actual reductions in expenditure, only putative ones. They proved particularly misleading by swamping other more *real* savings.

Whilst the Northumbria Police model, on which the Kirkholt assessment was based, provides a useful starting point for cost benefit analysis by identifying the kinds of monetary costs involved in responding to crime, additional information is required to get some sort of sense of the monetary benefits which might accrue from localised crime reduction. A monitoring exercise to measure the extent of police, probation and social services inputs to the study area over time, for instance, could show how these inputs respond to crime rate fluctuations. (There seems little point in doing this kind of exercise for courts or prisons as they are only likely to be affected by widespread crime reductions over many years.)

In the absence of any such monitoring exercise (of which there do not appear to be any examples), the Kirkholt-type assessment may provide a useful illustration of the kinds of spin-off benefits which are often overlooked but there appears to be no justification for combining the figures produced with *actual* monetary savings.

Savings for residents

Residents may benefit directly in terms of reduced losses of and damage to property. The proliferation of easily portable household items such as video recorders means that average losses from burglaries are likely to run into hundreds of pounds, even in relatively poor areas. Low levels of home insurance in some heavily victimised areas mean that many residents bear the full loss themselves. Vehicle related theft and damage is also likely to mean average losses of many hundreds of pounds, although most vehicle owners will be covered by insurance. Before and after surveys which ask residents about the net value of losses and damage from property crimes (ie taking account of property recovery) can be used to estimate the total monetary value of reduced crime for the study area's residents.

Levels of insurance need not influence calculations of the total monetary value of reduced crime. Insurance cover may mitigate the losses incurred by residents of the study area but these are still met by the wider community through premiums - and premiums reflect crime levels on a reasonably localised basis.

Victims may also have to take time off work (or suffer other kinds of disruption of planned activity), and some may lose income, to deal with the after-effects of crime - for example, time off to deal with the police, to effect repairs or, in the case of violence, to recuperate from injuries. It may be possible to quantify changes over time, through the use of before and after surveys, where victims have lost income directly. However, the *opportunity costs* to employers of staff absence are not likely to be accessible.

Other 'community' benefits

A range of other monetary benefits may flow from reduced crime levels. There may be fewer calls on the health services - the Nottingham Crime Audit estimated that casualty department cost associated with the **treatment** of assaults was £100,000 per annum. There may also be increased local business activity and local community facilities may attract more custom.

It may be possible to identify changes in the use of health services, for instance, through repeated residents' surveys and, if the value of health service *units* is known, these changes can be translated into monetary values. However, as was the case for criminal justice system costs, any savings may be putative or notional rather than actual.

Reduced crime may encourage new businesses (such as shops) or improve the performance of existing businesses, providing a monetary benefit for the local business community (the same would apply to local income raising community facilities). Measuring this monetary benefit is not easy. It is possible to argue that there is merely a transfer of business into the study area and that there is no overall monetary benefit to the wider community. However, some new expenditure may be generated - particularly in the area of leisure where locally generated activity may replace inactivity.

The data collection difficulties in this area are considerable and it may be that these kinds of community benefit are more easily treated as non-monetary benefits.

Step 2 - Establishing quantifiable non-monetary costs and benefits

Refinements to methodology

The *Estate Action Handbook* suggests that some non-monetary costs and benefits can be quantified by allocating numerical values to the factors under investigation and converting those numerical values into indices. For instance, repair performance can be measured by allocating numerical values to repair response times (one week, two weeks, three weeks and so on) and these can be converted into indices - with 100 representing the most favoured position. Similar exercises can be carried out for other factors, such as proportionate reductions in crime, and all the scores can be added up (and weighted if necessary) to produce an overall score. This appears to be an acceptable methodology for comparing different options for improvements (the handbook's main focus). The method is not so suitable for our purposes, although it may be possible to use it in a modified form to compare changes over time in a study area if, say, borough-wide indices were assumed to represent the most favourable outcome.

Another way of quantifying non-monetary costs and benefits is to ask those affected to ascribe a monetary value. This can be done on the *willingness to pay* principle - asking people to say how much they would be prepared to pay to avoid or gain some particular feature. Birmingham City Council, for instance, asked tenants in high rise blocks how much they would be prepared to pay in extra rent for the benefit of a concierge service, although the City was really only interested in how much extra rent it could charge to offset the costs of the service. There are difficulties with this approach to quantification. There may be a tendency to under-estimate the value if people feel that their responses are likely to be used to determine what they are actually going to pay. On the other hand, how real are responses going to be if the people concerned know that they will not have to pay come what may - for example, if their rents are met through housing benefit. Furthermore, some would argue that all this principle really demonstrates is that better-off people can pay more and one could easily conclude from this kind of approach that unpleasant outcomes in poor areas have a low social cost or, conversely, that improvements in poor areas have a low social benefit.

Another approach is the *compensation principle* - asking people what monetary compensation they would expect for a particular event. However, apart from the obvious danger of people inflating values beyond what is really meaningful, this principle is open to wide fluctuation on the basis of personal circumstances.

A variation on the *willingness to pay* principle, which on the face of it seems more *real,* involves assessing the value of a particular local feature by comparing the market value of properties affected with other similar but unaffected properties. For instance, it could be argued that the value of a concierge service can be measured by the rents tenants are prepared to pay as compared with similar blocks without a service. The main difficulty with this approach is that there are likely to be other features differentiating the blocks concerned - at the very least they will be in a different location - and these may also explain rent differences.

A rather different approach to non-monetary quantification would be to develop some of the ideas being pursued by the Applied Population Research Unit (APRU) at Glasgow University for measuring quality of life through surveys. APRU has established a list of *perceptual indicators* of the quality of life, such as health provision, climate, pollution and crime; respondents are asked to provide a score (on a scale of 1 to 5) for each indicator and scores are added together, with weighting on the basis of the priority given to each indicator, to provide an overall score (Findlay et al., 1988; Rogerson, 1989). Although this approach has been used to rank towns and cities in terms of quality of life, the techniques used appear to be applicable to smaller areas such as housing estates.

Our view is that the *perceptual indicator* approach has most to recommend it on a number of grounds. Firstly, it is firmly rooted in the perceptions of those most affected by changes on the ground. The *Estate Action Handbook* approach is purely quantitative and does not allow, for instance, that the nature of the crime problem may worsen even if actual numbers of incidents reduce. Secondly, it avoids the artificiality and guess work involved in trying to ascribe monetary values to what are essentially non-monetary outcomes. Finally, it is able to assess costs and benefits from different points of view. For instance, separate exercises can be carried out to measure the perceptions of residents, housing staff and other local agencies.

Further work would need to be carried out on developing the *perceptual indicator* approach for the purposes of housing improvement schemes. The indicators used would need to be tested out along the lines of the APRU piloting of city/town indicators (Rogerson et al., 1988).

Measuring the non-monetary but quantifiable benefits of crime reduction	The *Estate Action Handbook* describes reduction in the numbers of crimes as a quantifiable non-monetary benefit and advocates the allocation of numerical values to proportionate changes in crime levels as a method for measuring benefit (see above), However, it is questionable whether a reduction in the actual numbers of crimes committed is, in itself, a benefit. Rather, it is changes in the impact of crime which can be described as beneficial or otherwise, and that impact may not necessarily be related to numbers. Changes in the impact of crime can be measured in monetary terms (for example, in terms of victims' losses from burglary), or in non-monetary terms. Examples of the non-monetary benefits of crime reduction might include:

- Reduced fear of crime (and different types of crime) amongst residents or, for that matter, amongst those who work in the area;

- Increased preparedness to become involved in social and recreational activity, particularly after dark;

- Increased agency confidence in area and preparedness to improve/increase services;

- Increased business activity;

- Increased employer confidence in residents as potential employees;

- Reduced stigma;

- Greater insurability;

- Improved appearance (through less vandalism).

All of these benefits may be quantifiable through the use of *perceptual indicators* and it should be possible to construct overall measures of crime reduction benefit through the use of before and after surveys of residents, housing staff and other local *players*.

Step 3 - Establishing unquantifiable costs and benefits Refinements to methodology	The *Estate Action Handbook* describes typical unquantifiable costs (for example, disruption to estate caused by works) and typical unquantifiable benefits (for example, reductions in the fear of crime). However, if *perceptual indicators* form the basis of quantification, as we advocate above, the only real bar to measurement is an absence of survey data. Where there is no survey data, it may be possible to obtain some indication of costs and benefits by asking key individuals (such as housing managers, tenants' leaders and police beat officers) to make retrospective subjective assessments.
Step 4 - Making a final judgement Refinements to methodology	The *Estate Action Handbook* is principally concerned with value-for-money which, it says, can only be achieved if there is 'an overall excess of expected benefits over costs'. Our view is that, in the housing related crime prevention field, this sort of calculation may not be possible because the variety of methods used to arrive at different types of cost and benefit and the likely distribution of costs and benefits amongst a very disparate group (not just the housing authority), tends to preclude their being added together to produce two sides of a balance sheet.

Our suggested approach involves four basic stages:

Establishing the net price of the scheme to the producer

The scheme *producer,* the housing authority in most cases, will initially be concerned about its own net financial outlay - how far the monetary benefits (other than putative ones) compensate for the monetary costs for the producer. Invariably, it will have a clearer idea of the costs of a scheme than its benefits, because assessments of the latter are likely to require more in the way of data generation. Some form of discounting will be required to take account of the fact that costs and benefits occur at different points in time. Having established, as far as it can, the net price of the scheme (costs will invariably exceed benefits), the scheme *producer* will then be in a position to assess what this has *purchased* in terms of benefits.

Establishing the net benefits 'purchased'

The scheme may be expected to bring about other benefits but may also accrue other costs. What we are looking for are *net* benefits and this inevitably means making some kind of judgement over the weight of positive and negative outcomes for each factor assessed. For example, a scheme may lead to increased tenant satisfaction for a majority of tenants, but to reduced satisfaction for a key sub-group such as the elderly. It may be that the extent of difficulty generated by the scheme for that sub-group is so great that is judged to outweigh its effect on the majority. Similarly, a scheme may create additional work for other departments in some ways but reduce it in other ways.

The benefits *purchased* by a scheme will take a variety of forms (note that in most cases any negative outcomes will have to be balanced against positive outcomes to derive a *net* benefit):

- Other benefits to the *producer* - putative monetary benefits from, say, reduced staff time spent on dealing with crime, which may turn into actual savings if changes are widespread and long term; and non-monetary benefits from, say, improved staff satisfaction;

- Benefits to the *consumer* - actual monetary benefits for residents from, say, reduced burglary losses; and non-monetary benefits for residents from, say, improved quality of life.

- Benefits to others - actual monetary benefits for other departments or organisations from, say, reduced damage to their property; putative monetary benefits for other departments and organisations from, say, reduced staff time spent on dealing with crime; and non-monetary benefits from, say, improved business confidence.

The distinctions above are not always clear cut. What constitute benefits to the *producer* (often described as *private* benefits) will often be dictated by the terms of reference of the project. For instance, consumer satisfaction may be a project objective and therefore counted as a *private* benefit. It is clear, however, that *external* benefits or *externalities* are an important issue for housing related crime prevention because many of the benefits of reduced crime do not accrue directly to scheme funders. The benefits *purchased* should not be combined into a single calculation of benefit but, rather, should be listed separately. Whether the accrued benefits justify the costs of the scheme will inevitably be judged on *political* rather than mathematical grounds, as certain ends of benefit (such as tenant satisfaction or direct savings to the scheme *producer*) are likely to be given higher weighting than others.

The assessments of costs and benefits need to be sensitised to broader trends. It may be that some of the monetary savings on which the net price of the scheme is based reflect general trends - for example, there may have been a borough-wide re-organisation of repair services. And it may be that some of the benefits *purchased* would have accrued without the scheme - for example, burglary rates may have reduced in the rest of the police division. For these reasons, the assessment of costs and benefits associated with the scheme should be considered relative to broader changes either in the locality or elsewhere if appropriate. For instance, if expenditure on repairs and maintenance has reduced in both the study area and borough-wide, then estimates of reductions in the study area which can be attributed to the scheme need to assume that the study area would have followed the borough trend and only the difference (if any) taken into account. Strictly speaking, deteriorating benefits or increasing costs associated with a scheme can also be evidence of *gain* if they compare favourably with the comparison data, the argument being that even greater disbenefits or costs would have resulted if the scheme had not been introduced. There is, however, a question mark over whether those involved would count the initiative a success.

In many respects, the contextualisation issue creates most of the data collection problems as it precludes the possibility of relying on special data collection arrangements for the study area itself.

Judging cost effectiveness

Having established the net price of the scheme and the benefits *purchased* (which should be listed rather than added together), a judgement can be made on whether the expenditure was worthwhile. It need not have been worthwhile - the benefits may have been judged to be small in relation to the size of expenditure, there may have been other cheaper options for expenditure which would have derived similar outcomes, or the money may have been more productively spent elsewhere.

Data collection issues

Little of the data required to carry out a systematic cost benefit assessment will be readily available and some will not be retrievable at all. Inevitably, the best which can be achieved is an approximation of the costs and benefits and, as a general rule, it is better practice to use conservative estimates of the benefits which might accrue.

Judgements will also have to be made, in the light of the resources available for data generation (which has an *opportunity cost* of its own), about information gathering priorities. If the scheme *producer* is the housing authority, it is likely to focus on its own interests and prioritise the collection of data on the impact of the scheme on the housing service. It may be interesting, if only at a broader policy making level, to determine the external costs and benefits of a scheme - for example, in relation to the criminal justice system - but a housing authority may not feel able to justify spending any of its own money on the data gathering required and may not be able to persuade other agencies to do so. On the other hand, if the project *producer* is (at least partly) national government, other aspects of the scheme may be of more interest. This is illustrated well in the case of the Home Office sponsored Kirkholt Burglary Prevention Project (see p.140) where the cost benefit assessment focused on *obvious* expenditure on crime prevention and relied heavily on putative or notional benefits for the criminal justice system, whilst largely ignoring the costs and benefits associated with the large scale local authority refurbishment programme.

The use of before and after surveys of residents (and others) which we advocate as a means of obtaining data on non-monetary benefits is, on the face of it, an expensive option. However, it is now common for local authorities to undertake pre-surveys (of residents in particular) when planning improvement schemes and the prevalence of post-surveys is increasing. Some additional research would be required, however, to test out the operation of *perceptual indicators* as a means of measuring changes in the quality of life and, what might be described as, the 'quality of safety' in study areas.

Summary and conclusions

This report brings a spotlight to bear on *housing-related* crime prevention. This field of crime prevention accounts for a large part of crime prevention theory and practice and occupies much of the attention of policy makers. Doing something about crime in residential areas, where its impact is most obviously damaging to the public, has tended to take precedence over crime related to work, travel and leisure.

The report is in two parts. *Part One - Review of Research and Information* is a review of published (and occasionally unpublished) material on the topic, mostly from the UK but referring to American and continental European publications where appropriate. A framework for evaluating crime prevention initiatives is put forward as a guide to the various approaches and the evidence they present. Conclusions are drawn on the value of this evidence and the lessons for future initiatives.

Part Two - Assessing Costs and Benefits is a review of cost benefit analysis and cost effectiveness assessment as it has been applied in the crime prevention and related (public sector) fields. Various attempts to determine the costs of crime to public bodies and the community are described. A methodology is put forward for assessing costs and benefits in the housing-related crime prevention field.

Crime and housing

Our understanding of the extent and distribution of crime has been increased by the more widespread use of crime surveys, although the limitations of crime surveys need to be borne in mind. In particular, and in common with recorded crime data, crime survey data will tend to understate the distribution of violent offences because of under-reporting and under-counting (see Genn, 1988; Stenko, 1988; Young, 1988). One could argue, therefore, that our picture of crime is largely based on the extent and distribution of property crime.

Certain types of residential area have been shown to suffer higher rates of criminal victimisation. High risk areas tend to be the 'poorest council estates', 'multi-racial areas' and 'high status non-family areas' (Hope and Hough, 1988). Council tenants are more often victims of residential crime than homeowners and, related to this, so too are residents of purpose-built flats and maisonettes (Hope, 1990; General Household Survey, 1986).

People on low incomes, black people and young adults are more often victims of crime and, when sexual assault and domestic violence are taken into account, young women are more vulnerable to violence than young men (Hough and Mayhew, 1985).

Fear of crime tends to increase with crime levels (Hough and Mayhew, 1985). However, it may be that some environmental factors, such as high level walkways between blocks, evoke fear where crime levels are low (Safe Neighbourhoods Unit, 1988a). Visible signs of neighbourhood deterioration are said by some to affect residents' perceptions of their areas, reduce informal controls and contribute to increases in crime (Wilson and Kelling, 1982), but others are wary about ascribing any causal relationship (Hope and Hough, 1988).

However, whilst clear relationships have been established between crime levels and a range of environmental and social factors, outwardly similar residential areas can have remarkably different crime profiles.

Assessing the evidence

Claims have been made about the success of various crime prevention initiatives. The evidence put forward to substantiate those claims varies from, at one end of the spectrum, the subjective judgement of those closely involved to, at the other, seemingly comprehensive and exhaustive evaluations carried out by independent researchers.

In the light of the wide variation in evaluation *methodology* used to assess crime prevention initiatives, how can we draw conclusions about the efficacy of particular initiatives? In this report, we have developed a set of criteria against which to assess whether project reports contain sufficient information to make a judgement about their crime prevention effects. In developing the criteria we were guided by practical considerations of what it is possible to achieve given the methodological constraints of having to operate in the real world rather than the laboratory.

Notwithstanding the claims which are made about the success of particular crime prevention initiatives, we can never say with complete certainty that they did work. We can only be more or less confident about the evidence presented by the *evaluators,* and the research methods they used to arrive at their conclusions.

Central to the argument over what constitutes evidence of success is the tension between scientific and pragmatic approaches to evaluation. Scientific procedure is founded on the principle of the null hypothesis and the burden of proof entices the scientist towards the conclusions that 'nothing works' and a good deal of evidence is needed to persuade the scientist otherwise. Practitioners and policy-makers, on the other hand, devote substantial resources to their programmes and policies and want researchers to confirm their effectiveness.

It is clear that a balance needs to be struck between the two agendas.

The assessment structure we developed in order to provide a framework for judging existing published evidence is summarised below.

Evidence of reduced crime problems

We are interested in evidence of reduced incidence of crime and confirmation that fewer crimes means a reduced problem. This evidence may be presented in a variety of forms including: *recorded crime statistics* - which need to be supported by other crime-related data, except (with caution) where the *size of reduction* is judged to outweigh reservations about reporting and recording artefacts - and *crime survey data* - which are best looked at in conjunction with recorded crime statistics and should also indicate *changes in the severity of crime* and *the variable impact on different groups* in the community.

Evidence of initiative's effect

We are interested in evidence that the initiative was responsible for the reduction in crime problems rather than some other external factor. We need, for instance, *control group data* - from the wider locality or from a control estate/neighbourhood, to show that reductions in crime problems were not just part of a local trend - and *demographic data* - from surveys or agency statistics, to show that reductions in crime problems were not due to changes in the composition of the local population.

Evidence of effect of individual measures

We are interested in evidence that any individual measure(s), within the overall package, accounted for the reductions in crime problems. For this purpose we need, ideally, *continuous monitoring data* - from recorded crime statistics or other recorded data, to show more clearly when crime reductions took place - and *descriptive accounts of implementation* - to show when and how particular measures were implemented.

Evidence of permanence

We are interested in evidence to show that the improvements will not be short-lived, which means a *follow-up period of a minimum of 12 months* to provide an *adequate period for data collection* and *ideally 36 months or more to indicate some permanence.*

Evidence of replicability

We need to know whether there are any features of the initiative which reduce its potential for implementation elsewhere. *Descriptive accounts of implementation* should indicate whether there are any special local circumstances which may not be found elsewhere and *details of capital and revenue costs,* with *cost benefit evidence* if available, should provide guidance on its general applicability.

Theory into practice

The report distinguishes between crime prevention initiatives on the basis of the theoretical framework they appeared to have adopted. Initiatives are classified according to the main type of intervention. Five types are identified based on their reliance on:

- design changes;

- management changes;

- security measures;

- social measures;

- policing measures.

In reality, of course, many initiatives employ a range of measures, regardless of how they were originally conceived or continue to be described. Some initiatives, most notably the Priority Estates Projects, were not devised as crime prevention initiatives, did not include crime prevention in their original objectives and have only been assessed in these terms retrospectively.

Design

Design-led crime prevention has been described as *creative demolition* on the basis that, once executed, design changes are invariably permanent. For this reason it might be expected that practitioners and policy makers would be slow to pursue expensive design changes. Paradoxically, there are many examples of practitioners wholeheartedly embracing the notion of designing out crime.

Research on the relationship between design and crime is rooted in ideological assumptions and has often led to tentative conclusions with numerous qualifications attached. Unfortunately, when practitioners are considering design changes on estates or in areas with high crime levels, the assumptions and qualifications are often forgotten. Publicity can turn specific research conclusions into an accepted *common sense* quite removed from a single study or drawing from a number of different, if not contradictory, theories.

In the report we try to separate out the main strands of thinking about the link between design and crime.

Management

In recent years, a number of authors have underlined the importance of taking management considerations into account when assessing problems of crime and fear of crime on housing estates. Some have questioned research and practice which, in their view, overemphasises the relationship between estate design and crime. It may be true that certain types of estates (for example, those with large, interconnected linear blocks) are rarely successful; but there are estates of similar design, located in different areas, perhaps with a different history, mix of tenancies or management which work well and where design features exercise less of an effect. The effects of design on crime may have been exaggerated in some areas where housing departments have not developed appropriate styles of management for particular types of property. (Osborn and Bright, 1989)

The initiative which has most clearly aimed to demonstrate the importance of effective local housing management in the regeneration of run down estates is the Department of the Environment's Priority Estates Project (PEP). Power (1987a) describes in detail the beneficial effects which the existence of an estate office, together with associated initiatives, is claimed to have had in terms of reductions in crime and vandalism and feelings of security among tenants on 20 estates surveyed in 1984.

Security

Physical security or situational measures appear to offer a tangible and flexible approach to problems of crime, particularly acquisitive crime such as theft and burglary. However, physical security is often applied with little reference to the social situation. There is a tendency to assume that physical measures are somehow unproblematic and generalisable to quite different social situations.

Discussion of the social dimension of physical crime prevention measures has generally been limited to the problem of displacement. Displacement occurs when a measure causes crime to shift to other neighbourhoods, to different times of the day, to other offence types or to different groups in the same neighbourhood. Situational crime prevention is referred to by some as *primary prevention* or *opportunity reduction* (Bennett, 1986). Atkins (1989) suggests a more comprehensive definition which goes beyond the *locks and bolts* approach: situational crime prevention 'aims to reduce the opportunities for crime by changing the environment or context in which criminal activity takes place'. Hough et al. (1980) emphasise that situational crime prevention is 'directed at highly specific forms of crime', but there are differences in opinion between those who feel situational crime prevention is limited to reducing acquisitive offending, such as burglary, autocrime and, possibly, robbery and those who believe it may also be helpful in respect of *expressive* crimes such as those involving violence, for example, murder, rape and racial harassment.

Social development

Social measures to prevent crime are typically aimed at tackling the causes of crime and the motivations of individuals to offend. It could be argued that all areas of social policy have a bearing on crime but most often cited are housing, education, employment, youth, health and family policy.

This approach has not been fashionable in the last ten years or more but is now beginning to emerge again. In particular, the situation of young people in poor neighbourhoods is getting more attention.

An investigation of social measures taken at the estate or neighbourhood level presents difficulties. Firstly, social measures are usually conceived of in broad programme terms rather than in relation to specific geographical locations and a good deal of the literature ignores the community dimension. In fact, it is difficult to see how some kinds of social measure could be introduced locally in isolation from or in conflict with national or regional policy developments. Secondly, social measures which have an impact on crime are not necessarily introduced with crime prevention in mind and may be considered in these terms only in retrospect or not at all. Consequently, there is little relevant material in the crime prevention literature.

In the report we have attempted to summarise the main themes which underpin community-based social measures and to locate, where possible, practical examples of the different kinds of measures which have been implemented

Policing

There is considerable public support for increased police patrolling of residential areas on the assumption that formal surveillance deters potential offenders by providing a constant threat of apprehension. The key to effective local policing is increasingly being seen in terms of greater police visibility and accessibility, improved liaison with the community and other organisations and longer term commitment to areas on the part of individual beat officers. There is little evidence that this *community policing* model (if it can be called a model, given the wide variety of activities described in this way) is any more effective in reducing crime. Weatheritt (1987) concludes that there is little or no sign that they have made any measurable difference. And yet questions remain over whether *community policing* has actually been tried (see Smith, 1987).

Particular problems have been experienced with the policing of public housing estates and, more especially, the large high-density multi-storey developments. Concern has been expressed over the logistical difficulties of patrolling, in terms of the problems of access to *private* spaces (such as corridors) and design-induced lack of visibility, over conflict of responsibility between police and any estate security personnel, over the very high rate of turnover of beat officers and over the high profile and sometimes insensitive policing provided by mobile police units; there has also been concern over what precisely local beat officers should do on estates other than random and often invisible patrolling (see Osborn and Bright, 1988).

Reviewing the evidence

Overall, the published evidence is disappointing. Using the assessment criteria we had developed as a kind of yardstick against which evidence of success could be judged, it is fair to say that none of the initiatives we reviewed completely satisfied those criteria. In fact, as a general rule, the *best* evaluated initiatives produced the *worst* results, and vice versa. This in itself was not surprising. The more thorough evaluations are often carried out by researchers who, as we have said, tend to err on the side of caution. The least thorough evaluations tend to be carried out by practitioners, who may not have the time or the inclination to search for further evidence and for whom least is often best.

A number of questions are asked of the housing-related crime prevention initiatives in this report. Not only do we want to know whether crime was reduced and became less of a problem, we also want to know whether the initiative was responsible and, if so, whether the effect lasted and could be replicated elsewhere. The assessment criteria provide a framework for asking those questions. We did not expect initiatives to provide all the information required to satisfy the assessment criteria (although we expected more than we got). We did believe, however, that it would have been practical for them to provide that kind of information given the right circumstances.

An extensive search for examples of *evaluated* crime prevention schemes revealed far fewer examples than we had anticipated. Most surprisingly, given the frequent claims made about their value, few examples were located of design-led, security-led or policing-led schemes which provided any more than anecdotal evidence in support of their *evaluations*. There were at least as many examples of *evaluated* schemes which concentrated on social measures. The greatest number of examples of *evaluated* schemes was obtained from the management-led category and, on the whole, the evidence presented by these schemes was more persuasive.

The preponderance of *evaluated* management-led schemes is partly a reflection of the existence of long-term national programmes (the Priority Estates Project, NACRO and Safe Neighbourhoods Unit) which have had an interest in describing initiatives, collecting data and reviewing progress. They also account for the majority of examples in the social category. Remarkably, details on 15 of the 21 schemes identified in the two categories came from these sources.

On the basis of this review, we were able to identify a number of schemes which, on the balance of evidence, appeared to have been successful and to draw from these schemes a number of lessons about the key elements of successful schemes.

Assessing costs and benefits

Very few attempts have been made to quantify the benefits deriving from housing-related crime prevention or, for that matter, from the broad range of housing based improvement schemes. The difficulties of cost benefit analysis are well known. The methodology is complicated, there are considerable data collection problems to overcome and it is difficult to quantify the non-monetary benefits which are essential to the process.

In practice, the monetary costs of any initiative are likely to be seen to outweigh the monetary benefits. The assessments made for the Mitchellhill and Highgate concierge schemes illustrate this well. Even after taking account of savings from reduced repairs, increased rent income and other management savings, the schemes are not self-financing - at least from the housing department point of view. No attempt was made to assess the savings which may have accrued to residents from reduced victimisation or to any savings made by other departments or agencies. No data was gathered on the non-monetary benefits which may have derived from reduced fear of crime and increased resident satisfaction, but these kinds of benefits are likely to be the key to final judgements about the balance of costs and benefits.

Of particular interest in the field of crime prevention is the savings which the police and other parts of the criminal justice system may derive from reduced crime. Some progress has been made in recent years in establishing the costs of crime to the criminal justice system (see Home Office, 1988). However, it is not possible to derive figures for savings from reduced crime on this basis.

The conclusion drawn from a review of cost benefit models in the public sector was that the model adopted by the Estate Action Handbook of Estate Improvement (Department of the Environment, 1989) for *option appraisal* was a good starting point for the development of a methodology for housing-related crime prevention.

Conclusions
Successful crime prevention schemes

On the basis of the review in Part One of the report it was possible to come to some conclusions about the effectiveness of crime prevention schemes. In every case there are reservations about the evidence of their success in reducing local crime problems - questions left unanswered and additional data it would have been useful to obtain. However, a reasonably strong case was made for the following schemes.

- *Pepys Estate, Lewisham*

  A management-led initiative (described as a *co-ordinated estate improvement programme*) where a range of design, management, security, social and policing measures were introduced and where recorded crime rates dropped dramatically in the mid-1980s and where the reductions have been sustained to the present time.

- *Broadwater Farm, Haringey*

  A management-led initiative (described as an *estate based management initiative*) where a range of management, design, security and social measures were implemented and where recorded crime rates dropped dramatically in the mid-1980s and where reductions have been sustained to the present time.

- *Gloucester House, Brent*

  A management-led initiative (described as a *multi-storey block management and security initiative*), where a concierge service and associated physical works were introduced and where vandalism and the costs of maintaining the block were subsequently reduced.

- *Mitchellhill, Glasgow*

  A management-led initiative (described as a *multi-storey block management and security initiative*), where a *dispersed* concierge service and associated physical works were introduced in the late 1980s and where recorded crime (mainly burglary) and the costs of maintaining the blocks were subsequently reduced.

- *Highgate Estate, Birmingham*

  A management-led initiative (described as a *multi-storey block management and security initiative*), where a *dispersed* concierge service and associated works were introduced in the late 1980s and where recorded crime (mainly burglary) and the costs of maintaining the blocks were subsequently reduced.

- *Kirkholt Estate, Rochdale*

  A difficult to classify scheme which we have described as a *burglary prevention scheme* (target hardening with some social measures) on the basis of the Forrester et al. study (1988, 1990) of the Home Office sponsored burglary prevention project but which has much in common with the management-led initiatives on the Pepys Estate and Broadwater Farm. Recorded burglaries were substantially reduced in the late 1980s, which was the main objective of the Home Office sponsored project, but there are indications that the overall crime rate has remained unchanged and, most recently, that the burglary rate is rising once more.

- *Cunningham Road Estate, Halton*

   A difficult to classify scheme which is usually described as a *social* or *community development scheme* but which, as the forerunner of the programmes established by the Priority Estates Project, NACRO and the Safe Neighbourhoods Unit, contained elements of their programmes and could be described as a *co-ordinated estate improvement scheme,* although management changes were not a prominent feature of the scheme. Before and after surveys of residents in the late 1970s revealed a substantial reduction in crime, although recorded crime figures did not confirm this trend.

- *Bushbury Triangle, Wolverhampton*

   A difficult to classify scheme, similar to the Cunningham Road Estate scheme, which is usually described as a *social* or *community development scheme* but which, for the reasons outlined above, could be described as a *co-ordinated estate improvement scheme.* Recorded crime figures, before and after surveys and quota groups confirmed a marked reduction in crime in the mid-1980s.

- *Golf Links Estate, Ealing*

   A difficult to classify scheme which had all the hallmarks of a *management-led co-ordinated estate improvement scheme* (similar to the Pepys Estate scheme) when it was originally conceived in the early 1980s but which, after a series of implementation failures, brought social measures for young people to the forefront as the most prominent element of the scheme. Recorded crime dropped dramatically in the mid-1980s but began to rise again in the late 1980s when the youth project closed.

- *Possil Park, Glasgow*

   A *security scheme* established in the late 1980s as a community business with a very narrow objective of reducing damage to and theft from void properties. The costs of void management were substantially reduced as a result. The scheme did not aim to have an impact on other crimes and recorded crime figures did not indicate any significant changes.

These initiatives have many features in common and, from these, it is possible to develop a composite picture of the successful scheme:

- *Planned and researched*

   Every initiative went through a fairly lengthy planning stage and involved the collection of substantial amounts of data to inform the development of improvements.

- *Management-led*

  The approach taken by most schemes could be described as management-led, involving changes to estate management and maintenance services, often including localisation of services.

- *Inter-agency co-ordinated*

  Most involved a number of departments or agencies working together to develop a response to local problems. It is worth noting, given the current plethora of inter-agency initiatives, that this is a relatively new phenomenon and that as recently as the early 1980s it was not at all common for different agencies, or even departments of the same agency, to work together on the same initiative.

- *Independently enabled*

  In a majority of cases, an independent agency was called in to, play an enabling role, mediating between residents and local agencies and driving the initiative forward.

- *Multi-problem orientated*

  Most recognised the need to tackle a range of problems, and crime was not always the main priority.

- *Multi-solution orientated*

  A package of measures was introduced in all but one case (Possil Park). Most involved some design changes, nearly all involved a local management initiative, all involved some security measures, most involved social measures (for young people in particular) and a majority involved changes to policing arrangements.

- *Consultation based*

  Most recognised the need to consult residents in the target area and to develop responses on the basis of their priorities. Some also involved consultation with staff responsible for delivering services. Some consultations allowed for a wide range of proposals (eg Pepys Estate), but others presented limited options for negotiation (eg Mitchellhill).

- *Committed to participation*

  Most recognised the need for residents' participation in local decision making. In most cases this meant ongoing consultation during the course of improvements and liaison with residents' organisations.

- *Ring-fenced*

  All the schemes had dedicated budgets which were effectively ring-fenced from spending on competing areas of activity. All had some form of central government support in terms of funding through Estate Action (or its predecessor) or the Urban Programme (including the Possil Park Scheme which had Urban Programme support via Strathclyde Community Business). Many had advice and support from government funded programmes such as the Priority Estates Project.

Of course, these features are also evident in a number of *unsuccessful* schemes and cannot be treated as guarantees of success.

Perhaps the strongest conclusion from reviewing the evidence was the finding that schemes which set out to reduce crime problems through introducing just one type of measure did not generally lead to successful outcomes.

Permanence of success

A part of the *nothing works* view of interventions is the notion that any gains made are likely to be short term. We know that most, if not all, of the initiatives we have described were not by any means the first to be tried in the areas concerned and that they are unlikely to be the last. There is certainly a school of thought which says that areas with serious problems require special attention at regular intervals. The transience of any success is easy to explain:

- Local interventions are not able to influence the socio-economic conditions of residents to any significant degree and these are likely to continue to leave them vulnerable to crime and a range of other problems. National policies often seem to conspire against local initiatives. In this context, it could be argued that it is only possible to manage the crime problem more effectively, rather than to reduce it, by making a special (and usually unsustainable) effort.

- Local interventions are not always (or even usually) able to affect the way in which agencies generally deliver their services. Agencies participating in local initiatives are often willing to modify their service delivery for the project but this is often regarded as an exceptional and/or temporary measure which may be withdrawn when the project is over and the situation returns to *normal*. For example, the neighbourhood policing project on the Pepys Estate in Deptford has been under consistent pressure for replacement with a more conventional police service since its inception. Also, it is clear that new ways of working which emerge during the course of projects, and which may lead to permanent improvements in service delivery, are not effectively disseminated within organisations in most cases. This may be because only a small number of individuals are involved in an intervention and because the absence of evaluation leaves the lessons of the initiative unrecorded.

- Local interventions are often conceived of as time-limited projects and resources are withdrawn at the end of the period without concern for the effect. This is particularly an issue where measures are resourced from central government programmes. For example, the Golf Links youth project was funded through the DHSS Opportunities for Volunteering scheme whose criteria required withdrawal of resources after a maximum of three years.

- Local interventions do not necessarily *empower* local people and enable them to manage their own affairs. Without this it is difficult to see how improvements can be sustained and, equally important, new ideas developed once the special attention of local and outside agencies is withdrawn.

The case for evaluation

A great deal of attention has been paid in this report to the evaluation of crime prevention initiatives. Most of the schemes in this report have been retrospectively evaluated and the limitations of this are easily exposed. In particular, the lack of description available on the implementation of initiatives makes it very difficult to establish when and how measures were put into effect, whether they were introduced as originally intended, or whether external factors conspired to confuse the results. And the potential for rescuing data retrospectively is severely limited - much will have been lost for all time.

How do we ensure that evaluations are properly planned and executed? There are strong arguments for making evaluation a condition of access to funds. Central government has a definite role in this regard. There is also a strong case for greater collaboration between practitioners and researchers in the development of evaluations.

Crime prevention is not the only goal

We would like to conclude by remarking on the potential dangers of over-emphasising the crime prevention outcomes of local initiatives. Irrespective of whether design changes, new management arrangements and social improvements reduce crime problems, they often contribute to greatly enhanced living conditions. Crime prevention is just one aspect of the quality of life which residents will be concerned about and need not be their major concern. A preoccupation with crime prevention may create the kind of heavily fortified environments in which people (given a choice) do not want to live. And the kinds of environments they prefer (witness the premium on private houses whose gardens abut parks) may lead to increased chances of victimisation which they are willing to tolerate.

References

Adams J R (1973), 'Review of Defensible Space' in *Man Environment Systems*, 3, pp.267-268

Allatt P (1984a), 'Residential Security - Containment and Displacement of Burglary' in *The Howard Journal*, 23, pp.99-116

Allatt P (1984b), 'Fear of Crime - The Effect of Improved Residential Security on a Difficult to Let Estate' in *Howard Journal*, 23, pp.170-182

Altman I (1975), *Environment and Social Behaviour - Privacy, Personal Space, Territory Crowding*, Monterey, California, Brookes Cole

Anderson S, Smith C, Kinsey R and Wood J (1990), *The Edinburgh Crime Survey*, Edinburgh, Scottish Office

Angel S (1968), *Discouraging Crime through City Planning*, Working Paper 5, Berkeley, California

Architect's Journal, 26 March 1986

Association of District Councils (1990), *Promoting Safer Communities - A District Council Perspective*, ADC

Association of Metropolitan Authorities (1990), *Crime Reduction - A Framework for the Nineties?*, AMA

Atkins S T (1989), *Critical Paths - Designing for Secure Travel*, The Design Council

Audit Commission (1986), *The Crisis in Council Housing*, London, HMSO

Bagley C (1965), 'Juvenile Delinquency in Exeter - An Ecological and Comparative Study' *in Urban Studies*, vol. 2, 1964/5

Bailey S and Lynch I (1988), *The Cost of Crime*, Newcastle, Northumbria Police

Baldwin J and Bottoms A (1976), *The Urban Criminal - A Study in Sheffield*, London, Tavistock Publications

Ball C, Knight B and Plant S (1990), *New Goals for an Enterprise Culture*, London, Training for Enterprise

Bannister J (1988), *The Impact of Environmental Design upon the Incidence and Type of Crime*, Central Research Unit, Scottish Office

Barr J and Pease K (1990), in *Crime and Justice - An Annual Review of Research*, Tonry M and Morris N, University of Chicago Press, vol. 12

Bartlett School of Architecture (1989), *A Study of the Spatial Pattern of Crime*

Bennett T and Wright R (1984), *Burglars on Burglary - Prevention and the Offender*, Farnborough, Gower

Bennett T (1986), 'Situational Crime Prevention from the Offender's Perspective' in *Situational Crime Prevention - From Theory to Practice,* Heal K and Laycock G, Home Office Research and Planning Unit, London, HMSO

Bennett T (1988), *An Evaluation of Two Neighbourhood Watch Schemes in London,* Cambridge, Institute of Criminology

Birenbaum R (1983), 'Crime Prevention through Environmental Design' in *Habitat*

Birmingham City Council (1988), *Security Measures in High Rise Blocks,* Report of City Housing Officer, 13 October 1988

Birmingham City Council (1990), *Evaluations of the Group Concierge Scheme at Highgate,* Research Report No 2, City Housing Department

Birmingham City Council (1991a), *Cost Breakdown and Other Supplementary Information,* Special Tabulation, February 1991

Birmingham City Council (1991b), *Assessment of Lift Breakdowns, Vandalism and Minor Repairs Call Outs at Highgate,* Special Tabulation, February 1991

Brantingham P J and Brantingham P L (1975), 'Residential Burglary and Urban Form' in *Urban Studies*

Brent Council (1983), *Census Data for the Chalkhill Estate*

Bright J A (1969), *The Beat Patrol Experiment,* Home Office Police Research and Development Branch, unpublished

Bright J and Pettersson G (1984), *The Safe Neighbourhoods Unit - Community Based Improvements on Twelve Inner London Housing Estates,* Safe Neighbourhoods Unit

Bristol City Council (1989), *Report to Planning, Highways and Transport Sub-Committee,* 31 January 1989

Broadwater Farm Youth Association Co-op Ltd (1987), *Broadwater Farm Skills Survey, Human Resources and Tenants Consultation*

Broadwater Farm Youth Association Co-op Ltd (1990), *Report of Questionnaire Survey of Manston, Lympne and Kenley Blocks, Broadwater Farm Estate*

Burbidge M (1984), 'British Public Housing and Crime - A Review' in *Coping with Burglary - Research Perspectives on Policy,* Clarke R and Hope T

Burrows J (1980), 'Closed Circuit Television and Crime on the London Underground' in *Designing Out Crime,* Clarke R and Mayhew P (eds.), London, HMSO

CAPITA (1990), *Priority Estates Project Cost Effectiveness Study - Interim Report 1988-90,* for Department of the Environment

CAPITA (1991), *Data on voids, management costs and rent arrears for Phase 2 of study*

Central Housing Advisory Committee (Flats Sub-Committee) (1952), *Living in Flats,* HMSO

Chambers G and Tombs J (eds.) (1984), *The British Crime Survey Scotland,* Scottish Office Central Research Unit, Edinburgh, HMSO

CIPFA (1981), *Cost Benefit Study - Coventry Home Help Project*

City of Glasgow (1988), *Concierge Provision in Multi-Storey Flats,* Report by Director of Housing, 14 October 1988

City of Glasgow (1990a), *Concierge Information Package*

City of Glasgow (1990b), *Mitchellhill Concierge Service Monitoring Information,* Report by Director of Housing, 16 May 1990

City of Glasgow (1991), *Mitchellhill Arrears Analysis February 1991,* Housing Department

Clarke R (ed.) (1978), *Tackling Vandalism,* Home Office Research Study, no. 47, London, HMSO

Clarke R and Hough M (1984), *Crime and Police Effectiveness,* Home Office Research Study, no. 79, London, HMSO

Clarke R and Cornish D (1983), *Crime Control in Britain - A Review of Policy and Research,* Albany, State University of New York Press

Cleveland Constabulary (1990), *Policing of Housing Estates,* Cleveland Constabulary

Cloward R and Ohlin L (1960), *Delinquency and Opportunity - A Theory of Delinquent Gangs,* Glencoe III, Free Press

Coleman A (1985), *Utopia on Trial,* London, Hilary Shipman

Cornish D and Clarke R (1986), 'Situational Prevention, Displacement of Crime and Rational Choice Theory' in *Situational Crime Prevention - From Theory to Practice,* Heal and Laycock (eds.), Home Office Research and Planning Unit, London, HMSO

Crawford A, Jones T, Woodhouse T and Young J (1990), *The Second Islington Crime Survey,* London, Middlesex Polytechnic

Crouch S (1990), *Improving Doors to Flats in Multi-Storey Blocks - Practical Security Guide 5,* Safe Neighbourhoods Unit

Curtis L (1987), 'The Retreat of Folly - Some Modest Replications of Inner City Success' in *Policy to Prevent Crime - Neighbourhood, Family and Employment Strategies,* Curtis L (ed.), The Annals of the American Academy of Political Science, vol. 494

Curtis L (1988), 'The March of Folly - Crime and the Underclass' in *Communities and Crime Reduction,* Hope T and Shaw M (eds.), London, HMSO

Curtis L (1990), *Youth Investment and Community Reconstruction - Street Lessons on Drugs and Crime,* 10th Anniversary Report of the Milton S Eisenhower Foundation, Washington, Eisenhower Foundation

Department of the Environment (1973), *Children at Play,* London, HMSO

Department of Environment (1981), *Security on Council Estates - Report of the Housing Services Advisory Group*

Department of the Environment (1981), *Families in Flats,* London, HMSO

Department of the Environment (1989), *Handbook of Estate Improvement - Vol. 1 - Appraising Options,* Estate Action

Department of the Environment (1991), *Handbook of Estate Improvements - Vol. 2 - External Areas,* Estate Action

Dickens P (1988), 'Architecture, the Individual and Social Change' in *Housing Studies*

DuBow F and Emmons D (1981), 'The Community Hypothesis' *in Reactions to Crime,* Lewis D (ed.), Newbury Park, CA, Sage Publications

Durant M, Thomas M and Willcox H (1972), *Crime, Criminals and the Law,* London, HMSO

Farrington D and Dowds E (1985), 'Disentangling Criminal Behaviour and Police Reaction' in *Reactions to Crime - The Public, the Police, Courts and Prison,* Farrington D and Gunn J (eds.), Chichester, John Wiley

Field S and Hope T (1989), 'Economics, the Consumer and Under-Provision in Crime Prevention' in *Policing, Organised Crime and Crime Prevention,* Morgan R (ed.), report of British Criminology Conference 1989, vol. 4

Findlay J, Bright J and Gill K (1990), *Youth Crime Prevention - Handbook of Good Practice,* Crime Concern

Findlay A, Morris A and Rogerson R (1988), 'Where to live in Britain in 1988 - The Quality of Life in British Cities' in *Cities,* 5, pp.268-276

Fleming R (1987a), 'Lighting Design - A Major Element in the Fight Against Crime' in *Lighting Journal,* December 1987

Fleming R (1987b), 'Lighting and Crime, the Facts not the Fiction' in *Lighting Today,* September 1987

Fleming R and Burrows J (1987), *The Case for Lighting as a Means of Preventing Crime,* Home Office Research and Planning Unit

Forrester D, Chatterton M, Pease K (1988), *The Kirkholt Burglary Prevention Project,* Home Office Crime Prevention Unit, paper 13

Forrester D, Frenz S, O'Connell M and Pease K (1990), *The Kirkholt Burglary Prevention Project - Phase 2,* Crime Prevention Unit, paper 23, London, HMSO

Fowler F and Mangione T (1986), 'A Three-Pronged Effort to Reduce Crime and Fear of Crime: The Hartford Experiment' in *Community Crime Prevention - Does it Work?,* Rosenbaum D (ed.), Sage Criminal Justice System Annuals, vol. 22, Beverley Hills, Sage

Garafalo J and McLeod M (1985), *A National Overview of the Neighbourhood Watch Programme,* paper presented at Annual meeting of the American Society of Criminology, San Diego

Gardiner R A (1978), *Design for Safe Neighbourhoods - The Environmental Security Planning and Design Process ,* Washington DC, GPO

General Household Survey 1986, Table 7.3

Genn H (1988), 'Multiple Victimisation' in *Victims of Crime - A New Deal,* Maguire M and Pointing J (eds.), Open University Press

Gibberd F (1955), 'High Flats in Medium Sized Towns and Suburban Areas' in *High Flats,* report of Symposium, 15 February 1955, RIBA

Gifford et al. (1986), *The Broadwater Farm Enquiry*, Karia Press

Gifford et al. (1989), *Broadwater Farm Revisited*, Karia Press

Glasgow City Council (1987), *Possil Park Community Security Business*, Report by District Housing Manager to the North Area Management Committee, 26 February 1987

Glasgow City Council (1990), *Report by Director of Housing on Possil Park Milton Office for North Area Management Committee*, 14 May 1990; and *Report by Director of Housing on Possil Park for the Sub-Committee on Programme Management*, 31 May 1990

Glasgow City Council (1990), *Housing Sub-Committee Report on Mitchellhill Concierge Service*, 16 May 1990

Graham J (1990), *Crime Prevention Strategies in Europe and North America*, Helsinki, HEUNI

Graham I (1991), Data supplied by *Safe Castlemilk* for purposes of case study, January 1991

Graham I, unpublished report on Safe Castlemilk initiative

Greenberg S, Rohe W and Williams J (1985), *Informal Citizen Action and Prevention at the Neighbourhood Level*, Washington DC, US Government Printing Office

Harrison A and Gretton J (eds.) (1986), *Crime UK*, Newbury, Berks, Policy Journals

Heal K and Laycock G (eds.) (1986), *Situational Crime Prevention - From Theory to Practice*, Home Office Research and Planning Unit, London, HMSO

Hedges A, Blaber A and Mostyn B (1980), *Community Planning Project - Cunningham Road Improvement Scheme - Final Report*, Little London, Chichester, Barry Rose

Hill N (1986), *Prepayment Coin Meters - A Target for Burglary*, Home Office Crime Prevention Unit, paper no. 6, London, Home Office

Hillier B (1987), *Against Enclosure*, paper presented to British Criminology Conference 1987

Hillier B et al. (1983), 'Space Syntax - A New Urban Perspective' in *Architect's Journal*, London, 30 November 1983

Hillier B and Hanson J (1984), *The Social Logic of Space* , Bartlett School of Architecture and Planning

Hillier B and Penn A (1986), *The Mozart Estate Redesign Proposals*, Unit for Architectural Studies, Bartlett School of Architecture and Planning

Hillier B et al. (1989a), *The Architecture of Maiden Lane Estate - A Second Opinion* , Bartlett School of Architecture and Planning

Hillier B et al. (1989b), *The Spatial Pattern of Crime on the Studley Estate* Bartlett School of Architecture and Planning

HM Treasury (1984), *Investment Appraisal in the Public Sector - A Technical Guide for Government Departments*

Hoggett P and Hambleton R (1987), *Decentralisation and Democracy - Localising Public Services*

Home Office (1985), *Crime Prevention Initiatives in England and Wales*, Crime Prevention Unit, Home Office

Home Office (1988), *The Costs of Crime*, Report of Working Group, Home Office Standing Conference on Crime Prevention

Home Office (1989), *Five Towns Initiative*, London, Home Office

Home Office (1989), *Tackling Crime*, London, Home Office

Home Office (1990), *Partnership in Crime Prevention*, London, Home Office

Home Office (1991), *Safe Communities - The Local Delivery of Crime Prevention through the Partnership Approach*, Report of Working Group, Home Office Standing Conference on Crime Prevention

Hope T (1986), 'Council Tenants and Crime' *in Research Bulletin 21*, London, Home Office Research and Planning Unit

Hope T (1990), *1988 British Crime Survey - Special Tabulation*, Home Office Research and Planning Unit, unpublished

Hope T and Dowds L (1987), *The Use of Local Surveys in Evaluation Research - Examples from Community Crime Prevention*, paper to British Criminology Conference

Hope T and Hough M (1988), 'Area, Crime and Incivilities - A Profile from the British Crime Survey' *in Communities and Crime Reduction*, Hope T and Shaw M (eds.), London, HMSO

Hope T and Shaw M (1988), 'Community Approaches to Reducing Crime' in *Communities and Crime Reduction*, Hope T and Shaw M (eds.), London, HMSO

Hough J M, Clarke R V G and Mayhew P (1980), 'Introduction' in *Designing out Crime*, Clarke R V G and Mayhew, P (eds.), London HMSO

Hough M and Mayhew P (eds.) (1982), *Crime and Public Housing*, Research and Planning Unit, Paper 6, London, Home Office

Hough M and Mayhew P (1983), *The British Crime Survey - First Report*, Home Office Research Study, no. 76, London, HMSO

Hough M and Mayhew P (1985), *Taking Account of Crime - Key Findings from the 1984 British Crime Survey*, Home Office Research Study, no. 85, London, HMSO

Hurley N (1991), *Communities and Enterprise in Scotland*, Report for Scottish Office, CENTRIS

Husain S (1988), *Neighbourhood Watch in England and Wales - A Locational Analysis*, Crime Prevention Unit, no. 12, London, Home Office

Hyder K (1988), 'Heart Beats' in *Time Out*, 8-15 June 1988

Institute of Housing and Royal Institute of British Architects (1989), *Safety and Security in Housing Design - A Guide for Action*

Institute of Housing (1983), *Trends in High Places*

Institute of Lighting Engineers (1990), *The Lighting and Crime File*

Jacobs J (1961), *The Life and Death of Great American Cities* , London, Jonathan Cape

Jeffrey C R (1971, revised 1977), *Crime Prevention through Environmental Design*, Beverley Hills, CA, Sage

Jenks M (1987), *Housing Problems and the Dangers of Certainty*, paper given to Rehumanising Housing conference (1987)

Jones F M (1987),'Technological Social Needs' in *Rehumanising Housing*

Jones T, Maclean B and Young J (1986), *The Islington Crime Survey*, London, Middlesex Polytechnic

Kaplan S (1973), Review of 'Defensible Space' in *Architectural Forum*

Kelling G, Pate T, Dieckman D and Brown C (1974), *The Kansas City Preventive Patrol Experiment*, Washington DC, Police Foundation

Kendrick T and Pilkington E (1987), *A New Deal for Tenants or Papering over the Cracks?*, Hoggett and Hambleton (1987)

King M (1988), *How to Make Social Crime Prevention Work - The French Experience*, London, NACRO

Kinsey R (1984), *Merseyside Crime Survey*, Merseyside County Council

KPMG Peat Marwick/Safe Neighbourhoods Unit (1990), *Counting Out Crime - The Nottingham Crime Audit*

KPMG Peat Marwick/Safe Neighbourhoods Unit (1990), *Nottingham Crime Audit*, unpublished

LAMSAC (1987), *A report on Criminal Damage to Public Property*, London, LAMSAC

Lavraskas P and Bennett S (1988), 'Thinking about the implementation of citizen and community anti-crime measures' in *Communities and Crime Reduction*, Hope T and Shaw M (eds.), London, HMSO

Lavraskas P and Kashmuk J (1986), 'Evaluating Crime Prevention Through Environmental Design: The Portland Commercial Demonstration Project' in *Community Crime Prevention - Does it Work?*, Rosenbaum D (ed.), Sage Criminal Justice System Annuals, vol. 22, Beverley Hills, Sage

Laycock G (1985), *Property Marking - A Deterrent to Domestic Burglary?*, Home Office Crime Prevention Unit Paper, no. 3, London, Home Office

Laycock G (1986), 'Property Marking as a Deterrent to Domestic Burglary' in *Situation Crime Prevention*, Heal K and Laycock G (eds.), London, HMSO

Laycock G (1989), *An Evaluation of Domestic Security Surveys*, Home Office Crime Prevention Unit, Paper 18

Lea J et al. (1988), *Preventing Crime - The Hilldrop Environmental Improvement Survey*, London, Middlesex Polytechnic

Lewis D, Grant J and Rosenbaum D (1985), *The Social Construction of Reform - Crime Prevention and Community Organisations,* Final Report, vol. 2, to the Ford Foundation, Evanston, Ill, Northwestern University, Centre for Urban Affairs and Policy Research

Lewis D and Salem G (1981), 'Community Crime Prevention - An Analysis of A Developing Strategy' in *Crime and Delinquency,* 27

Lindsay B and McGillis D (1986), 'Citywide Community Crime Prevention - An Assessment of the Seattle Program' in *Community Crime Prevention - Does it Work?,* Rosenbaum D (ed.), Sage Criminal Justice System Annuals, vol. 22, Beverley Hills, Sage

LLoyd R and Wilson D (1989), *Inner City Street Lighting and its Effects Upon Crime,* paper presented at Institute of Lighting Engineers Conference, 1989

Locke T (1989), *The economic impact of crime on a local area,* Leicester Polytechnic School of Business

Lohman P and Van Dijk A (1988), *Neighbourhood Watch in the Netherlands,* The Hague, National Crime Prevention Bureau

London Borough of Ealing (1983-88), *Minutes of the Golf Links Steering Committee*

London Borough of Ealing (1985), *Report on Youth Provision on the Three Estates,* October 1985

London Borough of Ealing (1986), *Golf Links Estate - Provision for Young People,* March 1986

London Borough of Haringey (1976), *Report on Broadwater Farm,* presented by Borough Housing Officer October 1976

London Borough of Haringey (1989) *Report on Borough Housing Officer to Broadwater Farm Sub Committee 4/9/1989*

London Borough of Haringey (1990a), *Report of the Director of Housing Services on Estate Action Concierge Scheme to Housing Services Committee,* July 1990

London Borough of Haringey (1990b), *Report to Service Management Team, Housing Department, on Management of Concierge Schemes,* October 1990

London Borough of Haringey (1990c), Report of the Director of Community Services, *Broadwater Farm Youth Association - Review of Progress,* to Community Services Sub-committee, December 1990

Lurigio A and Rosenbaum D (1986), 'Evaluation Research in Community Crime Prevention - A Critical Look at the Field' in *Community Crime Prevention - Does it Work?,* Rosenbaum D (ed.), Sage Criminal Justice Systems Annuals, vol. 22, Beverley Hills, Sage

Lynch G and Atkins S (1988), 'The Influence of Personal Security Fears on Women's Travel Patterns' in *Transportation,* 15, pp.257-277

MacFarlane R (1990), *Using Local Labour in Urban Renewal - A Good Practice Study,* Business in the Community

Manchester City Council (1985), *Deck Access Disaster - The Hulme Conference*

Mayhew P (1979), 'Defensible Space - The Current Status of Crime Prevention Theory' in *Howard Journal of Penology and Crime Prevention*

Mayhew P (1984), 'Target Hardening - How Much of an Answer?' in *Coping with Burglary,* Clarke R and Hope T, Boston, Kluwer-Nijhoff

Mayhew P and Clarke R (1982), 'Crime Prevention and Public Housing in England' in *Crime and Public Housing,* Hough M and Mayhew P (eds.), Research and Planning Unit, Paper 6, London, HMSO

Mayhew P, Elliott D and Dowds L (1989), *The 1988 British Crime Survey,* Home Office Research Study, no. 111, London, HMSO

Metropolitan Borough of Rochdale (1984), *Kirkholt Report,* Rochdale MBC Housing Department, May 1984, unpublished

Metropolitan Borough of Rochdale (1984-1991), *Reports to and Minutes of the Kirkholt Estate Committee,* unpublished

Metropolitan Police (1984), *Neighbourhood Policing Programme,* unpublished, A2(3) Branch

Metropolitan Police (1985), *Estates Policing,* unpublished, A2(3) Branch

Metropolitan Police (1991), *Recorded crime figures for Chalkhill Estate,* unpublished

Moffatt R E (1983), 'Crime Prevention through Environmental Design - A Management Perspective' in *Canadian Journal of Criminology*

Montgomery S (1988), *Niddrie House Multi Feasibility Study*

Morgan P and Makeham P (1978), *Economic and Financial Analysis of Sheltered Employment,* Research Paper, no. 5, Department of Employment

MORI (1990), *Tenants Survey - Research Study Conducted for Brent Borough Council*

Musheno M C, Levine J P and Palumbo D J (1978), 'Television Surveillance and Crime Prevention - Evaluating an Attempt to Create Defensible Space in Public Housing' in *Social Service Quarterly*

NACRO (1975), *Housing Management and Crime Prevention,* Conference Report

NACRO (1983), *The Thirlmere Report,* London, NACRO

NACRO (1984), *Report of the Golf Links Estate Project,* August 1984, NACRO Ealing Neighbourhood Development Unit

NACRO (1986), *An Evaluation of NACRO's Crime Prevention Programme by Tavistock Institute of Human Relations - NACRO's Response,* NACRO

NACRO (1987), *Survey Report - Westminster Road Security Improvements,* NACRO

NACRO (1988a), *Growing Up on Housing Estates - A Review of Play and Youth Provision,* London, NACRO

NACRO (1988b), *The Golf Links Youth Project,* London, NACRO

NACRO/SOLACE (1986), *Crime Prevention and Community Safety - A New Role for Local Authorities,* London, NACRO

National House Building Council (1986), *Guidance on How the Security of New Homes can be Improved*, NHBC

Newman O and Franck K (1982), 'The Effects of Building Size on Personal Crime and Fear of Crime' in *Population and Environment*, vol. 5, pp.203-220

Newman O (1972), *Defensible Space - Crime Prevention through Urban Design*, New York, Macmillan

Newman O (1976), *Design Guidelines for Creating Defensible Space*, National Institute of Law Enforcement and Criminal Justice, Washington DC, GPO

Niddrie House Planning & Rehabilitation Group (1990[1]), *Annual Report*

Niddrie House Planning & Rehabilitation Group (1990[2]), *Report to Edinburgh District Council*

O'Connell M (1990), *The Cost Benefit Analysis of the Kirkholt Crime Prevention Project*, Greater Manchester Probation Service, unpublished

Osborn S (1986), 'Phone Entry Systems and the South Acton Estate' in *NACRO Neighbourhood News*, December 1986

Osborn S (1989), *Safe Communities 1989 - Local Government Action on Crime Prevention and Community Safety*, London, Safe Neighbourhoods Unit

Osborn S and Bright J (1988), *Policing Housing Estates*, London, NACRO

Osborn S and Bright J (1989), *Crime Prevention and Community Safety - A Practical Guide for Local Authorities*, London, NACRO

Osborn S and Shaftoe H (1991), *Safe Communities in the 1990s*, Safe Neighbourhoods Unit

Painter K (1988), *Lighting and Crime Prevention - The Edmonton Project*, Middlesex Polytechnic

Painter K (1989a), *Crime Prevention and Public Lighting with Special Focus on Women and Elderly People*, Middlesex Polytechnic

Painter K (1989b), *Lighting and Crime Prevention for Community Safety - The Tower Hamlets Study 1st Report*, Middlesex Polytechnic

Parliamentary All Party Penal Affairs Group (1983), *The Prevention of Crime Among Young People*, Chichester, Barry Rose

Percy Johnson-Marshall & Partners (1988a), *Niddrie House Rehabilitation Social Survey*

Percy Johnson-Marshall & Partners (1988b), *Niddrie House Rehabilitation Feasibility Study*

Police Foundation (1981), *The Newark Foot Patrol*, Washington DC, Police Foundation

Polytechnic of the South Bank and Institute of Housing (1985), *Tower Blocks*

Power A (1982a), *Priority Estate Project 1982*, Department of the Environment

Power A (1982b), *Report on Tulse Hill Estate*, June 1982

Power A (1984), *Local Housing Management - A Priority Estates Project Survey*, Department of Environment

Power A (1987a), *Property Before People - The Management of Twentieth Century Council Housing*, London, Allen & Unwin

Power A (1987b), *The Priority Estates Project Model - The PEP Guide to Local Housing Management*, Priority Estates Project, Estate Action 1 DoE/WO, HMSO

Power A (1987c), *The PEP Experience*, Priority Estates Project, Estate Action 2 DoE/WO, HMSO

Poyner B (1982), *Design against Crime - Beyond Defensible Space*, Butterworths

Poyner B (1991), *What Works in Crime Prevention - An Overview of Evaluations*, paper presented at the British Criminology Conference at York University, 25 July 1991

Poyner B, Webb B and Woodall R (1986), *Crime Reduction on Housing Estates - An Evaluation of NACRO's Crime Prevention Programme*, Tavistock Institute of Human Relations

Poyner B et al. (1986),*Walkway Demolition, Lisson Green Estate*, Tavistock Institute for Human Relations

Priority Estates Project (1986), *Broadwater Farm Estate, Haringey - Background and Information Relating to the Riot on Sunday, 6th October 1985*, PEP/DOE

Priority Estates Project (1987), *The PEP Guide to Local Housing Management*

Priority Estates Project (1988), *Broadwater Farm, Project Profile*

PSLG (Public Service and Local Government) (1989), 'Privatised Protection' in *Issue*, May 1989

Riley D and Mayhew P (1980), *Crime Prevention Publicity: an assessment*, Home Office Research Study no.63, London, HMSO

Rock P (1988), 'Crime Reduction Initiatives on Problem Estates' in *Communities and Crime Reduction*, Hope T and Shaw M (eds.), London, HMSO

Rogerson R (1989), *Measuring Quality of Life - Methodological Issues and Problems*, Glasgow Quality of Life Group, Applied Population Research Unit, University of Glasgow

Rogerson R, Findlay A and Morris A (1989), 'Indicators of Quality of Life - Some Methodological Issues' in *Environment and Planning A*, 20

Safe Neighbourhoods Unit (1982), *Pepys Improvement Project - Estate Profile and Action Plan*

Safe Neighbourhoods Unit (1984), *The Safe Neighbourhoods Unit - Community Based Improvement Programmes on 12 Inner London Estates*

Safe Neighbourhoods Unit (1985), *After Entryphones - Improving Management and Security in Multi-Storey Blocks*

Safe Neighbourhoods Unit (1986a), *Crime and Safety on Lansdowne Green*, London, Safe Neighbourhoods Unit

Safe Neighbourhoods Unit (1986b), *Crime and Security in Trellick Tower*, London, Safe Neighbourhoods Unit

Safe Neighbourhoods Unit (1986c), *The Safe Neighbourhoods Unit Report 1981-86*

Safe Neighbourhoods Unit (1987), *Coming Home to Trellick - Improving the Management and Security of a Multi-Storey Block*

Safe Neighbourhoods Unit (1988a), *The Mozart Survey Part 1 - A Study of Design Modification and Housing Management Innovation,* unpublished

Safe Neighbourhoods Unit (1988b), *Beyond the Barrier - Improving Management and Security on Southwyck House, Brixton*

Safe Neighbourhoods Unit (1988c), *Lighting up Brent - A Survey into Lighting and Safety on Chalk Hill, Stonebridge and South Kilburn Estates*

Safe Neighbourhoods Unit (1989a), *The East Spitalfields Report,* London, Safe Neighbourhoods Unit

Safe Neighbourhoods Unit (1989b), *Stockwell Park Estate - A Study of Security, Design and Management Issues,* unpublished

Safe Neighbourhoods Unit (1989c), *Barbot Street Estate Tower Blocks - A Survey into Improvement of Tower Block Security*

Safe Neighbourhoods Unit (1990), *The Milton Court Report,* London, Safe Neighbourhoods Unit

Safe Neighbourhoods Unit and Birmingham City Council (1990), *Securing a Future for High Rise Living*

Schneider A (1986), 'Neighborhood-based Anti Burglary Strategies - An Analysis of Public and Private Benefits from the Portland Program' in *Community Crime Prevention - Does it Work?,* Rosenbaum D (ed.), Sage Criminal Justice System Annuals, vol. 22, Beverley Hills, Sage

Scottish Office (1990), *Castlemilk Partnership Strategy Report,* Edinburgh, HMSO

Shapland J and Vagg J (1988), *Policing by the Public*

Sharpe, Dame Evelyn (1955), 'Opening Remarks' in *High Flats,* report of symposium, 15 February 1955, RIBA

Shaw C and McKay H (1942), *Juvenile Delinquency and Urban Areas,* Chicago, University of Chicago Press

Silberman C (1978), *Criminal Violence, Criminal Justice,* New York, Random House

Silloway G and McPherson M (1985), *The Limits to Citizen Participation in a Government Sponsored Crime Prevention Programme,* presented at Annual meeting of the American Society of Criminology, San Diego

Skilton M (1986), *Making an Entrance - Improving Living Conditions in Tower Blocks,* London Borough of Brent

Skilton M (1988), *A Better Reception,* Department of Environment

Skogan W (1984), 'Reporting Crimes to the Police - The Status of World Research' in *Journal of Research in Crime and Delinquency,* 21, 113-137

Smith D (1987), 'The Police and the Idea of Community' in *Policing and the Community,* Wilmott P (ed.), London, PSI

Smith S J (1987a), Design Against Crime? Beyond the Rhetoric of Residential Crime Prevention, *Journal of Property Management*

Smith S J (1987b), Review of 'Utopia on Trial - Vision and Reality in Planned Housing' in *Urban Studies*

Sparks R, Genn H and Dodd D (1977), *Surveying Victims,* London, John Wiley

Spicker R (1987), Poverty and Depressed Estates - A Critique of Utopia on Trial, *Housing Studies*

Stenko E (1988), 'Hidden Violence Against Women' in *Victims of Crime - A New Deal,* Maguire M and Pointing J (eds.), Open University Press

Stollard P, Osborn S, Shaftoe H and Croucher K (1989), *Safer Neighbourhoods,* Safe Neighbourhoods Unit and Institute of Advanced Architectural Studies

Stollard P and Warren F (1988), *Safe as Houses,* a review of the importance of housing design and layout in achieving security, Institute of Advanced Architectural Studies, University of York

Taub R, Taylor D and Dunham J (1984), *Paths to Neighbourhood Change - Race and Crime in Urban America,* Chicago, University of Chicago Press

Taylor R B, Gottfredson S D and Bower S (1980), 'The Defensibility of Defensible Space' in *Understanding Crime,* Hirschi T and Gottfredson M (eds.)

Taylor R B and Gottfredson S (1986), 'Environmental Design, Crime and Prevention — An Examination of Community Dynamics' in *Communities and Crime,* Reiss A J Jr and Tonry M (eds.)

Tebay S, Cumberbach G and Graham N (1986), *Disputes Between Neighbours,* Applied Psychology Department, Aston University

Teymur N (1987), The Pathology in Housing Discourse, *Rehumanising Housing*

Tien J and Cahn M (1986), 'The Commercial Security Field Test Program: A Systemic Evaluation of Security Surveys in Denver, St Louis, and Long Beach' in *Community Crime Prevention - Does it Work?,* Rosenbaum D (ed.), Sage Criminal justice System Annuals, vol. 22, Beverley Hills, Sage

Tien J, ODonnell V, Barnett A and Mirchandani P (1979), *Street Lighting Project,* National Institute of Law Enforcement and Criminal Justice, Washington DC, GPO

Trojanowicz R (1986), 'Evaluating a Neighbourhood Foot Patrol Program: The Flint, Michigan, Project' in *Community Crime Prevention - Does it Work?,* Sage Criminal Justice System Annuals, vol. 22, Beverley Hills, Sage

US Department of Housing and Urban Development (1980), *Interagency Urban Initiatives Anti-Crime Programme - First Annual Report to Congress,* Washington DC, Government Printing Office

van Dijk J (1989), *Crime Prevention - Practice and Prospects in the Netherlands,* paper presented to ISTD conference on Crime Prevention in Europe, 27 November 1989

Waller I and Okihiro N (1978), *Burglary - The Victim and Public,* Toronto Press

Walker C and Walker S (1989), *The Victoria Community Police Stations - An Exercise in Innovation, Victoria,* Canadian Police College

Wallis A and Ford D (1980), *Crime Prevention through Environmental Design - An Operational Handbook,* National Institute of Justice, Washing DC, GPO

Weatheritt M (1987), 'Community Policing Now' in *Policing and the Community,* Wilmott P (ed.), London, PSI

West D J (1982), *Delinquency - Its Roots and Prospects,* London, Heinemann

West Midlands Police (1991), *Analysis of Crimes in Beat Area 17, including Highgate, for 1988/89 and 1989/90,* Special Tabulation, February 1991

Wilson J and Kelling F (1982), 'Broken Windows - The Police and Neighbourhood Safety' in *The Atlantic Monthly,* March 1982

Wilson S (1980), 'Vandalism and Defensible Space on London Housing Estates' in *Designing Out Crime,* Clarke R V G and Mayhew P (eds.), London HMSO

Wilson S (1978), 'Vandalism and Defensible Space on London Housing Estates' in *Tackling Vandalism,* Home Office Research Study, no. 47

Wilson S (1981), *Reducing Vandalism on Public Housing Estates,* HDD Occasional Papers, London, HMSO

Wilson S, Kirby K, Curtis A and Burbidge M (1980), *An Investigation of Difficult-to-let Housing - Volume 1, General Findings*

Winchester S and Jackson H (1982), *Residential Burglary - The Limits of Prevention,* Home Office Research Study, no. 74

Yin R (1986), 'Community Crime Prevention - A Synthesis of Eleven Evaluations' in *Community Crime Prevention - Does it Work?,* Rosenbaum D (ed.), Sage Criminal Justice System Annuals, vol. 22, Beverley Hills, Sage

Young J (1988), 'Risk of Crime and Fear of Crime' in *Victims of Crime - A New Deal,* Maguire M and Pointing J (eds.), Open University Press

Zipfel T (1989), *Estate Management Boards - An Introduction,* Priority Estates Project

Printed in the United Kingdom for HMSO.
Dd. 0296026, 4/93, C16, GP 3396/6, CCN 16268.